PRAISE FOR *GETTING BACK IN THE GAME*

"*Getting Back in the Game* crystallizes Paul Heinbecker's impressive experience and analysis at the active centre of Canadian foreign policy for more than thirty years. His book is informed, fluent, often blunt, and both realistic and optimistic about a Canada that can matter in the world, and a United Nations that is 'innovative, effective, and important.'"

—The Right Honourable Joe Clark, Scholar,
Statesman, Former Prime Minister of Canada,
and Secretary of State for External Affairs, 1983–91

"Paul Heinbecker has served a variety of prime ministers and foreign ministers as a thoughtful and clear-spoken analyst of Canadian foreign policy. In this, a veritable 'playbook' in Canadian foreign policy past and present, he shares his insight with the Canadian public, and we will all benefit from his intelligent and provocative but always committed rendering of the active role that Canada can play in the world."

—Dr. Lloyd Axworthy, President of the University of Winnipeg;
Canada's Minister of Foreign Affairs, 1996–2000

"This is an impressive and comprehensive review of Canada and its place in the world: past, present, and future. It is a highly readable and sensible Canadian foreign-policy treatise well rooted in experience and wisdom."

—John Manley, President and CEO, Canadian Council of Chief Executives;
Canada's Minister of Foreign Affairs, 2000–02;
and Deputy Prime Minister, 2002–03

To Ayşe

GETTING BACK IN THE GAME

A FOREIGN POLICY PLAYBOOK FOR CANADA

PAUL HEINBECKER

DUNDURN
TORONTO

Design: Alison Carr
Printer: Marquis

Library and Archives Canada Cataloguing in Publication

Heinbecker, Paul, 1941-
Getting back in the game : a foreign policy playbook for Canada / Paul Heinbecker.

ISBN 978-1-55470-298-5 (bound). – ISBN 978-1-45970-165-6 (pbk.)

1. Canada--Foreign relations--21st century.   2. Canada--Foreign relations--1945-.
I. Title.

FC242.H45 2011   327.71009'0512   C2010-901800-1

1   2   3   4   5   15   14   13   12   11

We acknowledge the support of the **Canada Council for the Arts** and the **Ontario Arts Council** for our publishing program. We also acknowledge the financial support of the **Government of Canada** through the **Canada Book Fund** and **Livres Canada Books**, and the **Government of Ontario** through the **Ontario Book Publishing Tax Credit** and the **Ontario Media Development Corporation**.

Printed and bound in Canada.
www.dundurn.com

Dundurn 3 Church Street, Suite 500 Toronto, Ontario, Canada M5E 1M2	Gazelle Book Services Limited White Cross Mills High Town, Lancaster, England LA1 4XS	Dundurn 2250 Military Road Tonawanda, NY U.S.A. 14150

CONTENTS

PREFACE TO THE SECOND EDITION

Since publication of the first edition of *Getting Back in the Game*, much has happened—the proverbially good, bad, and if not ugly, at least incalculable—that will affect Canadian foreign policy.

Under the "bad" heading, Canada failed to win the United Nations Security Council election in the fall of 2010. From William Lyon Mackenzie King to Jean Chrétien, we had won the coveted seat every time we sought election, once a decade since 1948. The loss diminished our international standing and, equally bad, deprived us of an important, albeit temporary, instrument for promoting our ideas and protecting our interests.

The reasons for the loss were clear. Stephen Harper's government had scarcely concealed its contempt for the UN, abandoned Canada's commitments on climate change, shifted Canada's aid policy focus from the relatively poorer Africa to the relatively richer Americas, gave largely uncritical support to Israel's deepening occupation of the West Bank and its blockade of Gaza, and mismanaged relationships with China, Mexico, the United Arab Emirates, and others.

The loss matters because it constitutes a remarkable indictment of the Harper government's foreign policy. While the UN, with its universal membership, has a few tyrants and thug states among its adherents, the great majority of its 192 members are free or partly free democracies, according to Freedom House, the bipartisan

American monitor of international democratic progress. On the decisive ballot, Canada got just seventy-six votes.

The loss matters also because the Council, the world's top security body, handles the big issues of peace and war. In the last decade, while the Council has sometimes been divided, it has outlawed co-operation with al Qaeda, authorized military action in Afghanistan, declined to authorize the Bush administration's attack on Iraq, ended the bloody conflict between Israel and Hezbollah, toughened sanctions on nuclear violators North Korea and Iran, and imposed a no-fly zone to protect Libyans from their psychopathic leader. All of these issues affected Canadians' interests directly or indirectly. It is better to be a policymaker or, at least, shaper, inside the Council chamber than a policy taker outside it, which is why Japan, Germany, India, and Brazil seek election to the Council as often as possible and why they campaign persistently for permanent status.

Among the potentially "good" developments for Canadian foreign policy was the election of a majority government that creates the opportunity to reset Canadian foreign policy. Prime Minister Harper, who is more comfortable in his international role than he was as a rookie in 2006 and who has the political capital to do more than simply be prime minister, has quietly authorized an internal re-examination of Canada's goals abroad.

Potentially good, as well, is the appointment of John Baird as foreign minister. Although his international experience is scant and not especially happy, e.g., on climate change and on air transport relations with the United Arab Emirates, he is a strong personality and is trusted by the prime minister. He has his own political standing and is therefore more capable than many of his predecessors of resisting "poaching" by cabinet colleagues with their particular agendas, and can bring needed coherence to Canadian policy. As Lester Pearson, Joe Clark, John Manley, and Lloyd Axworthy, among others, have shown, strong foreign ministers can make a significant difference. Baird has made a promising start, especially on China, Libya, and Mexico. What is not clear is what Baird himself thinks about foreign policy and how far he is welcome to make needed changes.

The government has an opportunity to recoup Canada's standing if it suppresses the likely strong impulse to keep on doing what has worked for it politically, i.e., privileging communications over substance, tailoring foreign policy to diaspora politics, lying low on climate change, and disparaging the UN. If Canadian foreign policy continues to be marked by the pinched vision, shrunken ambition, and political cynicism masquerading as principle and purpose of the first Harper administrations, it will only prove the H.L. Mencken adage that in a democracy, people get the government they deserve, and usually good and hard!

Regrettably, the early signs are not all promising. At the G8 summit in May 2011, the prime minister parted company with his partners, including the United States, and endorsed the Likud government's position on Israel's borders. In the 2011 Speech from the Throne, Harper promised to "stand up for Canadian farmers and industries by defending supply management," the protectionist agricultural policy that profits Ontario and Quebec farmers, including separatists, at other Canadians' expense and burdens Canada's negotiations with the European Union and even excludes Canada from the Trans-Pacific Strategic Economic Partnership, potentially the most important transpacific economic group. Further, the government has signalled that it will slow the growth of the defence budget, freeze aid spending at current levels, cut back on diplomacy, and subject all departments to "strategic" spending cuts. None of this is a prescription for a more effective foreign policy.

Currently "incalculable" but obviously crucial are the breathtaking rise of China, India, Brazil, and Mexico, the political disarray of the United States and the fiscal crisis in Europe, the disappearance of existential threats to Canada and the diminishing need for alliances, the spreading scourge of illegal drugs and crime, the Arab Awakening, and the acceleration of the digital age that is transforming the context of foreign policy and the conduct of diplomacy.

To succeed in this rapidly changing world, there is much the Harper government needs to do, including to:

- Abandon the alternative universe it created for itself in its first five years in office, a universe in which, to quote the 2007 Speech from the Throne, "focus and action rather than rhetorical posturing are restoring our influence in global affairs ..." In this universe, saying something makes it so, international affairs are played for partisan advantage, and principle is evoked to cover all manner of policy failings, errors, and chicanery.
- Bring coherence to foreign-policy formulation by recalibrating the budgets of Canada's international departments, re-empowering Foreign Affairs to manage foreign relationships in the common interest, realigning defence and foreign-policy purposes, reintegrating aid policy into foreign policy, and partnering more effectively with the millions of Canadians active internationally.
- Enhance Canada's competitiveness by shoring up our key economic partnerships, incrementally and pro-actively removing unnecessary obstacles to business between Canada and the United States, our indispensable strategic partner and natural ally, and by restoring constructive political and economic relations with Mexico, so damaged by the Harper government's self-inflicted visa fiasco of 2009.
- Urgently make China a top strategic priority. To position Canada better to profit more fully from Chinese growth, and to further diversify Canadian markets abroad, especially at a time when US demand for Canadian exports is flagging, the government should also press ahead with the Asia-Pacific gateway and pipeline and transport corridor infrastructure on and to the West Coast.
- Expand our increasingly vital relationships with the rest of Asia where we have not been able to complete a single free trade agreement. The government should redouble its efforts to join the nascent Trans-Pacific Partnership, and to participate in the East Asian Summit to put ourselves back on the Asia-Pacific map.

- Strengthen global governance: by rebuilding our relationship with the UN, in part by employing the best small armed force in the world in UN-sanctioned humanitarian missions to protect civilians, as we are doing in Libya; and by devoting increased diplomatic effort to reinvigorating arms control negotiations.

- Embrace "mini-lateralism by making the G20 effective and rendering Canada indispensable in this most important international governance innovation; and by drawing up strategies for political, economic, and cultural co-operation with each member of the G20, including the second tier.

- Strengthen Canada's sovereignty in the North by controlling the Northwest Passage, promoting co-operation through the Arctic Council, and resolving competing resource claims offshore diplomatically with the five riparian states under the Law of the Sea.

- Put Canada on the right side of history by actively embracing the Arab Awakening (the twenty-first century's equivalent of the end of colonialism and of the collapse of Communism), providing technical assistance in support of the development of democratic institutions, and giving political and financial backing for Canadian investment that will help give Arab citizens the prospect of better lives.

- Reground our position on the Israeli-Palestinian conflict in international law, human rights, fairness, and compassion. Ottawa should maintain its steadfast support for Israel's security and right to exist, but also join the growing international movement to recognize the Palestinians' right to exist, too, in a viable, secure, and democratic state, based on the 1967 borders with agreed land swaps. Given the ferment all around them, and the shifting demographic balance west of the Jordan River, those who consider themselves the Israelis' friends should help them to achieve peace while it might still be possible.

- Make a good-faith effort independent of the US Congress to address climate change, a problem whose mitigation only becomes more expensive as time goes by.

These are big steps for any Canadian government to take, but they would deliver dividends at home and lift Canada's standing internationally. And, thanks to Canadian voters and vote splits, the Harper government has a strong political hand to play. What remains is for the Canadian people to demand a foreign policy that enhances, not diminishes, them.

In my non-partisan career I have served as Prime Minister Brian Mulroney's chief foreign-policy adviser and speechwriter, and I have written foreign-policy speeches for Prime Minister Pierre Trudeau, Secretaries of State for External Affairs Mark MacGuigan and Joe Clark, and Ambassadors Allan Gotlieb and Derek Burney. As "political director" of the Department of Foreign Affairs and Trade, I have advised Lloyd Axworthy on Canada's human security agenda. I have served as Canada's political minister in our embassy in Washington, ambassador to Germany, and Permanent Representative to the UN in New York. The last assignment brought me into close contact with Foreign Minister John Manley and Prime Ministers Jean Chrétien and Paul Martin.

From inside Ottawa and on the diplomatic front lines I have seen what we, Canadians, are capable of doing when we have the vision, the self-confidence, and the will to make a difference. In the pages that follow I invite readers to agree with me that Canada can be, and should be, an effective and responsible global player, one that does not pine for a mythical golden age, one that acts, not just sits on the sidelines, one that can do good and well, both, in short, one that is not a superpower but is a super country.

PART I

THE CASE FOR CANADA

1

OPTIMISM BEATS PESSIMISM

It's not the size of the dog in the fight that matters;
it's the size of the fight in the dog.
—Mark Twain, General Dwight D. Eisenhower, and others

World affairs lend themselves naturally to pessimism, which often seems the more sensible attitude, especially in a time of global financial meltdowns, trade protectionism, climate change, weapons of mass destruction, failed states, psycho tyrants, refugee flows, international terrorism, drug gangs, global pandemics, and superbugs, not to forget lost jobs, personal bankruptcies and home repossessions, shrunken asset values, roller-coaster markets and bank crashes, and, not least, simple human folly. The cumulative negative effects of a twenty-four-hour news cycle and globalized news media magnify the pessimistic tendency. Bad news travels faster and further than ever, and is heard more often and by more people. Also, bad news trumps good news. One plane crashing at Pearson Airport will always be bigger news than 100,000 planes landing safely. Likewise, one bad recession obscures fifty years of economic progress.

Our steady diet of bad news masks the reality that we are living in the most peaceful, most prosperous, most healthy, and most promising time in history. The period since the end of the Korean "police action" of the early 1950s is the longest interval of uninterrupted peace among the major powers in hundreds of years. Further, the tide has ebbed on the eight long years of the unilateral-minded, military-oriented, national-security-obsessed administration of George W. Bush. The election of the cosmopolitan President Barack Obama signalled a floodtide of opportunity to address and alleviate, even solve, some of the world's more intractable problems, and to re-establish international law and co-operation as the basis for progress.

Pessimism might, therefore, be more compelling than optimism, but it is a terrible guide to policy making, public or private. Pessimism is a cousin to defeatism. If our European forebears had been pessimistic or defeatist or just realistic, they would never have risked ten weeks on the North Atlantic to get here, much less have decided to stay on through Canada's devastating winters. If the English and French of Canada, described by Lord Durham in 1839 as "two nations warring in the bosom of a single state" had been realistic, they would have given up on the entire Canadian enterprise and contented themselves with nursing their differences, letting their evident incompatibility abort the very idea of Canada. If the nascent Canadian state had been realistic in the 1860s, Canada might have folded at merely the thought of the mighty Union Army, the largest in the world following the American Civil War. Today, Ottawa would be an obscure logging town in northern New York State, and the British Columbia lower mainland, at least, would be part of the US West Coast. Later, if realism about Canada's colonial status within the British Empire had prevailed, Prime Minister Mackenzie King would have continued supplying young Canadian fodder for the British to feed to the cannons of the enemies of the empire, notably in the 1922 Chanak Crisis in Turkey.

If my parents' generation had decided to placate Nazism, rather than field a half-a-million-strong army to help fight the Nazis in Europe, we would live in a very different, much worse, world today. If my generation, facing a choice of "being Red or being dead," had been realistic, we might have found something to love about Communism. Instead, we helped the North Atlantic Treaty Organization (NATO) and the United States to contain the Soviet Union for forty dangerous years, until it collapsed under the weight of its own contradictions. More-contemporary generations would have shrunk from the rigours of trade liberalization and not even considered free trade with the United States, let alone with Mexico. Entrepreneurs like Jim Balsillie and Mike Lazaridis of Research in Motion (RIM) might have decided that it was folly to try to build a world-class business enterprise in Waterloo, Ontario. If I had been a realist, I would never have written the foreign service exam so many years ago.

Generations of Canadians throughout our history did not accept the limits inherent in pessimism or defeatism, much less realism. Instead, they created one of the most respected, prosperous, and successful states on earth. We are a compassionate, capable, and progressive people with every chance of doing good and doing well—both, if we want to.

Some deprecate our achievements, mourning a golden past, a time when Canada helped the world to create a system of global governance—the UN, NATO, the North American Aerospace Defense Command (NORAD), the World Bank, the International Monetary Fund (IMF), the General Agreement on Tariffs and Trade (GATT)—a major, comprehensive, institution-building enterprise of the 1940s and 1950s. The story of Canada's role in the creation of these global institutions has grown with the telling, and with it, the danger that our past achievements become less the shining legacy of an earlier generation and more an impossible standard for succeeding generations to match—not an indicator of promise so much as a reference point for decline. To make the "Golden Age" the gold standard of our diplomacy is to pre-program disappointment. Each generation has to be measured in its own context against the challenges of its own time. In the intervening years, we have performed strongly, most notably regarding the unification of Germany and international governance innovation, wielding influence that the architects of the "Golden Age" would have readily admired. In our self-deprecating way, we tend to downplay the impact we have made, which is greater than most Canadians recognize.

Paradoxically, we Canadians are also complacent. Our self-image as a UN peacekeeping nation is a couple of generations out of date; the peacekeeping monument we built in Ottawa is a tribute to a receding past, like European statues of otherwise forgotten generals. Even counting the exceptional performance of our troops in Afghanistan, we don't crack the top ten contributors to UN-authorized or UN-sanctioned military missions. We like to believe Canada is an environmental leader, but we rank seventh in the world in carbon gas emissions[1] and dead last among the major G8 economies in terms of reducing our CO_2 emissions.[2] We consider ourselves generous in helping the less fortunate, but we greatly overestimate the sums we donate—we currently rank fourteenth on the list of rich countries in terms of official assistance to poorer countries,[3] and falling. We regard ourselves as free traders, but that only applies to one side of our mouth—or, at least, one side of our country. With the other, we support supply management systems, which protect Quebec and Ontario milk and poultry producers from foreign competition, thereby paralyzing ourselves in trade negotiations, where we once truly played a leading role. Our government has come to equate leadership with just showing up, and to equate "declaring" with doing. Delusion is a poor base on which to build a foreign policy, and self-satisfaction never produces greatness. We risk becoming world class in complacency.

Yielding to any of these tendencies—pessimism, self-deprecation, and complacency—would condemn us to mediocrity and break faith with those who built the Canada we inherited. Some Canadians would give up any pretensions to a global foreign policy and concentrate Canadian effort and attention only on Washington. This is especially true as the border "thickens" and "hardens" into a real border, to paraphrase Janet Napolitano, US secretary of homeland security in the Obama administration, a consequence of the deep insecurity of an American nation longing for invulnerability. Get the US relationship right, our bilateralists argue, and everything else will take care of itself. If the United States is "the one indispensable country," as former US Secretary of State Madeleine Albright has said, and even some members of the Obama administration have echoed, by definition our contribution is dispensable. Should we not just look after our economic interests in Washington and leave the world to the Americans?

Others would look for a role everywhere *but* in Washington, seeking counterweights to American influence, condemning Canada in the process to the small ponds of international irrelevance. Both approaches would waste the potential that is evident everywhere around us and neither would respond adequately to the challenges and opportunities we face.

The experience of two world wars and sixty-five years of mostly successful diplomacy should have taught us three things. First, we can do a lot in the world if we want to. Second, the more we do in the world and the more effective we are at doing it, the more respect we get in Washington. Third, and conversely, the more respect we get in Washington, the more we can do abroad and the more effective we can be in pursuing our interests—both abroad and in Washington. A purposeful, independent foreign policy is a virtuous circle. Moreover, it is hugely in our interest to concern ourselves with the emerging multi-centric world and how it is to be managed. For a country our size, the more the rule of law governs international relations, the better off we will be. This is especially the case as American power recedes, at least relatively. If we are diplomatically savvy and agile, we can serve our own purposes, assist the Americans in the process, and make the world a better place to boot.

Living next to the United States is a challenge almost unique to Canadians, shared only in part by Mexico. A revealing contrast to Canada is Australia, a country with a parallel history to ours and comparable institutions and traditions, but located a long way from a giant, friendly neighbour. Australia's geography mandates self-reliance, which, in turn, produces disproportionate shares of (summer) Olympic medals and films. But it does not guarantee security. In Australia, therefore, the default instinct vis-à-vis the US has been to stick close to the Americans politically.

In Canada, by contrast, our security is greater, and our governments often stiff-arm Washington—sometimes rightly, but, also, sometimes stupidly. They do this despite the fact that the US has not only *not* threatened Canada with its vast power in over 150 years, but, with the important exceptions of one or two rogue administrations, has helped us ensure our prosperity and security, while taking the lead in the development of the liberal, progressive world order in which we thrive. Were it not for Bill Clinton's thumb on the scale, for instance, the 1995 Quebec referendum might have been lost. Most countries would trade places with Canada in a heartbeat, happy to live in a shadow, if that shadow was American and meant living as well as we do.

It is also true that, at times, Washington has been a problem for Canada. American foreign policy, at least until the arrival of the Obama administration, has been ever more militaristic and unilateralist. Further, as American cultural wars deepened and partisanship grew more ferocious, serious Americans began expressing alarm about the country's ability to govern itself. As well, getting Washington's attention on bilateral problems has been difficult at the best of times. Some have considered this a blessing, cautioning against ever becoming an object of American foreign policy. In fact, played intelligently, Canada's close proximity to the US remains an enormous asset for us, the "great recession" of the recent past notwithstanding. Propinquity is not a liability, nor is it an excuse for provincialism either, or a reason to put all of our eggs in the American basket. We will need to adapt to the very major changes in the international system that the "great recession" and the growth of other powers seem likely to induce.

Sir Wilfrid Laurier's galvanizing optimism notwithstanding, the twentieth century did not belong to Canada, and the twenty-first century won't either. The US had a better, and prior, claim on the twentieth century than we did, and it has a better claim on the twenty-first, too, as does Asia. But we *can* prosper and we *can* help make the world a better place in the decades to come, hokey as that might sound. Canada has never been richer or more able to afford an effective, responsible foreign policy than now. To succeed in the world, we need to know who we are and what we want; to understand the world and where it is going; to believe in ourselves and invest in our ideas; and, then, to seize the emerging day.

2

CANADA:
The Size of the Dog in the Fight

How do we rank internationally? Actually, we are a pretty big dog by most international standards, bigger than we often realize. Living next door to the US has accustomed us to thinking of Canada as little. Being the smallest of the G8 economically advanced countries discourages delusions of grandeur. But globally, as Einstein might have said, it's all relative. There are 192 members of the United Nations, and our population ranks us thirty-second,[1] not a contender compared to India or China, but larger than 160 other UN member states. According to Statistics Canada, our estimated population in 2010 was 34,019,000. If that seems small, it is worth reminding ourselves that it is approaching the size of the United Kingdom at the height of the British Empire.[2]

Further, we are an extensively educated people. Of the thirty-three most industrialized economies and "emerging countries" surveyed by the Organisation for Economic Co-operation and Development (OECD, the respected intergovernmental think-tank in Paris), Canada ranked second after Russia (Japan was third and the US fourth) in the percentage of the population that has attained at least a university- or college-level education. According to the OECD, countries with high graduation rates at this level are the most likely to develop a highly skilled labour force, which is essential to international competitiveness. That degree of educational attainment helps us to punch above our weight economically. In addition, while some call for a national strategy on post-secondary education so that we do not lose ground internationally, the quality of our education is, nevertheless, comparatively good. According to the British Times Higher Education survey, our universities rank well vis-à-vis their counterparts abroad: eleven are in the top 200,[3] which ties us with Japan and the Netherlands for third place in the world. Three of our universities—McGill, Toronto, and British Columbia—are in the top fifty (Australia does better than we do with six in the top fifty). While these rankings have their methodological critics, it is, nevertheless, a fact that a respected independent non-Canadian entity has ranked our universities strongly. We should accept the judgment and stop being so self-deprecatingly Canadian about it.

Our high schools are getting even better results. More than 400,000 students from fifty-seven countries, making up close to 90 percent of the world economy, took part in the Programme for International Student Assessment (PISA) in 2006. Canadian fifteen-year-olds stood third in science proficiency, fourth in reading proficiency, and seventh in math proficiency, ahead of their counterparts in all G8 countries.

Canada currently ranks fourth on the annual UN Development Program Index of Human Development. We stand ninth in life expectancy[4] and seventh in the degree of globalization[5] across a range of factors (e.g., trade and investment, political co-operation with others, and the flow of ideas and information). The US ranked twenty-seventh. The 2009 HSBC Bank International survey of expatriates working in the twenty-six main expat destinations outside of their home countries found that those surveyed ranked Canada first in terms of quality of life and ease of integration into the local community (although we were considerably down the list in terms of incomes).

Our economy is the eleventh largest in the world,[6] larger than that of 181 other countries. Even if the newly emerging economies—

China, India, and Brazil among others—fulfill expectations and grow as strongly as anticipated, Canada will still rank no worse than sixteenth out of 192 countries in 2050, but even then, in terms of income per capita, we will rank fifth.[7] Income per capita is a much better indicator of influence than aggregate gross domestic product (GDP) because the latter does not say much about dynamism or inventiveness. Large numbers of peasant farmers add to a country's GDP, but a well-educated population delivers a lot more usable influence.

We are in the top half-dozen or so of trading nations[8] and are ninth in terms of competitiveness.[9] We might not be an energy superpower, as Prime Minister Harper has claimed (power resides in being able to turn the tap off, as Russia has occasionally done with gas exports, not just turn it on—although we stopped uranium exports to India after they made nuclear weapons), but we do have enormous stores of natural resources. Large reserves of conventional and non-conventional oil and gas, coal, uranium, and hydro make Canada one of the world's largest producers of most types of energy, and one of largest energy exporters, according to the research of the International Energy Agency (IEA). We are the largest supplier of petroleum products, gas, electricity, and uranium to the US. We rank second among OECD countries in the total production of energy, and our estimated reserves of 179 billion barrels of oil—the majority from the oil sands—put us second only to Saudi Arabia.

We do have our shortcomings. Our expenditures on research and development (R&D),[10] especially business R&D, are chronically low and likely to worsen with the demise of NORTEL, once Canada's top research performer. The OECD and other surveys rank our national R&D expenditures as mediocre, below the average of the world's twenty-seven most advanced economies. The foreign-owned automobile industry in Canada performs little research in this country—which is perhaps the reason why no foreign company has figured out how to defrost front windshields on cars as effectively as back windows—and is nowhere to be found on rankings of top R&D performers in Canada (Magna is third).[11] We rank eleventh among OECD countries in terms of access to a home computer and twelfth in terms of exports of information and communications equipment, despite the world-beating performance of RIM in Waterloo. We rank below the OECD average in terms of patents registered at the major patent offices in the United States, the European Union, and Japan.[12] Productivity in Canada has long been a concern. (It was a feature of the Mulroney government's foreign-policy review that I helped to write in 1983.) Child poverty remains stubbornly high, and the resolution of First Nations' problems has defied federal governments' efforts going back many years. Still, while we obviously have a lot of work to do, our balance sheet remains impressive.

On top of all this, we have other strong points that are often overlooked. First, we speak two of the world's leading languages. The English language is to international communication what the US dollar is to international trade and finance. Where others have to learn English to conduct business abroad, our business leaders can work in their native tongue or, at least, in their second language. And French is widely spoken around the world, giving bilingual Canadians a further advantage. These advantages are also enjoyed by the many thousands of Canadians working abroad with civil society groups. The advantage also benefits our academics, whose publications reach a much wider audience than those of many of their foreign counterparts who write, for example, in Urdu or Turkish.

Our strength in the arts, especially literature and music, is a further facet of the Canadian reality. A list of only a few of the most read Canadian authors is a statement of our excellence, as well as a reflection of our bilingual and multicultural makeup. In recent years, the list would include Margaret Atwood, Neil Bissoondath, Roch Carrière, Austin Clarke, Mavis Gallant, Barbara Gowdy, Margaret Laurence, Yann Martel, Anne Michaels, Rohinton Mistry, Alice Munro, Michael Ondaatje, Jane Urquhart, and Guy Vanderhaeghe. These are authors whose appeal transcends Canada, and there are many others. They are read not just in their original English and French, but often in translation as well. As ambassador to Germany, I personally saw the very strong demand for the works of Canadian authors at the giant annual Frankfurt International Book Fair.

Canadian music has also generated uncounted prizewinners and singers, from Neil Young, Bryan Adams, Michael Bublé, Jon Vickers, and Ben Hepner, to Measha Brueggergosman, Diana Krall, k.d. lang, Céline Dion, Nelly Furtado, Avril Lavigne, and Shania Twain, to name only a few (a complete list would be very long). They are living, performing testimony to Canadian creativity. And let's not forget excellence in sports; the fourteen gold medals at the Vancouver 2010 winter Olympics are the most any country has ever won.

Few countries are better placed to thrive in the multi-centric, globalizing world to come. Our population comes from every corner of the globe.[13] Nearly 150 of the world's languages are spoken in Canada, including those of the major economies such as Cantonese, Mandarin, Hindi, Punjabi, Arabic, Urdu, Russian, German, Italian, Spanish, Portuguese, and Turkish (Statistics Canada). In Toronto, 46 percent of the population was born in another country, making Toronto probably the most cosmopolitan major city in the world. People from 169 countries now call the Greater Toronto Area (GTA) home. Almost 90,000 new immigrants move to the GTA every year. The ability of Canadians to speak so many languages and to understand the cultures they express is an enormous advantage to Canada in terms of understanding foreign cultures, improving international governance and doing business abroad. Employees of RIM, for example, speak Hindi, Punjabi, Gujarati and Marathi, Cantonese and Mandarin, and Spanish and Portuguese. We are in a better position to develop co-operative relations with emerging economies than are most other countries.

When it comes to understanding Americans, we have a further advantage—one that no one else has, including the Mexicans. Speaking the same language, watching the same television programs, reading the same press, having access to the same media—including social media—give us a perspective on the US that others, even Americans themselves, do not have. As the Canadian-born comedian and producer David Steinberg once observed, when Americans watch television, they just watch television. When Canadians watch television, they watch *American* television (at least a substantial part of the time), which gives them a perspective on the US at one remove, a view that reveals more of the forest and fewer of the trees. This provides Canadians with a capacity to "read" Americans that other nationalities do not have. It also helps to explain the prevalence and prominence of Canadian comedians in the US. That does not make every Canadian an expert on the US— probably not more than one Canadian in a thousand, to be generous, could accurately explain the US budget process. However, it does mean we have insights into the American character that are invaluable when developing our own policies in the world.

A further major advantage is that Canada is a mature democracy that delivers stability, the rule of law, and (mostly) good governance to its citizens. Although we think of ourselves as a young country, we have been in existence as a nation longer than 160 other members of the UN, and we rank among the handful of oldest continuous democracies. The instruments of the Canadian state, including the bank regulators, work effectively. As a result, when the 2009 monetary crisis laid waste to financial institutions around the world, our banking system came through largely unscathed.* In the US and Europe, banks failed left and right, but not in Canada.

At the same time, we are not so small that we can be ignored, nor so large, thanks in part to federalism, that we become muscle-bound or immobile. We are, to use a football metaphor from my old days with the Wilfrid Laurier University Golden Hawks, a corner-linebacker or a running back of a nation. Or, to continue the canine metaphor, we are undoubtedly not a Doberman, but we are not less than a Labrador.

---

* Canada has the soundest banking system of the 133 countries surveyed in the Global Competitiveness Report of the World Economic Forum, which runs the Davos meetings of world leaders. The US ranks 108th.

HARD POWER, SOFT POWER, AND SMART POWER

Militarily, although we tend to think of ourselves as small, we still rank thirteenth in the world in spending,[14] ahead of 179 other countries. Lieutenant General Andrew Leslie, former chief of the Land Staff, is quoted in *Vanguard* magazine as saying that the Canadian Army is "the best army in the world for its size," and that might well be true. Several years of increased expenditures on weaponry have considerably strengthened our military capability. We do not have nuclear weapons, having made the judgment at the end of the Manhattan Project in the 1940s that we were safer without them, but we certainly have the industrial and resource capabilities to produce them, in the, hopefully, remote chance that one day that would seem a good idea.

In his widely read and highly regarded essay in the autumn 1990 issue of *Foreign Policy*, Joe Nye of Harvard University, who has also served as the chairman of the US National Intelligence Council and Assistant Secretary of Defense for International Security Affairs in the Clinton administration, coined the term "soft power." It was an attempt to comprehensively explain the elements of power and influence. Soft power derives from the respect that societies generate for themselves by virtue of their success and their values. In the case of the US, it means, effectively, the influence the US derives from others reaching the conclusion that a given US policy or practice is worthy of emulation—or at least of co-operation. This is co-optive power, in contrast to coercive power. Soft power was, and is, not an alternative to hard power, but a complement to it; Nye was writing, after all, about the United States. Nye cited as evidence for his theory the observation of the late Ralf Dahrendorf, German-British sociologist, philosopher, and political scientist, that it is relevant in international relations that millions of people around the world would move to the US if they could. According to a poll conducted by Gallup from 2007–09 of over 75,000 people around the world in 148 countries who would like to migrate, the United States remains the most attractive destination.

Soft power is very much a Canadian asset, as well. The idea has, however, become hopelessly muddled in Canada, with the US often portrayed as standing for nasty hard power and Canada depicted as standing for nice soft power. In this confused light, the Americans are about coercion, gunboats, and boots on the ground, whereas Canada is all diplomacy, "blue helmets," and foreign aid. In fact, Canada has both soft power and, in certain circumstances (for example, arresting foreign fishing boats or fighting insurgents in Afghanistan), hard power too—just not as much as the US does. The proof is in Dahrendorf's observation about the US, which is similarly true for Canada: many millions of people around the world would come here every year if Canada would have them, and not just the world's "huddled masses," either. According to the same Gallup survey, Canada is more attractive than the US, or anywhere else, to better-educated people in every age group above the age of twenty-four. In a survey conducted by Ipsos Reid for the Historica-Dominion Institute in May 2010, 30 percent of Americans polled said they would move to Canada if they had the choice.

Soft power is genuine. When I was Canada's Permanent Representative to the UN, I invariably received a ready and respectful hearing in the Security Council and the General Assembly. Canada was one of a very few countries that was able to play a constructive role on the Council, even when we were not a member of it. For example, when the Bush administration tried to hobble the International Criminal Court and give itself a permanent exemption from the court's jurisdiction, I called for an open meeting of the Security Council to discuss the issue. Sixty countries answered that call, and in the subsequent Council debate they were almost unanimous in expressing views similar to our own. I also received a willing hearing and much encouragement around the UN—and privately even from American and British officials—when I proposed a compromise to avoid the Iraq War that would have, if accepted, saved the US and the UK, as well as the UN, much grief. It was not because of my blue eyes that I got these positive responses, but rather because of how Canada is, or was, perceived.

The term "soft power" has evolved since it was first used; the Obama administration now talks of "smart power," a term first coined by Professor Fen Hampson of Carleton University in Ottawa. In her confirmation hearing before the US Congress in January 2009, Secretary of State Hillary Clinton said:

> We must use what has been called "smart power," the full range of tools at our disposal—diplomatic, economic, military, political, legal and cultural—picking the right tool or combination of tools for each situation. With smart power, diplomacy will be the vanguard of our foreign policy.

The same can be said for Canada, if we have the imagination to see beyond the traditional constructs of policy.

This glance at our assets and strengths is enough to see that we have a good-sized dog in the fight. As the late President François Mittérrand once told Prime Minister Mulroney during a meeting I attended in Paris on the 200th anniversary of the French Republic, Canada is one of a handful of states that matter. We are hardly a "middle power," a term that once signified substantial authority and capacity, but now, sixty-five years after the term was first coined, means much less. It was one thing to be a middle power during the Golden Age, when there were a mere fifty-one member states of the UN. It is another thing when the number of states has risen to 192. We court irrelevance when we call ourselves a middle power these days.

HOW OTHERS SEE US AND WE SEE OURSELVES

To paraphrase the Scottish poet Robbie Burns, to see ourselves as others see us saves us from many a blunder. How do others see us? Having represented Canada abroad much of my adult life, I have come to realize that most of the rest of the world sees Canada very positively, if sometimes rather impressionistically, occasionally a bit generously, and, usually, at least somewhat retrospectively. National reputations are created cumulatively over time.

Canada in the Eyes of Americans

Obviously, how Americans see us is crucial. So, how do they see us? We have had our critics. Al Capone, the 1930s Chicago gangster, dismissed us with the comment, "I don't even know what street Canada is on." Former Secretary of State Dean Acheson* once famously called Canada "the stern daughter of the mother of God." An acerbic American diplomat once asked me, since Sweden had joined the European Union, whether Canada would apply for the job of world's mother-in-law. Successive administrations, but especially the Reagan administration, criticized us for free riding on defence. Pat Buchanan, a former Nixon speechwriter, conservative commentator, one-time Republican, and Reform Party candidate for President in the 2000 presidential election, coined the term "Soviet Canuckistan," in reference to our presumed socialist and un-American impulses. Further, we were far from being Washington's preferred ally during the George W. Bush administration's eight years in office—although in much of the world's eyes, that is a credit to us, not a debit.

As depicted by the cultural warriors on the Fox cable network, Canadians personify what Americans should never become. For the loony American right, we are too liberal, too welcoming of the world's huddled masses, insufficiently concerned about the world's clear and present dangers, ungrateful for American protection, keepers of a porous border, even harbourers of terrorists, and proponents of a socialized medicine that is dangerous to American health, or at least to American health maintenance organizations (HMOs). The cartoon show, *South Park,* captured the point ironically with the lyrics: "Blame Canada / They're not even a real country anyway."

Fox and *South Park* notwithstanding, when average Americans

---

*Acheson's mother was a Gooderham of the Canadian Gooderham and Worts Distillery family.

look northward at all, which is rare—usually only on those occasions when a US president pays a visit to Canada or the US health insurance lobby drags up a disgruntled Canadian or a misplaced premier to deprecate our health system—they mostly see us benignly, if obscurely. To many of the sons and daughters of the American Revolution, Canadians are artifacts of an earlier time, an American-like people inexplicably, and a little lamely, somehow still tied to the British Crown. We are somewhat distant cousins, a polite, self-effacing, boring version of their more assertive, adversarial selves. (How do the inventors of baseball and four-down football think they can get away with portraying the inventors of ice hockey and basketball as boring?)

More important than the name-calling is the bouquet President Barack Obama gave Canada during his first visit here: "I love this country and I think we could not have a better friend and ally." And CBC still occasionally plays the clip that begins with the president saying, "I think that Canada is one of the most impressive countries in the world." The quote continues:

> ...the way [Canada] has managed a diverse population, a
> migrant economy. You know, the natural beauty of
> Canada is extraordinary. Obviously there is enormous
> kinship between the United States and Canada, and the
> ties that bind our two countries together are things that
> are very important to us . . . in the midst of this
> enormous economic crisis, I think Canada has shown
> itself to be a pretty good manager of the financial system
> in the economy in ways that we haven't always been here
> in the United States.

There was, as well, the "postcard" from the Olympics sent to us by the distinguished anchorman, Tom Brokaw, in a six-minute segment on NBC, painting as favourable a picture of Canada as anyone could ask for, mentioning world-class cities, majestic scenery, good neighbourliness, and Canada's participation and losses in the Second World War and Afghanistan. Former president

Bill Clinton's public compliments to Canada at the World Economic Forum in Davos regarding Canadians' extraordinary response to the earthquake in Haiti undoubtedly added to our reputation. Canadian Chrystia Freeland, while she was the US managing editor of the *Financial Times*, extolled the virtues of the Canadian banking system to her readers. And Fareed Sakaria, noted author and respected CNN commentator on the best foreign-affairs show on television and also in *Newsweek*, praised us for our fiscal management. Such third-party endorsements by respected, credible public figures are literally invaluable. You can't buy publicity like that. And it does have an effect.

At about the same time as President Obama visited Ottawa, Gallup polled Americans on their attitude towards "some foreign countries." Fully 90 percent of Americans said they had a favourable attitude towards Canada, putting it at the top of the list as their most-favoured country. Great Britain came next at 89 percent, but the next country, Japan, was down nine percentage points at 80 percent. Gallup repeated the poll a year later, with identical results for Canada.

Both polls were taken before the Vancouver Olympics, although it is hard to see how the results could have been more flattering than they already were. The findings are consistent and very positive. Clearly, the coolness evident after Canada declined to support the US invasion of Iraq in 2003 has dissipated. According to a 2008 survey by the Chicago Council on Global Affairs, 53 percent of Americans rank Canada as "very important" to the US, second only to the UK in the world. If they all had known that we are the US's principal foreign supplier of energy, the numbers would probably have been even higher. Our standing has slipped recently, according to a BBC/GlobeScan poll in January 2010. Still, for most Americans, we are a pretty good neighbour, a good ally in Afghanistan—while we stay, a welcome supplier of energy, and a source of pharmaceutical drugs (and some other less legal substances).

Canada in the Wider World's Eyes

To the wider world, which views Canada from a more distant perspective than the Americans—and more impressionistically— Canadians are the other Americans, the fortunate citizens of one of the more prosperous countries on earth, bordering on one of the world's richest markets and strongest democracies, the inhabitants of a cold and frozen land. Voltaire, the French Enlightenment philosopher, dismissed Canada as a few acres of snow (philosophers are more known for perspicacity than imagination). Many in the Third World,* and even some in Europe, presume Canada is a junior partner in the overall US enterprise, not quite a distinct country. Once, when I was making the case for a compromise at the UN to forestall the catastrophe that the Iraq War was to become, an Egyptian diplomat, marvelling at Canada's independence and, by extension, my own, asked tongue in cheek if I knew which country I was representing. The Canadian decision to stay out of Iraq was, in fact, a landmark of Canadian foreign-policy independence and, although that was not the intention, brought us enormous respect from a world profoundly in disagreement with the Bush administration, much as our independence on Vietnam did a generation earlier.

In any case, my years at the UN in New York left me in no doubt that the world really does respect us for our prosperous, bilingual, multi-ethnic, law-abiding, cultivated, and compassionate society. The world sees that Canada values diversity and integrates foreigners into national life and purpose—not perfectly, but as well or better than anyone else. We are known as a country that tries, and mostly succeeds, to respect human rights and to protect minorities (although Muslims are likely revisiting that judgment), a country worthy of emulation, albeit one that ought to do better

---

*"Third World" is the term often used to denote the countries that were neither part of the West nor part of the Communist world during the Cold War. The term continues to be used as a convenient shorthand, although the countries of the Third World are scarcely homogeneous.

by its aboriginal population. We are recognized for a culture that generates remarkable excellence in literature, the arts, and science, and for an economy that delivers an enviable quality of life and a very high standard of living. Internationally, we are respected for our constructive, capable, compassionate, and—prior to the Harper government, at least—fair-minded approach to global affairs. We are considered to be capable and constructive in the conduct of our international relations, especially in multilateral diplomacy, and in our contribution to international security—or we were. Canada is regarded as having the capacity and, sometimes, the will to make a difference diplomatically and militarily. Former UN Secretary General Kofi Annan told the Canadian parliament on a visit in 2004 that Canada's "multicultural character and bilingual tradition give it special qualifications as an exemplary member of our organization."

While our reputational balance sheet is undoubtedly positive, the perceptions of the public do tend to lag behind reality. In the trenches of international diplomacy, changes are discerned long before they meet the public eye. This is the case for our largely unquestioning, pro-Israel stance on the Israeli-Palestinian conflict, our foot-dragging on climate change, our shift of emphasis and aid resources from Africa to Latin America, and our mishandling of Muslim Canadians, including Maher Arar, Abdullah Almalki, Ahmad Elmaati, Muayyed Nourredine, Abousfian Abdelrazik, and Omar Khadr, all of whom were abused, to say the least, by their captors, and all of whom were treated deficiently by successive Canadian governments. It has also not escaped international attention that we turned over detainees in Afghanistan to local authorities without adequately satisfying ourselves that they would not be tortured, a violation of our obligations under the laws of war and the Convention against Torture. Over time, these perceptions can be expected to temper the very positive views others hold of us, especially if our practices do not change. Nevertheless, the bottom line, for now, is that we continue to be strongly respected for what we have made of ourselves and for what we have done internationally.

In a poll published by WorldPublicOpinion.org in 2007, Canada was ranked first in terms of positive influence in the world, Japan was second, and the US was eighth. In the WorldPublicOpinion.org 2010 survey, we had slipped to fourth. In a 2009 Gallup International "Voice of the People" poll, Canada came out on top, again. Almost half of the people polled around the world had a positive opinion of Canada, and less than 10 percent had a negative opinion. Nevertheless, in a BBC/GlobeScan survey published in February 2010, our standing had diminished. According to GlobeScan, this was the first time in five years of tracking that Canada's image around the world had worsened, and they tended to attribute blame to the negative media coverage of Canada's policies on the environment. Clearly, when it comes to the environment, we have our critics. George Monbiot, a columnist for *The Guardian* newspaper in the UK, called Canada "a petro-state" and "the nation that has done most to sabotage a new climate change agreement." If you Google "Monbiot Canada," you get over 75,000 hits.[15] While some say there's no such thing as bad publicity, that kind of press cannot be good for Canada.

Canada in the Eyes of Canadians

Canada's home-grown critics on the Right criticize Canada for "sanctimony," "moralizing," "holier-than-thou preaching," "Boy Scout imperialism," "feel-good rather than do-good policies," and—the all-purpose putdown—"naiveté." Allan Gotlieb, my friend and much-revered boss at the Canadian embassy in Washington, called Canadian foreign policy "romantic," which he did not mean as a compliment.[16] Two former trade officials of the Department of Foreign Affairs and International Trade, Michael Hart and Bill Dymond, writing in *Policy Options* in 2004, argued that Canadian foreign policy was a Potemkin village, stuck in "a nostalgic time warp" over the past decade.[17] That decade coincides broadly with the time that Lloyd Axworthy was Canada's foreign minister; it appears to be Axworthy's human security agenda that elicited—and, in some cases, still elicits—such animus.

Why this agenda has so riled, and still roils, the Canadian

Right is not clear. The agenda included several priorities—the Ottawa Landmines Treaty, the creation of the International Criminal Court, the adoption by the UN General Assembly and Security Council of the norm the Responsibility to Protect, as well as a Security Council resolution calling for the protection of civilians in armed conflict—that could hardly be regarded as sanctimonious, romantic, or just feel-good. For example, over 150 states have acceded to the Ottawa anti-personnel landmines treaty; a total of 85 states have completed the destruction of their stockpiles (64 states had no stockpiles), collectively destroying 43 million anti-personnel mines. Some 3,200 square kilometres of land have been cleared of mines and other explosive remnants of war so farmers in affected countries can use their land again. Millions of limbs and lives have been spared as a result. Thirty-nine countries—including China, India, Russia, and the US—have yet to join the treaty, but most are in *de facto* compliance with its key provisions, and only thirteen countries still produce landmines. There has not been any trade in landmines between states confirmed since 1999.[18] The Ottawa Treaty has also spawned a small-arms treaty and a cluster-bomb treaty. Unless the Canadian Right just likes landmines and cluster bombs, it is hard to see what they are upset about. The same is true for the UN norm the Responsibility to Protect, which is aimed at preventing widespread loss of life when governments are unable, or unwilling, to protect their own citizens. This principle was endorsed at the 2005 UN Summit by over 150 heads of government and another forty representatives. In April 2006, it was unanimously endorsed by the Security Council. I suppose that makes the entire world, including the former Bush administration, naïve, "romantic," and anti-American.

The adjective "anti-American" is bandied about very readily by Canadian mini-cons and theocons, the Canadian derivatives of the American neocons. It offers a built-in rationalization for ignoring disagreement, indeed for pressing ahead no matter what others think. If you can characterize those who criticize some aspect or other of US foreign policy as anti-American, their views can be deprecated or dismissed accordingly.

What is labelled in Canada as anti-Americanism is sometimes, in reality, pro-Canadianism or Canadian nationalism. For some, the simple fact of not being pro-American is interpreted as being anti-American. By this yardstick, the United Empire Loyalists were the original anti-Americans, although they would likely have thought of themselves as pro-Empire. Anti-Americanism seems to be regarded by some as endemic in Canada, even inherent in our national character. Writing in *Behind the Headlines* in 1996, Professor Jack Granatstein observed, "Anti-Americanism has been found, at differing periods and in differing intensities, across the entire spectrum of Canadian politics and in all segments of Canadian life."[19] More recently, he was quoted in the *National Post* as saying, "Obama is in this honeymoon period, but anti-Americanism is there just waiting to flare up again." Michael Hart, author of *From Pride to Influence: Towards a New Canadian Foreign Policy*, wrote, "[the] attention of Canadians to foreign policy is modest and intermittent, and the susceptibility to anti-American notions remains strong."[20]

But what actually is "anti-Americanism?" There are various definitions, but I prefer the one given by two distinguished American academics, Peter Katzenstein and Robert Keohane,[21] who describe it as "a psychological tendency to hold negative views of the United States and of American society in general," that is, it is a kind of unreasoned prejudice. Undoubtedly, there are certain countries and elites, and some Canadians, who can legitimately be described as anti-American by this or any other definition. But the more important point to be made is that to hold a negative view of certain US policies is not only not psycho, but actually quite sane— even commendable. To disagree with the Bush administration on going to war in Iraq or to lament the excesses of the health-care debate in the US is not anti-Americanism. The "Blame Canada First" gang, our home-grown mini-cons and theocons, nevertheless continues to view disagreement with US policy as essentially anti-American. Now that the Democrats are in charge of the White House, they are probably recalibrating their position.

On the Canadian Left, Canada is regarded as capitalist and

exploitative, a willing tool for corporate America and corporate Canada, an exploiter, through globalization, of less-developed countries and a ready accomplice of American imperialism. Canada is also accused of humiliating others, being a country of ugly Canadians (politically, at least), and miserliness towards the world's poor. The Left also thinks Canada is naïve, but for different reasons than the Right does. The Left has tended to view the North American Free Trade Agreement (NAFTA) as a betrayal of Canada. Their influence has ebbed since Communism retreated and NAFTA turned out not to be the economic and political catastrophe they feared (hoped?) it would be.

What do mainstream Canadians think of Canada? Everyone will have his or her own views and experience, but my "read" is that Canadians are, actually, very internationally minded, feel strongly connected to the world abroad, and want their country to be a responsible, constructive, and effective international player. Many want to be directly involved personally in international affairs, a judgment backed up by polling and anecdotally by my students.

There are some research sources from which some helpful insights and inferences can be drawn about Canadian "internationalism." Statistics Canada's 2006 Census reported that 20 percent of the population of Canada (6,186,950 people) were born abroad. Seventy percent of those people settled in Toronto, Montreal, and Vancouver. About 2.5 million Canadians study, work, or are retired abroad. About 50 million Canadians travel abroad each year.[22] Almost 67 percent of Canadians have visited the US in the past five years, 73 percent have travelled outside of Canada and the US at least once in their lives, 34 percent have visited Europe, 22 percent have been to Mexico and the Caribbean, and 10 percent to Asia. Two-thirds of Canadians feel a personal connection to a country or region abroad. Four in ten Canadians have donated to organizations or causes that address issues in other countries (projected to total $7.3 billion annually), and one in five has given financial help to family or others they know abroad (estimated at $20 billion annually).[23] These amounts sent by individual Canadians abroad dwarf the $5 billion in official development assistance in

Canada's 2010 budget. These Canadians follow international news nearly as closely as they do Canadian news. The point to be made is that Canadians are a very international people.

According to a Pew Global Attitudes Survey in 2005, conducted near the nadir of President Bush's presidency, Canadians were the second-most pro-American of the sixteen countries polled, although clearly unhappy with Bush; Poland was a narrow first. Four years later, after Barack Obama was elected president, Canadian support for the US had climbed back to near pre-Bush levels, although certain others, notably the French, Germans, and Indians, had grown even more positive towards the US in the interim than we had. Various surveys place Canadians in the upper reaches of those countries polled on attitudes towards the US, towards the American people, and towards President Obama. On Obama, Canadians ranked fourth in the world, considerably higher than Americans themselves who answered the same question.

According to the Canadian market research firm, Strategic Counsel, 90 percent of Canadians believe that Canada is the best country in the world, a figure only somewhat higher than the 83 percent of Americans who accorded such approval to their country in a Gallup International poll in the summer of 2009. In a Canada's World poll, Canadians said they believed their country could make a positive difference in the world and they wanted it to do so, especially with regards to peace, hunger, the environment, and human rights.

At the same time, Canadians have a paradoxical tendency towards self-deprecation, perhaps a natural consequence of living in the shadow of the most powerful nation since time began. It is not encouraging to measure yourself against a neighbour with a population nine times greater than your own that outspends you 31:1 on national security (in fact, spends nearly as much as the rest of the world combined on its military), that has won about 40 percent of the Nobel prizes ever awarded, whose universities continue to set international standards for excellence, whose culture is pervasive, whose market absorbs 78 percent of your exports, and provides nearly 60 percent of inward direct investment into your economy—in short, whose soft and hard power are literally without peer in the world, even after the "great recession." Thinking small in these circumstances is not surprising. But it is not smart.

Canada is not a budding superpower, but we are also not the "Little Canada" that Prime Minister Chrétien sometimes seemed to suggest, nor the quite dispensable country that Prime Minister Harper seems to believe. We invariably get a respectful hearing in the UN Security Council, the IMF, NATO, the G8, and the G20, for both who we are and what we do. Canada is one of the biggest, most bountiful, and most beautiful countries on earth. Our democracy is one of the oldest and most mature on the planet. Our arts are prolific; our writers are especially widely celebrated. Our economy is one of the richest, with disproportionately abundant resources, and our financial system is, perhaps, the soundest that exists. Our daily lives are enriched by immigrants from literally every other national culture extant. We have learned to value difference and harness diversity as well, or better, than any other country in the world. We are admired for our respect of minorities and for our integration of newcomers. And, despite legitimate criticism of our policies of late, our natural environment is still the envy of most. All of these attributes make us one of a small number of countries that can make a considerable difference, especially in the multi-centric world that is emerging.

The challenge for Canadians, as they put the noise on the Left and the Right out of their minds, is to hit the golden mean. That means recognizing that Canada does have the influence, the assets, and the skills to succeed in the world and make a positive difference. It means manifesting a reasoned confidence in Canada, while not slipping into complacency. Finally, it means, above all, exercising the will to act.

PART II

"THE PAST IS PROLOGUE"

—Shakespeare, *The Tempest*, and title of the memoirs of The Rt. Hon
Vincent Massey, first Canadian-born Governor General of Canada

Making intelligent foreign-policy choices starts with reminding ourselves not only of who we are, but where we came from, and understanding the factors and forces shaping our evolving world. Although Canada has been independent since 1867, it was only at the end of the First World War that we effectively took responsibility for our international affairs. Today's and tomorrow's foreign policy has its roots in Prime Minister Borden's insistence on a separate identity for Canada at the peace talks that ended the First World War, and in Prime Minister King's consolidation of that independence following that war. With the outbreak of the Second World War, we found ourselves once again expected both to give enormously of our blood and treasure, and meekly to accept the wisdom of our "betters" in their conduct of the war and the shaping of the peace. It was really only with the end of the Second World War, in an extraordinarily successful period of Canadian diplomacy under the leadership of Lester B. Pearson that came to be called in Canada "the Golden Age," that we found the diplomatic confidence and ambition to employ our considerable assets and pursue our interests in the wider world with vision and purpose. Successive Canadian prime ministers built on the legacy of Borden, King, and Pearson and the Golden Age to expand our policy independence, to develop our capacity to generate ideas, to contribute constructively to world affairs, and to raise our standing abroad, thus allowing us to become one of a few countries that can, and often does, make a positive difference, setting the stage for tomorrow's foreign policy. The following chapters will discuss what these prime ministers did and how they did it.

3

A FOREIGN POLICY OF OUR OWN

Canada got nothing out of the war except recognition.
—Robert Borden, *Dictionary of Canadian Biography Online*

It is what we prevent, rather than what we do,
that counts most in government.
—William Lyon Mackenzie King, *First Among Equals:*
The Prime Minister in Canadian Life and Politics

Canadian independence was earned in the trenches of Passchendaele, at Vimy Ridge, and in all of the other bloody battles that Canadians fought in the First World War, and it was progressively asserted in the negotiation of the peace to end the war that had taken so many Canadian lives. Prime Minister Robert Borden saw it as his duty to achieve autonomy for Canada and recognition of Canada's right to sign the Treaty of Versailles, to have full membership in the League of Nations, to play a leading role in development of the nascent Commonwealth, and to pursue its own external policy. In his own words, "Canada got nothing out of the war except recognition."[1] It was more than enough.

Prime Minister Mackenzie King consolidated and expanded those gains by withstanding British pressure in 1922 to send

Canadian troops to Çanakkale, Turkey, to fight resurgent Turkish nationalists,* asserting that the Canadian parliament, not Whitehall, would decide where Canadians fought; by signing Canada's first international treaty, the Halibut Treaty, independently of the UK; and by helping to draft the Balfour Declaration of 1926, which recognized the Dominion of Canada and other dominions as "equal in status [with the UK], in no way subordinate to one another in any aspect of their domestic or external affairs," thus effectively recognizing Canada's sovereign independence. This independence was codified formally in 1931 in the Statute of Westminster.

While developing Canadian independence, King feared being drawn into international commitments, which is not surprising given the scale of Canadian losses in the carnage of the First World War, the national unity divisions that conscription had generated, and the nascent quality of the young dominion. King distrusted the League of Nations and did not want to get involved. He did little to make the institution work and, in fact, took positions that contributed to it not working—notably in opposing sanctions on Italy when the latter attacked Abyssinia. Like Wilfrid Laurier, he sought the least harm and disruption to Canada's internal order. Nonetheless, King knew from about 1936 onwards that war was more likely than not, and that it would involve Canada.

When war became inevitable, the King government underlined Canada's formal independence by declaring war separately, a week later than the British did. As in 1922, the point was made that it was the Canadian parliament that would decide when Canada went to war. Nevertheless, that Canada would support the British against the Germans was never in doubt.

Seen from today's perspective, that support was pretty much a one-way street. The British and the Americans, whose war efforts

---

*The "Chanak Crisis." After defeating occupying Greek forces in Asia Minor, Turkish nationalist forces threatened the British occupation of the Dardanelles and Istanbul. The British called for Commonwealth troops to help against the Turks.

greatly outstripped Canada's, immense as ours were, saw little need for Canada to be at the table when they were developing the Allied strategy for prosecuting and concluding the Second World War, both in Europe and in the Pacific, and conceiving of post-war institutions. King considered himself to be close to Washington, and was described by Roosevelt as a personal friend. Nevertheless, King was on the outside looking in at war planning conferences, even at the two that Roosevelt and Churchill held in Quebec City in 1943 and 1944. King's polite request for the Canadian military to be present at those particular meetings, at which the British and the Americans discussed matters likely to implicate Canadian forces in combat, was rebuffed by Roosevelt on the grounds that the Brazilians, Chinese, and Mexicans, as well as other Commonwealth countries, would expect similar treatment, which would complicate and delay decision-making (see page 48).[2]

Roosevelt indicated he would prefer meeting with Churchill alone in Bermuda to having Canadians present at the meetings in Quebec. It did not seem to occur to Roosevelt, or fully to Churchill, who was comfortable speaking on behalf of an empire that, by that point, scarcely existed, that Canada was in a different category from the other countries, supplying well over a million personnel to the war effort, training vast numbers of Allied airmen, providing enormous economic support to Britain, and playing an indispensable role in protecting Allied shipping in the North Atlantic. Nor did our allies acknowledge that Canada was to play an important part in the conflict in Italy and the liberation of northern France and the Netherlands, and, ultimately, to occupy northern Germany. The other countries whose sensitivities so worried Roosevelt could make no comparable claim.

Canada's marginalization was partly our own fault, of course. King diffidently remained outside the meeting rooms, absent from substantive discussions, despite the fact that the meetings affected our interests and went on for weeks on Canadian soil. King's assessment was that the big decisions would be made by those with the big battalions.[3] King had little expectation of influencing the outcomes, and keeping clear of

Referring to your Number 377 of 23 July,[2] I cannot look with favor on the attendance of Canadian Staff officers at plenary meetings of the Combined Chiefs of Staff during the QUADRANT Conference for the following reasons:

(1) Inclusion of the Canadian Staff in "QUADRANT" will almost certainly result in an immediate demand from Brazil and China for membership on the Combined Staff in Washington.

(2) It will probably result in a similar demand from Mexico, our neighbor on the southern border, as Canada is on the northern border.

(3) We have until now succeeded in preventing the deterioration of our Combined Chiefs of Staff in Washington into a debating society by refusing membership to representatives of other Allied Nations.

(4) It appears certain that inclusion of Canada in "QUADRANT" with its unavoidable attendant publicity would make it extremely difficult, if not impossible, to exclude from the Combined Chiefs of Staff representatives of the other Dominions and the other Allied Nations.

I had a long talk with Leighton McCarthy yesterday and he went to Ottawa last night to explain the whole thing to Mackenzie King, who will, I think, understand. As you know, Mackenzie King is one of my oldest personal friends.

Rather than face the difficulties that would follow admitting the Canadian Staff to "QUADRANT" I would prefer to have the meeting elsevwhere say Bermuda.

The 17th is the earliest day I can make it, so let us decide on that.

ROOSEVELT

---

[2] *Supra.*

Roosevelt Papers: Telegram

Prime Minister Churchll to President Roosevelt [1]

MOST SECRET   LONDON, 25 July 1943.

878. Former Naval Person to President personal and most secret.

1. Operation QUADRANT. As Colonel Warden (see my immediately following) is going by the same method as last time,[2] he will have to arrive at "ABRAHAM" during the 10th and will await you there. I should be glad to know if your delay till the 17th means that you are cline to meet UJ. If this is so and you are not taking your staff with you, it has occurred to me that perhaps these might come to "ABRAHAM" a few days earlier so as to begin the discussions, which are always lengthy, with their opposite number. On military grounds, we are very anxious that the staffs should be in contact as soon as possible.

---

[1] Sent by the United States Military Attache, London, via Army channels.

[2] i.e., on the Queen Mary.

the top-level policymaking meant he could avoid being blamed if things went badly wrong. No one appears to have made the case effectively for a greater executive role for Canada until very late in the war.

King apparently contented himself with performing mostly protocol functions and participating in occasional tripartite, largely social, meals. King "dismissed the substance of influence abroad as a will-o'-the-wisp; far better ... to enjoy the appearance of influence, posing happily for the photographers at the Quebec Conference beside American President Franklin Roosevelt and British Prime Minister Churchill. Only King and his closest staff knew that the Canadians then left the scene."[4] With that sort of "leadership," it is not surprising that Canada did not get the credit it was due in the Second World War and its aftermath.

It was not only the British and Americans who ignored our contribution—subsequent French governments did so as well. While I was on a posting in Paris during the 1970s, I took my visiting mother around the City of Lights to see the sights, including to the Musée de l'Armée at les Invalides—with unexpected results. I can remember clearly my mother's very rare, tearful anger on leaving the museum, when she realized that the Canadian war effort in Normandy, a campaign in which she had lost friends and relatives, was not even mentioned in an extensive treatment of the subject. The people of Normandy were, fortunately, both more conscious of the sacrifices Canadians made in 1944 and more appreciative than their Parisian compatriots.

The Quebec conferences were not, alas, to be the only occasion on which Canada was expected to defer to its "betters." In fact, "great power" dominance was to remain the norm after the war, even if the power, specifically Britain's power, was not so great anymore and depended on the acquiescence and support of the Commonwealth. This is to say nothing of France's power at the time, which was non-existent.

The Americans, especially, and to a lesser extent the British, were loathe to share power, as were the Russians and even the Nationalist Chinese, even in cases where it should have been a "no-brainer" that Canada should have had a major leading part. Perhaps the most egregious case was the resistance against Canadian membership on the executive council of the UN Relief and Rehabilitation Administration, to which Canada was one of the largest contributors, second only to the US.[5] Canadian officials, including Lester B. Pearson (who was then at our embassy in the US), had to make the case, repeatedly, in Washington and London that Canada merited inclusion on the executive councils of such specialized agencies and boards by virtue of the size of its contribution. By war's end, Canadian officials were included in these organizations in one capacity or other, but not with the authority in proportion to the contribution expected of us. The norms and practices of international relations had not changed greatly.

After the war, the "great powers" continued to dominate, and Canada had to fight for influence. We still do. No one hands Canada our status on a plate. Too much of my diplomatic career involved pushing myself into rooms that our "betters" preferred Canada stay out of. For example, when a "contact group," comprising the US, the UK, France, Italy, and Russia, was established to run the diplomacy of the Kosovo War, all G8 members except Canada and Japan were included (the Japanese were expected just to help pay the bills as they had done in the Gulf War). We were the only two excluded. The first meeting of the group was held in Germany, and, as ambassador there at the time, I insisted on a place for Canada on the grounds that we had been part of the defence of Germany for the previous forty years at a very substantial cost, and our dedication to European security was evident in the cemeteries across Europe where Canadian soldiers lay buried. Probably out of embarrassment, the Germans reluctantly agreed. Ironically, Ottawa decided, for whatever reason—perhaps so that it could, King-like, avoid any heavy lifting if that became necessary—not to exploit this opening after attending the first meeting.

Ultimately, it was Russian officials who made it possible for Canada to be at the table when the Kosovo War was settled. They shrewdly decided to use the G8 framework to negotiate on Kosovo, recognizing that G8 membership mattered more to President Yeltsin than the Milosevic government did (not all Russian officials agreed), and that they needed a deal by the next G8 summit if they were going to remain part of the club.

4

FROM THE GOLDEN AGE TO THE MODERN AGE:
Lessons Learned

Prime ministers make foreign policy. To be sure, they do so on the advice of their cabinets, ministers of international portfolios, caucus, senior officials, international peers, pollsters, barbers, chauffeurs, donors, spouses, issue-specific lobbies, the media— especially the newspapers—and whoever talked to them last, not necessarily in that order. The history of our foreign policy is the history of their international successes and failures. Undoubtedly, their foreign ministers were more than accessories—most of them anyway—and many made their own marks on history, none more so than "Mike" Pearson, who was recognized with a Nobel Prize for his exceptional contribution. If there had been any justice, Lloyd Axworthy would have shared in the Nobel Peace Prize awarded to non-governmental organizations (NGOS) for the Ottawa Treaty, the anti-personnel landmines treaty, because without him, there would likely not have been a treaty. Other ministers also made significant contributions to the development of our policy and to the creation of our international reputation for constructive internationalism. But all of the ministers would likely agree that the support of their prime ministers for what they did was indispensable, and the influence their bosses had in the world was determinant. To help us navigate the changing world of the twenty-first century, we need to revisit the experiences of our leading prime ministers and mine their records for lessons we should learn for the times ahead.

"MIKE" PEARSON AND THE GOLDEN AGE

To sit in a back seat at the UN, acquiescent or critical, but in either case silent, was certainly not a policy.
—Lester B. Pearson, *Mike, Volume II*

With the experience and carnage of the Second World War still vivid in their minds, and notwithstanding the reticence of Prime Minister King, Louis St. Laurent, then secretary of state for external affairs and later prime minister, along with his talented officials, decided to take a hand in the building of the new international order.* This was a 180-degree turn in policy. According to Mike Pearson's memoirs,[1] King was uneasy about Canada taking so much responsibility for the building of the new international structure at the United Nations. "This was none of our business," thought Mr. King. But Pearson and St. Laurent pressed on because

> Canadian public opinion had come to realize that since
> Canada could not escape the effects of international
> storms by burying [its] head in the sand, [it] should play
> a part in trying to prevent the storms by accepting
> international commitments for that purpose.[2]

---

* The department was founded as the Department of External Affairs and later became the Department of External Affairs and International Trade. The department's name was changed to the Department of Foreign Affairs and International Trade in 1993, and formalized by an Act of Parliament in 1995. To simplify, I may sometimes refer to the department as Foreign Affairs, regardless of the era under discussion.

Pearson's words are as true now as they were then, arguably even more so. Active, effective engagement with the emerging multi-centric world is manifestly important if the world is to be run in a way that serves—or, at least, does not undermine and defeat—our interests.

In what was to become regarded as the (first) "Golden Age" of Canadian diplomacy, a time when Canada had relative economic strength, comparative military weight (ranking fourth in the world at the end of the Second World War), and, equally important, plenty of ideas, vision, and will, Canada engaged constructively in Washington, New York, London, and other key capitals. St. Laurent deployed his exceptionally capable corps of diplomats and senior officials to help change the world. And help change it they did—aggressively, imaginatively, and in the Canadian interest.

Canada helped to breathe life into the nascent United Nations and to create NATO, the IMF, the World Bank, the Colombo Plan (the first development assistance program, for former British colonies), the International Civil Aviation Organization (ICAO), and the GATT, which in later years became the World Trade Organization (WTO).

Not every initiative we undertook worked. In the lead-up to the Dumbarton Oaks and San Francisco conferences on the creation of the United Nations, Canadian representatives worked hard, but ultimately in vain, to persuade the four (soon thereafter to be five when France was added) major powers, and others, to acknowledge the contributions of the middle powers. At the UN, Canadian representatives developed the "middle power" theory. This theory held that, just as the great powers had to be recognized as such, so too did countries such as Canada, Australia, and India, which were markedly more powerful than, for example, Haiti, Iceland, and Lebanon, need to be recognized. Much was expected of the former who should, therefore, be accorded rights commensurate with the responsibilities they would inevitably be asked to bear. Further, the capacity of the middle powers at the time was, in some cases, not so far removed from that of the great powers.

With respect to Security Council participation, Canada

pressed the argument that the middle powers should make up a separate category of membership, in recognition of their large contribution to preserving the peace. The British, Americans, Russians, and Chinese had already awarded themselves permanent seats, with vetoes. The Russians and the Americans had made it clear that otherwise there would be no United Nations. They would not allow themselves to be outvoted on matters of war and peace.

In the end, the middle power idea did not fly, partly because the great powers did not want any false gods before them, and partly because of the difficulty of establishing acceptable criteria for determining which countries would qualify. Ironically, current efforts at reforming the UN Security Council aim at creating a new tier of permanent members, without vetoes. These would be middle powers in all but name, just as Canada conceived the idea long ago.

Regrettably, however, today this new tier might not include Canada because of the population size of the emerging countries, the need for more equitable geographic representation on the Council (there are presently no Latin American or African permanent members and only one Asian), and the fact that, in recent years, the efforts Canadian governments have invested to make the UN work have been inadequate. The contrast with the United Kingdom, which wants to retain its permanent seat, is instructive. The British play a leading role in UN affairs, making themselves indispensable—or at least too useful to do without. In contrast, in recent years Canada has been content to follow the lead of American neocons and to sit in judgment of the UN.

Canada had better results on a second idea it put forward. Hume Wrong, an ill-named person if there ever was one, was one of the brilliant cadre of public servants of the Golden Age who articulated "functionalism"—a second philosophy of international relations—in an attempt to codify and consolidate Canadian influence and responsibility in world affairs. Functionalism held that capacity, contribution, and expertise on an issue-by-issue basis, not just great-power status, should determine leadership and responsibility. It differentiated international power in a manner that was both realistic and equitable. On issues in which a nation had a major interest or was making a significant contribution or had special capacity, that nation should be accorded commensurate responsibility and influence.

The persuasiveness of this Canadian idea is evident in the eventual wording of Article 23 of the UN Charter, which establishes the essential qualifications required for membership in the Security Council. It states that, in choosing non-permanent members, due regard should "specially be paid, in the first instance, to the contribution of Members of the United Nations to the maintenance of international peace and security and to the other purposes of the Organization, and also to equitable geographical distribution." The geographic clause was added as a gesture to Brazil, among others. It was left up to the members of the General Assembly to decide who filled the bill.

Canadian influence was evident in other articles of the Charter, notably Article 44, which directs that member states be invited "to participate in the decisions of the Security Council concerning the employment of contingents of that Member's armed forces." One imagines that this was a lesson learned when Canada was excluded from decisions affecting its military at the Quebec conferences. The Security Council does not, in practice, compel other member countries to provide troops for missions these days, but the five permanent members (P5) still make decisions involving the troops of other members without consulting them. In 2000, India and Jordan pulled out of the Sierra Leone operation when the Council added a more dangerous task to their mandate without consulting them.

There were many other accomplishments during the Golden Age. At the Bretton Woods financial conference in 1944, British and American policymakers were the clear leaders of the negotiations, the "G2" of that era. However, Canadian officials, headed by Louis Rasminsky, later governor of the Bank of Canada, played central roles in the development of a new monetary system, brokering between the Americans and the British.[3] (Our finance ministers and Bank of Canada governors, who preside over one of the soundest financial systems in the world, are still regularly consulted by their British and American counterparts.) The International Civil Aviation Organization was established in Montreal, in large part because of the work of the diplomat Escott Reid. In the same year, another Canadian diplomat, Dana Wilgress, played a leading role in the creation of the GATT. On human rights, Canadian John Humphrey, a professor from McGill, is credited with writing the first draft of the UN Declaration on Human Rights, which was adopted in 1948 and laid the foundation for today's considerable international human rights architecture. Typically, Humphrey didn't get credit for doing so until long after his death. In 1950, the Colombo Plan was adopted. It was Canada's first major commitment to assist developing countries, and Pearson was one of its architects. In due course came the midwifery of Paul Martin Sr., bringing former British and French colonies into the UN in 1955 and paving the way for the universality of membership that is integral to the UN's continuing legitimacy.

Influential in Washington; Influential in the World

Canadian diplomacy, often personified—or, at least, fronted—by Pearson, enjoyed many successes in the UN. In testimony to his strong relations with the British and Americans, and the respect in which he was held in both capitals, Pearson was twice nominated to be UN secretary-general (and twice vetoed by the Russians). In 1952, he became the only Canadian ever elected to the presidency of the General Assembly and, of course, he led the effort to shut down the war initiated by the British, French, and Israelis against Egypt over the latter's nationalization of the Suez Canal. Pearson's success in doing so earned him the Nobel Peace Prize.

The United Nations was not our only focus. Canadian diplomats of the Golden Age were among the first to recognize the dangers posed by the resurgent Soviet Union, and the inability of the UN to offer adequate protection against them. Their solution was the creation of a collective defence alliance, NATO, of which Canada was a leading promoter. Convinced that the struggle with the Soviet Union and Communism was going to be as much about ideas as armies, the Canadians insisted that NATO should be more than a military alliance. They succeeded in inserting into the founding treaty Article 11, known as "the Canadian article." This promoted political, economic, and social co-operation among members in order to diminish the appeal of Communism to the war-ravaged survivors of Western Europe, especially in France and Italy, where Communist parties were strong. It was also evident that the government in Ottawa wanted the clause in order to show Quebecers that there was more to NATO than military commitments and the danger of another bloody European entanglement. It was in recognition of the effectiveness of Canadian diplomacy generally, the role Canada played in the creation of NATO, and the relations Pearson himself had developed with Washington and London, that he was offered the post of NATO secretary general, which he declined in order to pursue his domestic prospects.

The underlying point is that, against the background of the reticence of the King era, Canadians took a creative, direct, and effective hand in defining what NATO was to become (at one point the Americans wanted to do no more than issue security assurances to the Europeans, rather than create an alliance vis-à-vis the Soviets). Further, we persuaded Washington and the entire NATO alliance to endorse a central Canadian objective. We had come a long way from the Quebec conference in 1943. Pearson himself described Ottawa's success in promoting a new NATO as an important chapter in the history of Canadian diplomacy.

Canadian diplomats, although not achieving all that they wanted, left significant fingerprints on the most remarkably creative period of international governance the world has ever known. People around the world had come to agree that states would govern themselves co-operatively and multilaterally, insofar as possible. This created the conditions for Canada to exercise influence virtually across the diplomatic board on issues such as security, politics, economics, human rights, and international law.

Not everyone recognized our influence. In *An Act of Creation* (Westview Press, 2003), an examination of the establishment of the UN, noted US historian Stephen Schlesinger made no reference at all to the impact of St. Laurent or Pearson, or even Canada. He drew on sources that appear to be heavily, perhaps excessively, American, which might be part of the explanation. Margaret MacMillan's *Paris 1919* would have been a very different book, and much less illuminating, if she had used principally American (or Canadian or British or German) sources to develop her understanding of the times. Nevertheless, to one distinguished American historian, at least, Canada's influence was invisible. Some Canadian scholars (for example, Adam Chapnick in *The Middle Power Project: Canada and the Founding of the United Nations*, UBC Press, 2005) point out that in the Golden Age, mistakes were made and opportunities were missed. Nevertheless, considering the standing start Canada made in 1943, it seems fair to conclude that the Golden Age may have had silver and bronze undertones, but it was golden nonetheless.

The Golden Age was a period of extraordinary accomplishment by an exceptional group of Canadians who registered the fact of our nationhood and its significance in the diplomatic congresses of San Francisco and New York and in the chanceries of Washington, especially, and of London, Moscow, and Paris. The times demanded creativity and ambition, and Pearson and his colleagues provided both, helping to build a new system of global governance from the ground up, and making a difference still felt today. Pearson's Nobel Peace Prize symbolized the excellence and creativity of Canadian diplomacy, a chapter of our history of which Canadians are rightly proud. His legacy was still perceptible forty years later when I became Canada's Permanent Representative to the UN in New York.

The years from 1943 to 1957 were an extraordinarily productive time for Canadian diplomacy. It was all the more remarkable for having begun from that standing start. To quote Pearson, "We had come of age. The voice of Canada was now being heard and it was listened to seriously and with respect during those years." [4]

The Importance of an Independent Foreign Policy

On coming to prime ministerial office in 1963, following the tumultuous Diefenbaker years during which Canada-US relations deteriorated markedly, Pearson re-established co-operative links with Washington. Following President Kennedy's death, however, as the war in Vietnam consumed the Johnson administration and opposition to the war grew in Canada as well as in the US, relations between Ottawa and Washington slid back into a state of disappointment, distrust, and disagreement. (One major bright spot was the conclusion, in January 1965, of the Auto Pact, the agreement that facilitated the rationalization and integration of the auto industries on both sides of the border.)

Beyond performing a few diplomatic probes of North Vietnam on Washington's behalf, the Pearson government kept Canada out of the Vietnam War, a sound judgment that others, notably Australia, did not make. It was also an extraordinary exercise of independence. (Forty years later, that precedent was very much in my mind when I advised the Chrétien government to decline the American invitation to join in its attack on Iraq.)

Relations between Pearson and Johnson effectively ended in April 1965, when Pearson used an American venue, Temple University, to call for a pause in the US bombing of North Vietnam, challenging publicly, and on American soil, the direction of American policy on the most sensitive issue of the age. It was a modest challenge, but in Johnson's Washington at the time, any dissent was unwelcome in the extreme. Pearson's subsequent meeting with Johnson, in which Johnson accused Pearson of "pissing on his rug,"[5] has a prominent place in Canadian diplomatic history—and, indeed, in the international annals of diplomatic practice. As Andrew Cohen observed in his biography of Pearson,[6] his reputation derives from almost three decades of statecraft in forums large and small. About Pearson, Sonny Reston of the *New York Times* wrote, "Some Britons have accused him of being too pro-United States, and some Americans have said he is too pro-British. The truth is he is thoroughly pro-Canadian."[7] A fitting epitaph.

Pearson and his Nobel Peace Prize inspired an entire generation of young Canadians to join the public service, including me. I wanted to be part of a team that could do the kind of great things he had done. In fact, that is the answer I gave my interviewers, Gordon Osbaldeston, who went on to become Clerk of the Privy Council under Trudeau, and Jim Nutt, who was to become ambassador to NATO, when they asked why I wanted to join the foreign service. I must have been convincing. The fact that they were football fans and I was a university football player also probably helped. Fortunately for me, they were not opera buffs instead.

I had written the foreign service exam after football practice one October evening because it was raining too hard to go home, and I realized I was going to need a job if I didn't make it as a professional football player. I was an accidental diplomat; it took me a long time to consider myself part of that extraordinary group. I was not the only one who wondered if I belonged. In fact, my first boss thought me so manifestly unsuited to the profession that he called me in to tell me I should find another job. It probably had not helped that I used to lock my office door in the afternoons and take naps on my desk after late nights out with the departmental hockey team, or that I was suspended from the civil service hockey league for fighting, definitely conduct unbecoming an officer in Canada's diplomatic corps. "There are many honourable professions," he told me, "and you should find one." It was a real morale booster. Far from home, twenty-two years old, a football career passed up, and having no other job, I carried on.

All Things Considered

All good things come to an end, including the Golden Age. Institutions need only be constructed once. By the time the Liberal Party was defeated in the 1957 election, the period of post-war institution building was largely over, and the focus of diplomacy had shifted from the exciting challenges of creation to the workaday jobs of implementation. In the decades that followed the Golden Age, Canadian diplomacy did not sleep. It registered important achievements that Pearson and his colleagues would appreciate and respect.

There are many lessons to learn from Pearson's time as prime minister, but two in particular stand out for me. The first is that the two great arenas for Canadian foreign policy—the world, which in Pearson's day especially meant multilateral organizations and, particularly, the UN, and Washington—are reciprocally linked. Success in one facilitates success in the other. The inverse is also true; failure begets failure. Few Canadian leaders have had the influence in Washington and the world that Pearson did.

The second lesson is that it is not fatal to disagree with Washington on a major issue, in Pearson's case the Vietnam War. We always have a choice. The issue for Canada is not choice, but price—whether we are prepared to pay the costs of independence. The corollary is that the cost of disagreeing on a matter of principle has proven invariably affordable and of short duration, especially when the American position has turned out to be wrong.

It is testimony to Pearson's greatness that twenty-eight eminent Canadian historians and thinkers, assembled in 2003 by the Institute for Research in Public Policy and its publication *Policy Options,* chose Pearson as the best prime minister of the previous fifty years (Brian Mulroney was second).

PRIME MINISTER PIERRE ELLIOTT TRUDEAU

In the long run, the overwhelming threat to Canada will not come from foreign investments, or foreign ideologies, or even—with good fortune— foreign nuclear weapons. It will come instead from the two-thirds of the peoples of the world who are steadily falling farther and farther behind.
—Pierre Trudeau, University of Alberta, 1968

Pierre Trudeau had an expansive vision of Canada, an intellect to match, a style that transcended politics, and a self-confidence that shrank from nothing and no one. He knew the world and it did not scare him. Much as is the case with Obama and the US today,

Trudeau transformed Canada's international image in a kind of personification of public diplomacy. In the world's eyes, he made us exciting, independent-minded, and visionary. When, in the UN Security Council in September, 2000, nearly twenty years after he had left office, we marked his passing, I was struck by how many in attendance made a point of conveying their personal condolences to me.

Engaging the World, Independently

Trudeau deliberately downplayed the constructive internationalism of Pearson as regards both the UN and NATO. He even coined the phrase "effective power" as a more accurate way for Canada to describe itself than "middle power," which was favoured by Pearson and the diplomats of the Golden Age. He stressed a more hard-boiled and narrower "Canada first" calculation of Canadian interests,* cutting Canadian troops under NATO auspices in Europe in half. His foreign policy had two main thrusts, both of which created friction with Washington: development for the Third World and détente with the Soviet Union.

As my former colleague Jeremy Kinsman has observed, despite Trudeau's emphasis on Canadian interests, he consistently promoted a better deal for the world's poorer countries, augmenting the North-South quotient of Canadian foreign policy in the process, and opening up dozens of Canadian missions in newly independent, poorer countries, especially in Africa.[9] His efforts at doing so redounded to Canada's credit around the world, although the concrete results of his efforts on behalf of the Third World were, at best, mixed.

---

*Lester Pearson commented on the emphasis on national interests in Pierre Trudeau's Foreign Policy for Canadians that "a far better foreign policy is that which is based on a national interest which expresses itself in co-operation with others; in the building of international institutions and the development of international policies and agreements, leading to a world order which promotes freedom, well-being and security for all."[8]

Trudeau delighted in challenging conventional wisdom, and his foreign policy reflected a similar contrarian instinct, especially as regards the Soviet Union, vis-à-vis whom he strongly supported détente. Partly as a consequence, his relations with Washington were contentious—in the Nixon and Reagan years in particular. Official Washington considered him too soft on Communism and too friendly with Castro, and disapproved of a visit he paid to Moscow just three years after Russian tanks had churned through the Prague Spring (and a year before Nixon himself visited the Soviet Union). Trudeau considered the Americans too paranoid about Russia, and too ideological about Cuba. They saw him as an economic nationalist, and a socialist to boot. He saw them as mercantilist and overbearing. At the same time, he did not challenge the US on Vietnam.

Trudeau moved to shed the nuclear roles Pearson had accepted, and seemed initially disposed to give Moscow considerable benefit of the doubt on security issues. The Russian buildup of conventional military forces in Eastern Europe in the late 1970s and the stationing there of short-range nuclear weapons aimed at NATO Europe, as well as the invasion of Afghanistan on the eve of the 1980 Olympic Games, blunted that impulse, even if the American response to the last—a boycott of the Moscow Olympics and a wheat embargo—was not welcome in Ottawa.

Despite staunchly defending individual civil rights at home, notably delivering the Canadian Charter of Rights and Freedom, Trudeau's emphasis on national interests meant he engaged little in the promotion of human rights abroad and, indeed, avoided human-rights issues in contacts with other countries. According to the late Mark MacGuigan,[10] foreign minister in the latter stages of the Trudeau era, it was alien to Trudeau's world view to make human rights a central preoccupation of foreign policy. He tended to overlook Soviet human-rights abuses, which had been amply documented by the Nobel Prize winner Alexander Solzhenitsyn. Trudeau believed that pressing Moscow on human rights made

East-West détente more difficult to achieve.* Trudeau's handling of the Nigerian Civil War in the late 1960s, in which a million people perished from starvation in the would-be breakaway state of Biafra, was concerned more with legalistic issues of sovereignty than human solidarity. In fact, his approaches to human rights and humanitarian affairs abroad were followed by none of his successors until Harper.

Trudeau maintained comparatively close relations with Cuba, in spite of American anti-Communist reflexes—and, at least in part, because of them. Trudeau recognized the undoubted achievements of the Cubans in economic and social rights, particularly as regards health care and education, but he seemed to turn a blind eye to the Castro government's many civil- and political-rights violations. Trudeau made his own opening to China, months before President Nixon did, carrying through on an ambition of Pearson's.

There was a roller-coaster quality to the relations with Washington in Trudeau's time. Canada's assertion of Canadian sovereignty through the Arctic Waters Pollution Prevention Act was proven sound over time, and anticipated what became international practice, but initially mightily discomfited the US State Department and the powerfully connected US Navy. The roller coaster plummeted again on Nixon's economic measures in 1971, which sought to impose a surcharge on the importation of all manufactured goods, including Canada's. Things became worse when Ottawa realized that the impact on Canada was not accidental; ultimately, the measures were rolled back. In 1972, the roller coaster rose again, when Trudeau and Nixon signed the Great Lakes Water Quality Agreement.

---

*Nevertheless, Trudeau did not prevent Canadian diplomats, notably Michael Shenstone, Tom Delworth, and Bill Bauer, from doing exactly that, pursuant to the human-rights articles of the Helsinki Accords and the Conference on Security and Co-operation in Europe during the 1970s, which eventually became a factor in the collapse of the Soviet Union.

Personal Diplomacy

Trudeau respected Nixon's foreign-policy acuity and realism, if not his character. Nixon enthusiastically reciprocated, privately calling Trudeau "a clever son of a bitch," but also "a pompous egghead" and worse.[11] Trudeau got along well, however, with President Gerald Ford, who engineered Canada's entry into the G8 over the objections of French president Giscard d'Estaing, but with German support. Relations with France, still regarded with bitter suspicion in Trudeau's time—by Anglophone Canadians, at least—as a consequence of de Gaulle's ungrateful meddling, never rose above correct, though that was through no fault of Trudeau's. (I do still savour his withering put-down—"You speak French well, yourself"—of a self-absorbed French TV personality expressing surprise at how well Trudeau could speak French.) Trudeau got on well with US president Jimmy Carter who, despite the fact that he was one of the few American presidents not to visit Canada while in office, was, nonetheless, a good friend. Carter supported Canadian national unity as it was being challenged by René Lévesque, and on North-South issues, he was broadly of a similar mind with Trudeau.

With the arrival in office of Ronald Reagan, relations with the US tanked again. Like everyone else who met Reagan, Trudeau found it impossible to dislike the amiable, guileless man, but he also found it impossible to respect his simple-mindedness, especially on issues of East-West relations and his "profound ignorance . . . about circumstances in developing countries and his naïve belief in the ability of free market mechanisms to solve all problems."[12] According to Trudeau,

> [the] American view of the world catered to simplicity,
> passed off as old-fashioned values, and a "might-is-
> right" attitude that was pre-Hobbesian in its fierceness.
> To those who believed, deeply, as we did that the future
> of the human species would be overwhelmingly
> influenced by the attitudes and actions of the four-fifths
> of humankind who lived in the developing regions, the

Reagan mindset was more than disturbing, it appeared
to be seriously flawed and downright dangerous.[13]

Trudeau, believing that the world's burgeoning poor ought to
be a priority in foreign policy, embraced the need for a new
international economic order with interventionist, social-
democratic values and power sharing with the poorer countries of
the South. He co-chaired the unsuccessful North-South summit at
Cancun, Mexico in 1981. Trudeau's ideas ran straight into a new
conservative, markets-oriented ethos that had already begun to
materialize in President Carter's time, and it only strengthened
with the advent of Ronald Reagan in the US and Margaret Thatcher
in the UK. There was a woolly quality about his ideas, but they
might have fared better today in the wake of the harm done by the
excesses of free-market ideology.

Reagan, who was "unwilling to participate in intellectual
debate or address himself to facts outside his immediate personal
experience," projected an image of being "an instrument of others,
persons who never let him stray from their sight."[14] Prior to the
1981 Montebello summit, Richard Allen, a top White House aide to
Reagan, who was visiting Ottawa to "advance" Reagan's visit,
volunteered to us that Reagan was not some bicycle whose tires
they pumped up periodically and rolled out on stage. As none of
us had asked that question or imagined the metaphor, we
concluded that was exactly what they did. In Trudeau's view,
Reagan's limitations undermined the spontaneity of leaders'
interactions on major policy issues and, effectively, ruined the
Montebello summit in particular. At the 1982 G7 Versailles summit,
Trudeau mocked Reagan openly and publicly, deepening the
animosity towards Trudeau in Washington.

Trudeau enjoyed the respect of many other foreign leaders,
and seemed on especially good terms with Chancellor Helmut
Schmidt of Germany (who backed Ford on promoting Canadian
entry into the G7), Lee Kuan Yew of Singapore, Kenneth Kaunda of
Zambia, Michael Manley of Jamaica, and Julius Nyerere of
Tanzania, all renowned thinkers of their day (Lee Kuan Yew and

Helmut Schmidt are still dispensing wisdom today). Relations with Margaret Thatcher, whose intellect Trudeau respected, started out in conflict and only got worse, as she, like Reagan, pursued ideological economic and Cold War policies. She was helpful on the patriation of Canada's constitution.

Influencing Washington—Negatively

Following the Nixon Shock* of 1971, the Trudeau government conceived of the "Third Option" policy, as it tried to encourage greater control by Canadians over the Canadian economy, and to diminish Canadian exposure to US economic power. The policy advocated neither maintaining the existing relationship with the US (Option I) nor integrating further (Option II), but rather, deliberately seeking to reduce Canadian vulnerability to American policy and American business interests (Option III). Attempts to give substance to the policy and to create alternatives to the US in Europe and Japan failed in the face of the realities of geography, the dynamism of the US economy, and the propinquity of the people on either side of the border. Increasingly, while Canada and the US remained two independent countries, the North American economy proceeded to integrate, despite the international border running through it. For Canadian business, the American market was too rich, too close, and too open to pass up for political reasons. The "contractual link"—a sort of trade deal that Trudeau pursued with Europe to encourage diversification—was the diplomatic equivalent of pushing on a rope, and delivered little of value. Nearly forty years later, Canada is still looking for a deal with Europe that would complement our relationship with the US.

Two economic policy initiatives of the Trudeau government stirred profound antipathy, even hostility, in Washington: the 1974

---

* In which the US took a series of economic measures, including ending the convertibility of the US dollar to gold, thereby unilaterally terminating the Bretton Woods system, and imposing a 10 percent surcharge on imports, including, initially, imports from Canada.

Foreign Investment Review Act (FIRA) and the 1980 National Energy Program (NEP). FIRA was designed to limit and diminish foreign, particularly American, ownership of the Canadian economy. Canadian critics on the Left thought it too lenient; the business community and the Americans (and Europeans too, especially the Germans, as I was to learn when I took up my assignment there nearly twenty years later) thought it too obstructive. The NEP, introduced in the wake of successive Arab oil shocks and dramatically increased international oil prices, was designed to promote oil self-sufficiency for Canada, foster Canadian ownership of its own energy industry, promote lower, made-in-Canada prices, and increase federal government revenues from oil sales. The Americans interpreted the NEP as a retroactive confiscation of Americans' assets, to the point that US Ambassador Paul Robinson warned publicly in 1982 of a "gathering storm."

Perhaps because relations between Trudeau and Reagan were poor, on coming to office as secretary of state, George Shultz met his Canadian counterpart, Allan MacEachen, quarterly, a practice that was very helpful. The squeaky wheel gets the grease.* Shultz made it clear that he considered the bilateral relationship with Canada important, and he used the relatively frequent sessions to do the "gardening," by which he meant keeping Canada-US relations from being overgrown with problems.

I was the notetaker for most of these sessions. As MacEachen and Shultz were both notoriously slow speakers who used words as though they were going to be charged a dollar for each one uttered, I was able to capture every word said. Somewhere in the Canadian archives, there are word-for-word accounts of bilateral meetings. I hope the historians are grateful.

Arms control and disarmament were abiding interests of Trudeau. In 1978, he delivered a remarkably comprehensive policy proposal at the UN (developed by Foreign Affairs officials led by

---

* When Joe Clark succeeded MacEachen, he and Shultz continued the practice, but it ended after that.

one of Foreign Affairs' most powerful thinkers, Klaus Goldschlag) to "suffocate" the nuclear-arms race. Elements of the proposal remain in play to this day, notably a comprehensive test ban and an agreement to stop the production of fissile material for weapons purposes. Both are still the subject of negotiations, and priorities for the Obama administration, a sign of both their inherent difficulty and obvious necessity.

By the early 1980s, Trudeau was becoming increasingly concerned by the hard line being taken in Washington towards the USSR, as well as NATO's determination to counter Moscow's actions. He also worried about where Reagan's "Star Wars" space-based weapons program would lead, what it would do to the concept of mutual deterrence, and how the USSR would react. East-West tensions rose dramatically when, in 1983, the Soviet military shot down a Korean civilian airliner that had entered deep into Soviet airspace, accusing it of spying. Trudeau told the House of Commons that he did not believe that "the people in the Kremlin deliberately murdered or killed some 200 or 300 passengers ... it was a tragic accident."[15] Trudeau worried that the penalty for misjudgment could be a nuclear holocaust.

One day at the height of the Korean airliner crisis, I found myself in a small group of advisers in Trudeau's Parliament Hill office to discuss what he should do about it. The world was collectively holding its breath to see how the Americans would react. At our meeting, Trudeau said that Canada had the standing to promote a peaceful solution because we spent little on defence. He had told the CBC (November 1983) that "a country can be influential in the world by the size of its heart and the breadth of its mind, and that's the role Canada can play." I gathered up my courage, realizing that what I was about to say might result in my never seeing the inside of that beautiful panelled office again, and told Trudeau that, whatever the quality of our ideas, our not sharing the security burden equitably disqualified us as interveners in the eyes of many, including those in Washington who would decide how to react to the Russian act. My colleagues busied themselves counting ceiling lights and contemplating the carpets.

Rather than just throwing me out, Trudeau debated the point with me, and I was to return to that office many times in the years to come. Sometimes, there really is nothing to fear but fear itself.

Trudeau thought he had a duty to act; his political handlers also thought he had an interest in doing so. And so he launched the well-intended, but ultimately ill-fated, "Peace Initiative" to turn down the political temperature between East and West due to the Korean airliner incident. It turned out to be his last major foreign-policy initiative. Perhaps because of his own low estimates of Reagan's acuity and his awareness of the geriatric inadequacies of the Soviet leadership, and because of the hardheaded people surrounding both leaders, Trudeau initiated a program of international visits in an attempt "to call international attention to the danger . . . [and] to turn the trend line of the crisis."[16] The fact that the initiative was very popular with Canadians was also no political disincentive. Although cooler heads had already begun to prevail in Washington and Moscow, Trudeau persisted in what became an increasingly quixotic enterprise. Support came from Swedish prime minister Olaf Palme, among others, as well as from some surprising sources, including Margot Kidder and Barbra Streisand.[17] Neither the Russians nor the Americans felt that Trudeau was needed, however, to interpret one to the other or to tutor them on their handling of the incident. Following a few more speeches, the initiative ended with Trudeau's famous "long walk in the snow." *

All Things Considered

History has been appropriately much kinder to Prime Minister Trudeau for repatriating the Canadian constitution and creating the Canadian Charter of Rights and Freedoms than, so far, for his

---

* I wrote one of those speeches; it was significant more for its length than for its eloquence—Trudeau insisted it be sixty minutes long so there would not be time for opposition leader Mulroney to speak before lunch. Trudeau was not coming back afterwards.

foreign policy. At the end of his sixteen-year tenure, his government's contributions to global governance institutions were not plentiful, interactions with France were still tendentious— largely because of the French, bonds with the countries of the South were much enlarged and intensified, but relations with Washington were poor and not especially productive. In the words of Mark MacGuigan, he projected more anti-Americanism to the Americans in the Reagan era than was tolerable to them, and "was entirely indifferent to the personal element of foreign policy." [18] He left the government's finances in poor condition, necessitating cut backs in defence and diplomacy. Nevertheless, by force of intellect and charisma, he conveyed a progressive, independent image of Canada. Under his leadership, Canada was admitted to the most exclusive club in the world, the G7, an achievement the stars of the Golden Age could only dream of.

PRIME MINISTER JOE CLARK

Canada was effective internationally because we pursued two priorities at the same time. We worked hard on our friendship with the United States and the rest of the rich world. And we worked hard on an independent and innovative role in the wider world. . . . They are two sides of the Canadian coin.
—Joe Clark, speech at the University of British Columbia, May 2009

Joe Clark was prime minister for too short a time to have been able to create a major legacy. He is better known for his strong performance as secretary of state in the Mulroney government, especially for the fight against apartheid, and for his thoughtful reflections on Canadian foreign policy in recent years. He did, nevertheless, deliver one very significant accomplishment—the migration to Canada of 50,000 Vietnamese "boat people," refugees from the Vietnam War, who were fleeing by sea. The program was remarkable for the extraordinary engagement of ordinary Canadians with the boat people, who were received and sheltered by service groups, church groups, and municipalities across the country. This program demonstrated how willing Canadians are to respond personally to humanitarian need. It was a significant departure from attitudes of the Trudeau government.

PRIME MINISTER BRIAN MULRONEY

Our membership in [multilateral institutions] gets us no leverage and no particular place at the table. Our membership has to be personified in a way where other countries with the economic power to have an impact on our quality of life want to deal with Canada, because they believe the country and its leadership can make a contribution.
—Brian Mulroney, *Memoirs*

Brian Mulroney was the last prime minister who came to office with international ambitions for Canada that matched the country's potential. While he stirred strong antipathies among many Canadians which persist to this day—back-to-back electoral majorities notwithstanding—he stirred equally strong loyalties among those he worked with. Although his image has been eclipsed in the public mind by perceptions of scandal, he conducted an exceptionally active foreign policy, one arguably as successful as that of the Golden Age of the 1950s,* perhaps more so. There is an apples-and-oranges quality to such comparisons, but what *is* fair to say is that the achievements of each era significantly advanced Canada's interests in the world, and stand on their own.

Influence in Washington, Influence in the World
No one talked of Canadian decline or disappearance in Mulroney's day. He had influence at the top in Washington, London, Paris, Bonn, and Moscow, as well as many other capitals, unlike any Canadian leader before him had or has had since. He had the ear of George Bush Sr., and the confidence of Gorbachev, Yeltsin, Mittérrand, Kohl, Mandela, and many others. He also engaged

---

* Disclaimer: I was the chief foreign-policy adviser of Brian Mulroney, 1989–92.

actively with the United Nations, the Commonwealth, and la Francophonie. His standing in the world helped him in Washington, and the respect he enjoyed in Washington reinforced his effectiveness in the world.

As the epigraph above makes clear, Mulroney understood that international leadership was an important part of his job, and he worked at it—travelling extensively and working the phones intensively when at home. His international standing grew even as his domestic support flagged. Like his predecessors and his successor, national-unity imperatives demanded his attention, detracting from what, without them, could have been an even-more-eventful period of Canadian foreign policy. As noted earlier, of the nine post-war prime ministers, the IRPP placed Mulroney a strong second to Pearson. Much of that judgment rested on his foreign policy.

Mulroney differed from Trudeau in style and substance, and, most directly and consequentially, on relations with the United States. He promised better relations, "super relations," with the US, and to give the US, a friend, the benefit of the doubt, but—and this part was often forgotten by his critics—to maintain an independent foreign policy. Still, relations with Washington were "job one" for him. He met Reagan, Bush, and Clinton annually and at international summits, and used those meetings to keep close oversight of the relationship of the two countries and to press the Americans on bilateral and international issues of interest to Canadians.

Mulroney made it his business to know the people who mattered in Washington—not just the presidents, but also the influential members of Congress and members of the media, not least Katharine Graham, publisher of the *Washington Post*. I was at our embassy in Washington in the latter part of the 1980s, and I remember that Mulroney left us in no doubt that he expected the *New York Times* and the *Washington Post* to cover his visits to Washington, preferably on the front page and above the fold, because the most powerful people in the world read those newspapers. The visits of most foreign leaders scarcely rated a mention, even in the social-affairs sections of these papers, and then, only if their wives were wearing outfits by the leading couturiers. I saw first-hand the extraordinary efforts made by Ambassador Allan Gotlieb and our press officer, Bruce Philips, the former CTV anchor, to try to get that kind coverage.

In his relations with Washington, as with the United Nations, Mulroney turned the clock back to Pearson, whom he quoted approvingly in his memoirs as saying, "We should exhibit a sympathetic understanding of the heavy burden of international responsibility borne by the United States." In Mulroney's own words: "Having established a relationship of friendship, trust and mutual respect with the President of the United States, Canada's leader is uniquely qualified, through ongoing private dialogue, to influence decisions."[19]

Free Trade

The MacDonald Commission on the Economic Union and Development Prospects for Canada, appointed in 1982 by Trudeau, reported in 1985, recommending that Canada pursue a free trade agreement with the United States. Mulroney, a politician to the core of his being, reminded us more than once that free trade had cost Laurier the 1911 election and that, in the 1940s, the political risks of free trade had caused Mackenzie King to retreat from an agreement being negotiated. In 1985, Mulroney proceeded anyway.

In 1988, just four years after he took office, the Free Trade Agreement (FTA) with the US was signed, the most significant achievement of his nine-year tenure. Success took political will and courage on Mulroney's part, in the face of extensive worry in Canada about getting into bed with the elephant, and heavy criticism from his political opponents. It also took all of his renowned persuasive abilities and persistence with President Reagan, who, along with his administration, was deeply distracted by the Iran-Contra scandal*

---

* Senior US officials facilitated the sale of arms to Iran, the subject of an arms embargo, to generate off-budget funds for the "Contras" to fight the Sandinista government in Nicaragua.

and subject, as always, to persistent special-interest lobbying. President Reagan was also showing incipient signs of the Alzheimer's disease that was to afflict him later.

Some time after the FTA was concluded, a representative of then Mexican president Salinas came to Ottawa on a confidential mission and sat down with the prime minister's chief of staff, Stanley Hart, and me in the prime minister's boardroom, to notify us as a courtesy that, to our surprise, Mexico also wanted a free trade agreement with the US. We informed Mulroney, warning him that a separate deal between Mexico City and Washington would create a hub-and-spokes relationship, with Washington as the hub and Ottawa and Mexico City—and potentially other capitals—as the spokes. Recognizing the disadvantages for Canada in that sort of arrangement, Mulroney insisted that the FTA be made a trilateral agreement instead. In 1992, the North American Free Trade Agreement (NAFTA) was signed. Tellingly, the FTA was a highly contentious agreement in Canada and not in the US, while NAFTA was highly contentious in the US, but much less so in Canada.

NAFTA generated large increases of trade and investment, and has become integral to the residual abilities of all three countries to compete with offshore competition. Fifteen years after NAFTA came into effect, three-way trade had tripled to US$946 billion, and Canadian trade with its NAFTA partners had increased to US$571 billion. Inward direct investment from the other two NAFTA countries into Canada totalled US$240 billion.[20] Meanwhile, despite intense worries at the time, Canada's social programs, especially universal health care, remained intact. In fact, they were strengthened by the greater government revenues NAFTA generated than would otherwise likely have been available.

Personal Diplomacy

A defining characteristic of the Mulroney style was his gift for personal diplomacy. Personal diplomacy is important because it is one of the surest ways of getting important issues addressed and, possibly, resolved. That is the case with all countries, but it is particularly true with the United States. With a few notable exceptions (Berlin-Paris, Berlin-Moscow, possibly Beijing-Tokyo), every country's most important foreign relationship is with Washington, and consequently, there is tremendous competition for the president's time and attention. But while a president's responsibilities are truly global, like everyone else, he* has only twenty-four hours in his day, and his programmers are quite unsentimental in managing it. Some things, even important things, will therefore never come to his attention. To get your issue to the top of his agenda, especially if your issue matters more to you than it does to him, he needs to *want* to be helpful to you personally—or at least want not to harm your interests—and his programmers have to realize that. It helps a great deal if there are regular occasions when he will be meeting you face to face. Such contacts force bureaucracies to address issues and facilitate both stock-taking and decision-making. Personal relations are, therefore, vital, and the onus inevitably is on the smaller partner to take the initiative. In *Memoirs*, Mulroney recalls a conversation he and I had one day at 24 Sussex Drive, when he said other countries

> think we're decent and helpful, by and large, and we're listened to on occasion. But . . . that's not because of who we are or where we stand or the geopolitical framework. That's because of how hard we work to make sure we are noticed. That's what few people understand about the job a Canadian Prime Minister has. . . . Membership has to be personified. . . . [Others have to see that] the country and its leadership can make a contribution.†

---

* The male form is used for convenience; so far, only men have occupied that office.

† In his memoirs, Mulroney recalls saying these words to his chief of staff, Hugh Segal, but I distinctly remember the conversation.

To be sure, he was lucky in his interlocutors; Gorbachev, Mittérrand, and George Bush Sr. were easier to admire and work with than Brezhnev, de Gaulle, and Nixon. But, unlike Trudeau, Mulroney found a way to get along with Thatcher and Reagan, relations with the latter at least proving to be of significant benefit to Canada.

After the Shamrock Summit on March 17, 1985, when the two leaders sang "When Irish Eyes are Smiling," Mulroney was criticized for being too close to President Reagan. The fact is, that close personal relationship was indispensable in solving bilateral issues. Without that closeness, the Americans would almost certainly never have agreed to a free trade agreement (the little importance Americans attach to free trade with Canada was evident again in the 2008 presidential electoral campaign). The same is true for the acid rain agreement and for the understanding on the Northwest Passage (the Canada-US Arctic Co-operation Agreement of 1988), which stipulated that the US would not use the passage without Canada's consent, and that Canada would not withhold consent. Without Reagan's personal direction on this issue, the US Navy and other US interests would have opposed this agreement for eternity.

On the other hand, effective personal diplomacy does not have to imply sycophancy or holding your nose and acquiescing to the other side's views. Mulroney disagreed with Washington on Star Wars, on ballistic missile defence, on abrogating the Anti-Ballistic Missile Treaty, and on American policy towards Cuba, among other things.

What the critics were also missing when panning the Mulroney relationship with Reagan was that Mulroney practised personal diplomacy on all the leaders he considered important to Canada—Helmut Kohl, Mikael Gorbachev, Boris Yeltsin, Margaret Thatcher, and François Mittérrand especially. Mulroney assiduously cultivated Mittérrand, even literally and figuratively translating Mittérrand to Reagan and vice-versa. Mulroney's purpose was to develop a working relationship with Mittérrand that made it possible for him to appreciate that France had interests in Canada that went beyond Quebec, and for Canada and France to co-operate constructively again after twenty years of tensions. In the same vein, but more profoundly, Mulroney was trying to ensure that France did not meddle in Canadian constitutional affairs, particularly as regards the Meech Lake Accord and, subsequently, the Charlottetown referendum. As Sherlock Holmes might have said, there was a reason why that particular dog did not bark when the referendums were held.

Mulroney also used his personal relationship with George Bush Sr. to lobby on behalf of German unification. When the Berlin Wall came down suddenly in 1989 after forty-five years of Soviet occupation, ordinary Germans not surprisingly were ecstatic that their country would soon be united. Germany's European allies and traditional enemies, especially Gorbachev's Russia, were less ecstatic; in fact, they were not happy about it at all. Margaret Thatcher was particularly reluctant. Mulroney intervened with Bush, whose views would be decisive in NATO, arguing that, after decades of assuring Germans they would be united one day, it would be unfair and potentially dangerous to renege on what was widely understood by the German people to be a promise. It did not take an especially long memory to realize that disappointing the German people was not a good idea. Mulroney made the same argument to Gorbachev, Mittérrand, and Thatcher. Ultimately, they rallied to the side of reason and unification proceeded without serious controversy. In 1993, Kohl publicly singled out Bush, Gorbachev, and Mulroney as the three leaders who helped Germany most on unification.[21]

The relationship with Kohl extended beyond unification. In 1991, Mulroney, Helmut Kohl, Kohl's adviser, and I had lunch in the chancellor's office in Bonn. The Balkan conflict was under way, and Kohl was very worried about Serbian aggression. How, he asked, was he to persuade Germans who remembered when East Prussia was German that other borders in Europe were adjustable by force, but that Germany's were not?

Engaging the World through the UN

If "super relations" with the US were the first priority for Mulroney, strong support for the UN was a close second. At his insistence, Canada paid its UN dues in full and on time, one of the few countries that did. (The Americans were particularly dilatory.) Mulroney often made the point that he did not want the UN secretary-general to have to be an international mendicant. At Mulroney's explicit direction, I used to arrange for the delivery of a cheque covering Canada's fees and contributions to the UN on January 1. The UN was delighted to get the money in such a timely way (although the Canadian officer who delivered it and the UN official who received it would have been happy to wait a day—and quite possibly did). In Mulroney's time, Canada participated in every UN peacekeeping mission, including in Bosnia, supplying about 10 percent of the troops. (In the spring of 2010, we were supplying about 0.16 percent of all the troops on UN-commanded missions.)

When Saddam Hussein invaded Kuwait in 1990, Mulroney pressed Bush not to respond unilaterally, but to take the issue to the UN for authorization to intervene. There were several phone calls in that period between Washington and Ottawa in which the messages from the Ottawa side included the importance of going through the UN. In the end, the US got the authorization of the UN Security Council to "use all necessary means" to expel the Iraqis from Kuwait, which—after forming a broad-based coalition of the willing—they did. Mulroney's strong backing of the UN embellished the reputation Canada has enjoyed at the world body since Pearson's time.

During Mulroney's tenure, Canada was very active on security, human rights, and the environment at the UN. Partly as a consequence, Mulroney was approached in 1991 by the US, the UK, France, and Russia to accept the position of UN secretary-general. The Chinese would likely have agreed, although they were not pleased by Canadian condemnation of Chinese suppression of pro-democracy students in Tiananmen Square. After the failure of Meech Lake, Mulroney was tempted by the offer, whose pros and cons we discussed. In the end, on the grounds of pressing domestic obligations regarding the Charlottetown referendum, he declined.

The "Greenest Prime Minister"

In 2006, Mulroney was named the "Greenest Prime Minister" in Canadian history by a panel of environmentalists assembled by *Corporate Knights* magazine. Under his leadership, Canada's international environmental accomplishments were many, notably a bilateral acid rain agreement with Washington. That agreement, signed with George Bush Sr. in 1991, had been the subject of relentless lobbying by Mulroney, who raised it at every one of about a dozen meetings he had with Reagan and Bush.* Reagan persisted in his belief that acid rain came from trees, a position that suited the coal producers in West Virginia, Kentucky, and Pennsylvania, as well as the Midwest electricity generators upwind from Eastern Canada. Success came only after Canada took the initiative to launch a $300-million program to cut Canadian-generated acid rain in half, shaming Washington into reciprocating. Mulroney's "clean hands" approach contrasts starkly with that of the Harper government on climate change, which consists of waiting for Washington to act.

In 1987, Canada played a prominent part in the negotiation of the Montreal Protocol to protect the ozone layer. In 1988, the first international, high-level meeting on climate change, the World Conference on the Changing Atmosphere, was held in Toronto. In 1992, at the Rio Earth Summit, Mulroney and Canada played leading roles in establishing the United Nations Framework Convention on Climate Change. Further, Canada was the first industrialized country to sign the Biodiversity Convention that was opened for signature at Rio. At the time, Elizabeth May of the Sierra Club and subsequently leader of the Green Party, said, "Let's not be modest just because we are Canadians. Brian Mulroney

---

* I and countless others in Ottawa and at our embassy and consulates in the US had worked on this file for ten years. I lobbied numerous members of Congress and took speaking engagements, including in coal-mining states like West Virginia, to push our case. Fortunately, no one threw me down a mine shaft.

accomplished something really significant by being willing, within hours of Bush saying he wasn't going to sign it, to say Canada was."[22] Together with the "Green Plan," the Great Lakes cleanup, the creation of several national parks, and the prevention of drilling in the US part of the Arctic National Wildlife Reserve, Mulroney's tenure constituted a "green" Golden Age.

Apartheid

Apartheid in South Africa linked Mulroney with the Diefenbaker government of thirty years earlier, which had engineered the exit of South Africa from the Commonwealth. At the UN in 1985, Mulroney threatened "total sanctions" and the severing of diplomatic relations unless South Africa ended the loathsome racism of apartheid. (Note that there was no known South African diaspora in Canada whose votes he sought.) Mulroney also used Commonwealth summits for keeping the heat on South Africa, leading to legendary confrontations with Margaret Thatcher, including duelling press conferences and figurative head-on collisions inside the meetings. At the Commonwealth summit in Kuala Lumpur in 1989, where one evening the British renounced, on the BBC, the communiqué on apartheid that Mrs. Thatcher had accepted in the meeting room that afternoon, Mulroney confronted her in front of all the others, saying, "In Canada, you do not sign a deal at 5:00 and repudiate it at 6:00. . . . I do not quarrel with Mrs. Thatcher's right to speak her mind. I quarrel with the right to tell us one thing and then without warning to do another."[23]

With its substantial economic relationship with South Africa, Britain was loathe to irritate Pretoria. Thatcher took the view that increased economic sanctions were immoral, would hurt blacks most, and would be counterproductive with whites. Her strong beliefs in the functioning of the free market also disposed her to avoid direct action. Ronald Reagan agreed with her, especially about the free market, fearing as well that Mandela and his African National Congress (ANC) were Communists and terrorists. Mandela was not, but some others undoubtedly were. Helmut Kohl also supported Thatcher in these fights, but none of Thatcher's

Commonwealth partners shared her views, which only made her more convinced of her own rightness, not to say righteousness. Ultimately, Mulroney largely prevailed in a contest that lasted during the entire period he and Thatcher overlapped in office.

As the apartheid regime began to disintegrate, pressure mounted to abandon the sanctions. Mulroney instructed me to canvas Nelson Mandela's views through our ambassador in South Africa, Lucie Edwards, and Mandela was firm in saying the sanctions still mattered. Mulroney responded to those who advocated an ease-up by saying that when Mandela judged sanctions were no longer needed, Canada would relent—but not before. That was essentially the same stance he took on East Timor, when two prominent Canadian companies asked him to ease Canada's opposition to Indonesian occupation. Mulroney responded that Canada would relent in its opposition to Indonesian policies in East Timor when Indonesia ended its occupation.

Mulroney used his personal relationship with Robert Mugabe to lecture him empathetically, but firmly, on the need for Zimbabwe to protect human rights, including property rights, and to foster economic freedoms, pointing out that otherwise, the economy of Zimbabwe would be ruined. The conversation took place at Mugabe's residence in Harare, in the context of a Commonwealth summit, and Mulroney spoke in as direct and forthright terms as I have ever seen one leader use with another. It helped, a bit, for a while.

At that summit in Harare, Nelson Mandela, then the head of the ANC, asked for a bilateral meeting with Mulroney. We knew from our embassy in Pretoria that Mandela intended to request a Canadian donation to the ANC, and we knew that not everything about the ANC was above board. When we met, Mandela duly made his request, politely. Mulroney evaded it, politely. Mandela persisted, politely. Mulroney resisted, politely, and so on until, with the conversation becoming increasingly awkward, Mulroney finally relented. Mandela graciously accepted, and the meeting continued on through other subjects on the agenda to its conclusion. As he was leaving, Mandela turned at the door, with a twinkle in his eye, and said, "And, Brian, you will make that US dollars, won't you." When Mandela was gone, Mulroney asked me to find a way to make the donation so that it supported the legitimate activities of the ANC without also underwriting the organization's not-so-legitimate activities—which, with the help of our embassy in South Africa, we managed to do.

The Ethiopian Famine

Little noticed or remembered, but of transcending importance to the people concerned, was one of Mulroney's first initiatives on taking office in 1984, in response to the famine in Ethiopia. CBC correspondent Brian Stewart was bringing the situation to the world's attention, and, seeing Stewart's reporting, Mulroney directed Stephen Lewis, his new ambassador to the UN, to urgently generate and lead an international humanitarian rescue effort. Joe Clark and David MacDonald in Ottawa co-ordinated the Canadian contribution. The UN and Red Cross launched what was, at the time, the greatest single humanitarian relief effort in history: to save an estimated seven million people facing starvation in Ethiopia, along with a further twenty-two million across the continent. Stewart believes that Mulroney's timely intervention led to the saving of as many as 700,000 lives.[24]

There were other human rights achievements, notably the negotiation and conclusion of the UN Convention on the Rights of the Child, an international convention that set out the civil, political, economic, social, and cultural rights of children. Mulroney co-chaired the summit, the largest gathering of heads of government until that time. Every government in the world but the United States and Somalia has since acceded to it. Mulroney also foreshadowed the human security policy of the Chrétien government at a commencement ceremony at Stanford University, when he argued that the idea that a leader could abuse his people behind the shield of national sovereignty was as out of date and unacceptable as a man claiming he could beat his wife because his home was his castle. In that speech he also argued that if the countries of the Warsaw Pact adopted democratic systems of governance and values, they should become part of NATO, an idea that the British seemed to find particularly ill-advised right up to the time they embraced it as their own.

All Things Considered

Prime Minister Mulroney took it for granted that Canadian foreign policy should be active and constructive. He neither exaggerated Canadian influence nor underestimated it, but used it deliberately to advance Canadian interests in Washington and in other major, and not-so-major, capitals. Under Mulroney's leadership, Canadian foreign policy was engaged on the biggest issues of his era, a consequence of his belief in Canada and our capacity to make a difference in the world. He had reserves of ambition and determination, more than many Canadians were comfortable with, but these qualities helped greatly on foreign policy. In some ways a Pearsonian, albeit certainly not politically, he re-proved the thesis that influence in Washington and influence in the world are reciprocal and mutually enforcing. He felt a responsibility to make the UN work, and supported the institution strongly. He understood and sympathized with the burdens of the US, but never shrank from disagreeing with Washington when that was necessary. Nor did he seek to find differences for their own sake. He was a trusted counterpart of President George Bush Sr. on the unification of Germany and on the Gulf War, and he achieved more bilaterally with Washington—free trade, acid rain, the Arctic—than either his predecessors or his successors did.

PRIME MINISTER JEAN CHRÉTIEN

I believe that Canada's decision not to go to war in Iraq was one of the most important moments in our history. It proved to us and to the world that we are a proud independent nation.
—Jean Chrétien, *My Years as Prime Minister*

As prime minister, Jean Chrétien's style on foreign policy, as on government in general, was as hands-off as Mulroney's had been hands-on. Partly as a consequence, his personal foreign-policy legacy was limited, although his government's was significant, including Foreign Minister Lloyd Axworthy's human security agenda. Chrétien intervened only when he judged that things were going awry (for example, during the fisheries wars with Spain, with military action threatening, he intervened to lower the escalating temperature).

An Independent Foreign Policy: The Iraq War

Undoubtedly, Chrétien's most important decision was a negative one: to stay out of the catastrophic US war in Iraq. The US seemed to have taken Canadian support for the war for granted, despite ample evidence that Ottawa's support for the Americans on this issue was not a given. At a tête-à-tête meeting in Detroit in September 2002, Chrétien apparently told George W. Bush that if the US got a UN authorizing resolution, he would support US action.[25] In February 2003, a month before the invasion, Chrétien spoke to the Chicago Council on Foreign Relations, urging the Bush administration to work through the UN Security Council, which would strengthen Washington's hand, and the hands of those who might support the US. In New York at the UN Security Council, I was promoting a compromise that would have avoided war. None of these actions should have been interpreted as signs of a Canadian endorsement of invading Iraq. But, bent on war and deaf to disagreement, the Americans missed our signals. As Andrew Card, who at the time was Bush's chief of staff, told Chrétien subsequently, "It was our mistake not to take you seriously. We assumed that, at the last minute, a practical guy like Chrétien would decide to come along. That was our fault. We should have believed you."[26]

In the lead-up to the war in 2003, I informed Prime Minister Chrétien that, despite the assertions of Prime Minister Blair, among others, the Security Council would not authorize military action against Iraq because there was widespread doubt about the validity of the case that the Americans and British were making. [27] In going to war, the Americans and their allies were going to destroy the lives of a lot of innocent people, ruin their own country's standing in the world, do enormous harm to the United Nations, and damage international law in the process. I also thought it would lead to a prolonged period of instability and reprisals in Iraq and its neighbourhood. In fact, the war was to do all of that, and much more.

Ottawa was distinctly uncomfortable with the options it faced: either supporting our closest allies, who, the government feared, were about to commit a profound error, or opposing them—or, at least, not supporting them—with whatever repercussions that might bring for Canada. So, in typical Canadian fashion, we looked for the middle ground. We realized there could be no compromise between war, which the Americans and British wanted, and no war, which the French, Germans, Russians, and most others wanted. But we thought that perhaps the launch date of the war could be delayed to provide time for an acceptable solution to be found in the interim.

After consulting Hans Blix, the head of the UN's weapons inspectors, and with the encouragement of many delegations—including, privately, some members of the British and American delegations—I formally proposed in the Security Council in mid-February 2003 that the UN's weapons inspectors be given six more weeks to complete their assessment, at which time the Council would decide on a pass-or-fail basis whether the Iraqis were complying with Security Council directives—or not. "Pass" meant that the American and British would stand down on war, the weapons inspections would continue, and Iraq would remain contained. "Fail" meant that the French, Germans, and Russians would drop their opposition to British and American action. Blix had wanted ten weeks to do his work, but we thought that this was more than the political traffic would bear. As it turned out, even six weeks was more than it would bear.

We were fully conscious at the time that we probably had about a 5 percent chance of success with this compromise idea, but we gave it a 100 percent effort, because we were sure the consequences of war were going to be disastrous. Deep in hubris, the US insisted on its war, nevertheless, and the Germans, French, and others remained suspicious of any process that could trap them into approving war down the road. The long shot proved too long, and the war followed.

The Chrétien government's decision to stay out of the war was not well received by some in Canada, especially by the Alliance Party, precursor to the Conservatives, who argued, essentially, that we should support our ally right or wrong. Stephen Harper and Stockwell Day penned an op-ed in the *Wall Street Journal:*

> Today, the world is at war. A coalition of countries under the leadership of the U.K. and the U.S. is leading a military intervention to disarm Saddam Hussein. For the first time in history, the Canadian government has not stood beside its key British and American allies in their time of need. The Canadian Alliance—the official opposition in parliament—supports the American and British position because we share their concerns, their worries about the future if Iraq is left unattended to, and their fundamental vision of civilization and human values. Disarming Iraq is necessary for the long-term security of the world, and for the collective interests of our key historic allies and therefore manifestly in the national interest of Canada.[28]

Nor did many in the business community, notably the Canadian Council of Chief Executives, rally to the flag—at least, not to the Canadian flag.

The evidence of the wisdom of Chrétien's decision was not long in coming, as at least 100,000 Iraqis were killed in the conflict and its aftermath (estimates range as high as one million killed), regional politics were scrambled, and the Bush presidency consumed. Chrétien has called the decision not to go to war in Iraq one of the most important in Canadian history. He was right, and that decision was enough to ensure him an honourable place in Canadian diplomatic history.

Personal Diplomacy

Like Mulroney, Chrétien was very adept at personal diplomacy. In his relations with US presidents, he differed little from Mulroney in substance, but a lot in presentation. Publically, Chrétien took a visible distance from Clinton, maintaining that "business is business and friendship is friendship." In his campaign for office, he said that "[his] ambition was not to go fishing with the President of the United States,"[29] referring to Mulroney's visits with President Bush at Kennebunkport. Privately, Chrétien went golfing with Clinton, frequently, happily, and with little public comment or disapproval, during the eight years they overlapped in office. Fortunately for Canada.

It was with the promise of a golf match that Chrétien persuaded Clinton to speak to the Forum of Federations meeting at Mont Tremblant, at which Clinton delivered a brilliant, unscripted defence of federalism and a united Canada, visibly discomfiting Lucien Bouchard, who was sitting in the front row. Earlier, on the eve of the Quebec referendum of 1995, pursuant to a conversation with Chrétien, Clinton made a point of saying at a press conference how much the US valued "a strong and united Canada,"[30] thus putting a thumb on the scale of a Canadian referendum won by the federal side 50.5 percent to 49.5 percent. Chrétien's close relations with Clinton paid off.

As had been the case with Mulroney, Chrétien practised personal diplomacy on other leaders as well. One of the most significant for Canadian interests was President Jacques Chirac of France. Chirac had seemed sympathetic to the Quebec separatists' arguments in his early days in office, and had uttered an unhelpful, if vague, statement on what France would do if the separatists won the 1995 referendum. Chrétien confronted him later, and ultimately used the 1999 Francophonie summit in Moncton to show Chirac that there were French-speaking communities outside Quebec that had been free to preserve their language and culture, and they had not been suppressed or repressed. Following the summit, Chrétien took Chirac, a student of aboriginal art, to the Canadian North, where he cemented their personal relationship and showed him the magnificent heritage that belonged to Quebeckers in a united Canada as much as it did to Anglo-Canadians. As was the case with Mulroney and Mittérrand a decade earlier, the Chirac government subsequently refrained from endorsing separatist aspirations.[31]

Engaging the World, Carefully

Chrétien's dealings with other leaders, especially the leaders of major powers, tended to be low key. His experience as a legislator, negotiator, and minister of almost everything taught him that "[he] could often be most useful by playing a quiet, supportive role."[32] Sometimes, his unassuming style was a bit too diffident and unambitious, as when Li Peng of China visited Canada in 1995. Li, whose government had used the Chinese army to suppress students at Tiananmen Square, did not want to be dogged by protestors, and the attempts of the Canadian government to shield him from them proved very controversial. Chrétien's memoirs recall a Canadian journalist asking him whether he was being frank enough on human rights: "Be realistic," Chrétien replied. "I'm the prime minister of a country of 28 million people. He's the president of a country of 1.2 billion people. I'm not allowed to tell the Premier of Saskatchewan what to do. Am I supposed to tell the president of China what to do?"[33]

The answer is that it depends on how it is done. My own limited experience with the Chinese is that, if you manifest respect for what they have been able to achieve, and empathy for the size of the task that remains for them to do, they will be more receptive to advice that is meant to be helpful rather than critical.

At the same time, Chrétien assiduously courted the increasingly powerful China, leading "Team Canada" missions there and maintaining a steady rhythm of exchanges. His years in office were marked by the numerous Team Canada visits he led abroad to China (twice), Japan, Korea, India, Brazil, Chile, and the western US. Although Mulroney had headed trade and investment missions abroad, as had other foreign leaders—Chancellor Kohl of Germany led trade missions to India (during which he gave the Indians land in Berlin that had been earmarked for Canada's new embassy there)—Chrétien's innovation was to include provincial leaders as well. The governments on the receiving end were uniformly impressed by the effort Chrétien was making in building relationships and economic connections with them and their countries. Canadian business seemed to welcome the signal that was sent by such visits, and the doors they opened for them. The visits had domestic benefits as well, encouraging informal discussions among the Canadian leaders en route that were impossible in the fishbowl of federal-provincial politics in Ottawa, and generating solidarity among the premiers. What was less clear about Team Canada missions was their impact on economic relations and whether they generated sufficient business that would not have happened otherwise, to render the considerable cost justifiable. Chrétien's successors have not continued the practice.

Chrétien attended nine G7 summits, two of which he hosted. In Halifax, in 1995, he arranged for Boris Yeltsin's (nearly) full participation, transforming the group into a G7½. At the 2002 Kananaskis summit, which he chaired, he made Africa a major focus, devoting an entire day of leaders' time to it, and allocating $500 million to a special African fund. A year later, at the Monterey meeting on Financing for Development, Chrétien announced a commitment to double overseas development assistance by 2010, with half going to Africa. At Kananaskis, G8 members united to launch the Global Partnership Against the Spread of Weapons and Materials of Mass Destruction. Over US$20 billion was pledged to this program over a ten-year period. Canada committed $1 billion to the fund.

Human Security

A signature effort of Chrétien's time in office was Foreign Minister Lloyd Axworthy's human security agenda, a genuine made-in-Canada success story. In the light of the international community's failures in Rwanda, Bosnia, Kosovo, the Congo, and all the rest of the tragic catalogue of international neglect and indifference, the Chrétien government saw a pressing need for an idea to galvanize action to save innocent lives. That idea was "human security," and it was revolutionary in that it put the security of people, not states, at the centre of foreign-policy calculations. It also recognized that the security of states was necessary, though not sufficient, to ensure the safety and well-being of individuals. Further, it regarded such safety as essential to achieving international peace and security, and it brought innovations to diplomatic practice—for example, direct co-operation with civil society through the then-incipient Internet-based revolution.

It was, in essence, a people-protection agenda, and included remarkable achievements. At its heart was the "responsibility to protect," a new norm, and potentially a major accomplishment. Following the Rwanda, Kosovo, and Bosnia experiences, Foreign Affairs, led by Axworthy, became convinced that something had to be done about the apparent incompatibility of the UN Charter's proscription of interference in the internal affairs of states and the humanitarian imperative of saving people from destruction at the hands of their own governments. To think the matter through and to reconcile the incompatibilities, we created an international commission, including three Canadians—Michael Ignatieff, Gisèle Côté-Harper, and Ramesh Thakur. The commission re-framed the debate away from the colonialist-tinged "right to intervene" to the more neutral "responsibility to protect," shifting the focus from the rights of interveners onto the needs of people at risk. The commission recommended a high bar for intervention, specifically only "where a population [was] suffering serious harm, as a result of internal war, insurgency, repression or state failure" and where there was a "large scale loss of life, actual or apprehended, with genocidal intent or not . . . or large scale 'ethnic cleansing.'"[34] It was adopted at the 2005 Millennium Summit by over 150 heads of government and state. The human security agenda also included the Ottawa Treaty on anti-personnel landmines; the International Criminal Court; the Kosovo Intervention; the UN Protocol Against the Illicit Manufacturing of and Trafficking in Firearms; the protocol to the Convention on Child Rights, outlawing the use of child soldiers, child prostitution, and child pornography; a UN resolution on the protection of civilians in armed conflict; the promotion of women's roles in delivering peace and security; and, not least, through the extraordinary work of Canadian UN ambassador Bob Fowler, curtailment of the blood diamond trade in Angola and an end to the civil war there.

Misengagement

The basic operating style during the Chrétien years was comparatively low key, one of a government minding its own business. There was a tendency to wait to be asked, rather than to see a duty and take the initiative. There was also a need to balance the government's fiscal books, especially in the 1990s, when just paying the interest on the national debt was hobbling the government. Still, the capacity of Canada's military was allowed to run down, and money became very scarce for Canada's diplomacy. Partly as a consequence, Canada's international impact and standing diminished. Further, Chrétien declined an invitation to join a UN-authorized multilateral force to oust the Haitian general Raoul Cédras, on the grounds that "we didn't see deposing dictators as our role in the world."[35] Nor would he support NATO's bombing of Bosnian Serb positions in Bosnia.

The Chrétien government did little to try to stop the genocide in Rwanda. To be sure, the main responsibility for the tragedy lay with the Hutu *génocidaires*, and the main international responsibility to react to it lay with the UN Security Council, which turned a blind eye and a deaf ear to the slaughter until it was too late. Ottawa was aware of the unfolding tragedy, but it was slow to register the size and nature of the issue and the need to exercise leadership. An estimated 800,000 Tutsis died.

Perhaps as a consequence, Chrétien resolved to do something about it when a million refugees from the Rwandan war and genocide, captive in camps across the border in Zaire, were threatened with starvation. He volunteered Canadian leadership of an international rescue mission and worked to rally international support. The Americans, pursuing their own obscure agenda in the Congo, offered much advice but little assistance, and the

British, unwilling to play second fiddle to "colonials" and supporting the Americans reflexively, were actively unhelpful. Before the troops could be assembled and deployed into Zaire, however, the *génocidaires* who were occupying the camps fled into the bush, and most of the refugees streamed back into Rwanda. What triggered the abrupt end of the crisis was never clear. What *was* clear was that Canada did not then have the military capability itself to carry out a major combat operation half a world away.

There was a perceptible reluctance on the part of the Chrétien government and of the Finance Department, whose international interests rarely extend beyond their own geo-economic activities, to recognize that protecting people from violence required military capacity. Human security is not a pacifist doctrine; nor is it cost-free. It takes a lot of money to pay for the combat-capable ground forces on whom intervention to save lives often depends—as the ill-fated Canadian intervention in the Congo showed. The Chrétien government sometimes seemed to think that it was enough for Canada to be innovative diplomatically—Ideas Were Us! Muscles were someone else.

The Chrétien government also mishandled the Kyoto Protocol on climate change. In 1997, I led the delegation to Kyoto, where Canada agreed to a target of reducing greenhouse gases by 6 percent on average from 1990 levels, the base year for the treaty, largely because others, especially the Americans, were going to do their part. In 2000, the Republicans defeated the incumbent Democrats in the US federal election, and Bush repudiated the Kyoto commitment made by Clinton, leaving Canada out on a limb. In 2002, the government proceeded to ratify the treaty anyway, over the objections of the oil industry, in particular, and the province of Alberta. Neither Jean Chrétien nor Paul Martin implemented the deal, and the Conservatives renounced it on taking office in 2006.

All Things Considered

Chrétien's leadership will be remembered primarily for his declining of the American invitation to join in the invasion of

Iraq, a courageous decision, the wisdom of which was quickly validated. Notwithstanding its failure to act on the genocide in Rwanda, his government also won respect for its innovative human security agenda, which has been widely accepted abroad, albeit not by the neocons in Washington and their theocon derivatives in Canada. Chrétien developed an effective relationship with Clinton that paid off in spades on national unity. He also put relations with France on a constructive footing, reinforced ties with China, and launched major investments in aid to Africa and in the dismantling of weapons of mass destruction.

PRIME MINISTER PAUL MARTIN JR.

There is no contradiction between Canada doing well and Canada doing good . . . Canada benefits directly when the world is more secure, more prosperous, more healthy and more protective of the natural environment . . . we must take our responsibilities to the global community seriously . . .
—Paul Martin, *Canada's International Policy Statement: a Role of Pride and Influence in the World*, 2005

Paul Martin, Jr., learned foreign policy at his father's knee and had nine years of international experience as finance minister. However, his tenure in office as prime minister was too short and, as head of a minority government, too precarious, to have created a substantial record, although there were noteworthy decisions. He will likely be remembered for initiating the global governance innovation known as the G20 (the club of the major developed and developing countries). Before leaving office, he launched the idea that the G20, a finance ministers' group, which he himself had created during the Asian financial crisis of the late 1990s, should be replicated at the leaders' level. It would, effectively, expand the G8 to include China, India, Brazil, and other emerging market countries as full members. The idea was picked up by President Bush in desperation, in the face of the 2008 international economic meltdown, and adopted as well by President Obama. Leaders meeting on the financial crisis in Pittsburgh in 2009 designated the G20 to be the premier forum for international economic co-operation. This achievement might turn out to be major indeed, and Canadian fingerprints are much more visible on the G20 than they were on the UN Charter in the Golden Age.

PRIME MINISTERS AND FOREIGN POLICY FROM THE GOLDEN AGE TO THE MODERN AGE: LESSONS LEARNED

What have we learned from the experiences of our post-war leaders, from the Golden Age of Pearson to the modern day? In fact, countless lessons can be drawn from the experiences of our prime ministers to help illuminate the way forward for Canada in the emerging multi-centric world. Five strike me as particularly relevant for the times ahead.

1. Canada can accomplish a lot when vision and creativity are combined with political will, leadership, and hard work.
2. Personal diplomacy by our leaders is indispensable to success.
3. As in life, success comes to those who want it most; no one is going to hand the world to us on a platter. It is in Canada's interest that we engage constructively with the world, not just watch it go by.
4. The more influential we are in Washington, the more effective we are in the world and, vice versa, the more effective we are in the wider world, the more influential we are in Washington.
5. To make our way in a transforming world, foreign-policy independence is necessary, and also possible. We always have a choice; the real issue is cost, and whether we are prepared to pay it. The corollary is that the cost is always affordable.

PART III

MEANWHILE IN THE WORLD:
The Context for Canadian Policy

Foreign policy is a statement of intent, not a prescription, and the desired results are not pre-ordained. Others have their word to say, some more compellingly and more loudly than others. For the last seventy years, Washington's voice has been the most compelling and strongest of all. Partly for real security reasons—the threat of Communism, partly out of ideology and ambition, partly because of the self-interest of the military-industrial-congressional complex that Eisenhower warned about, and partly out of sheer capacity, the US has strongly predominated. In doing so, it has largely shaped the context in which Canadian foreign policy has been pursued.

Canada has agreed with Washington's goals, notably containing the ambitions of the Soviet empire, and tended to exercise its independence on the means, such as détente over confrontation, more than on the ends—sometimes, at the outer borders of consensus. As Ottawa's doubts about the US's national-security-obsessed foreign policy grew, so did our differences with Washington. With the election of President Barack Obama, more co-operative times may be back. US power remains the dominant reality of our time, but there has been a welcome change of tone—and, in some cases, substance—under Obama, as the US, too, copes with changing times and as the paradigm of international relations reshapes itself to accommodate new players.

Washington's voice has not been the only prominent one of course. From 1940 to 1990, Moscow's views were nearly as consequential. Since the end of the Cold War, other voices, notably those of Beijing, Brasilia, Brussels, and Delhi, have come to be heard, making our reality more complex. At the same time, the international organizations that the world has created to help govern itself have become indispensable—albeit sometimes inadequate—forums for deliberation and, where possible, decision-making. The UN is in a class by itself, establishing and maintaining the norms and rules by which countries interact and diplomacy is done. Its existence makes the job of other organizations easier. The UN has also become a proxy for those countries without seats at the top tables, speaking especially on behalf of the 170 or so countries whose voices are less strong and compelling, but which, nevertheless, need to be heard in the global discussion. Increasingly, the international discourse has been held in restricted groups such as the G20, as the powerful seek to address each other directly, avoiding the complexity caused by vast numbers of players, and end-running some of the obstruction to which large groups are prone. Meanwhile, "civil society," from Oxfam to the Gates Foundation, dissatisfied with the results governments achieve, are playing a larger and more direct role in world affairs, as well. At the same time, terrorism and organized crime are also out on the worldly field.

To understand what we can achieve in this increasingly complex world and to chart a successful course forward, we need to understand the context and the parameters that the institutions of global governance and American foreign policy have created for us in these past sixty-five years. Here's what they mean to us.

5

THE UNITED NATIONS:
The Motherboard of Global Governance in a Changing World

The UN was not created in order to bring us to heaven,
but in order to save us from hell.
—Dag Hammarskjöld, former UN secretary-general*

WHY WE STILL NEED THE UNITED NATIONS

Three generations have come to adulthood since the UN was born in San Francisco in 1945. The memory of the terrible losses of the two world wars and the misery visited upon hundreds of millions of survivors of those wars is fading as the ranks of veterans thin at cenotaphs each November, sadly but inexorably. With the loss of that memory goes the visceral understanding of the *raison d'être* of the United Nations. It is important to remind ourselves what it is.

---

* A similar comment is often attributed to Henry Cabot Lodge, former US delegate to the UN: "This organization is created to keep you from going to hell. It isn't created to take you to heaven." Perhaps they both said it.

In San Francisco, the gathered delegations gave the UN four crucial, transcendent missions:

1. to save succeeding generations from war;
2. to protect human rights;
3. to foster universal justice; and
4. to promote social progress and better standards of living.

By and large, the UN has succeeded in fulfilling all of these mandates. Or, more accurately, *we* the member states have done so, because the member states, acting together, are the UN. Over the decades, through the UN we have spawned an extensive body of international law, treaties, norms, practices, and institutions that govern most facets of interstate relations, bringing greater order, predictability, and progress to global affairs, and greater modernity, dignity, and security to people's lives.

The United Nations: What It Is and What It Is Not

In trying to get a mental grip on the UN and why it still matters to us as we transit into the future, it is necessary to recall what it is and, more importantly, what it is not. For people coming from the Westminster traditions of government such as ours, with parliament, cabinet, and executive functions, it is easy to misunderstand the United Nations.

The first thing to remember is that the organization is not a government, much less a world government. As Secretary of State Hillary Clinton put it, "The United Nations is a building. It is not able to act in the absence of the decisions made by member-nations."[1] The UN is not an independent entity, but rather a global governance club under the control of its members. The UN is *sui generis*, a thing unto itself.

The second thing to keep in mind is that no one is in charge of the United Nations. Literally. And no one is fully accountable for it.

The secretary-general is the public face of the UN, but he* is not the prime minister or president of the organization. His authority is deliberately circumscribed in the UN Charter. According to Article 97, he is the chief administrative officer of the UN, not the chief executive officer. He is more secretary than general, and is very much the servant of the membership, not its superior.

Third, the General Assembly is not the parliament of the world's people. It is a forum of states for states, usually represented by their "Permanent Representatives," diplomats who have been appointed by their governments for fixed periods. ("Permanent" means only that they live in New York for the duration of their assignments.) The UN Charter borrows from the language of the US Constitution, but speaks of "We the peoples . . ." not "We the people," of states, not citizens. There is not a single officer of the assembly that is elected directly by the world's people. It is the forum where states convene and deliberate on—and, where possible, dispose of—major issues on the international agenda. The assembly negotiates and concludes treaties, and establishes norms of international behaviour.

The UN Security Council is not the cabinet of the United Nations. Nor is it responsible to the General Assembly or even responsive to it in any meaningful way. It is a distinct body of the UN. The council currently has fifteen members: five permanent members, often called the P5—the US, the UK, France, China, and Russia—all with vetoes, and ten non-permanent members without vetoes. The latter ten are elected for two-year terms by a vote of the membership of the entire general assembly. (Canada has been elected once a decade since the late 1940s; at the time of writing, Canada was running for election for the period 2011–2012.)

The Council's writ covers only peace and security, fairly broadly defined. It does not make decisions on matters that are essentially about economic policy, monetary policy, trade, social

---

* So far, only men have held the office, although the first deputy secretary-general was a woman, Louise Fréchette, of Canada.

development, and the like—that is to say, the kinds of things that
national cabinets and other international bodies address routinely.
The council is, nevertheless, arguably the most important political
body in the world, equipped by Chapter vii of the un Charter
with the power to "legislate" in member countries, a power that
even the august g20 group of country leaders does not have. The
decisions of the council taken under Chapter vii are legally
binding on member countries, whether they are on the council at
the time or not. Major international political and security issues
continue to be brought to the un for deliberation and decision.
The Afghanistan conflict, the Iraq War, and the Iranian nuclear
program are high-profile examples.

The p5 members of the council have the power to veto
resolutions of the body, and they use it. According to the UK
Foreign and Commonwealth Office, the following is the tally of
vetoes cast from 1946 to 2008:

Russia/Soviet Union	119
The United States	82*
The United Kingdom	30
France	18
China	7

The Motherboard of Global Governance

With its Charter, and the international law and treaties built onto
the Charter, the un has become the world's central operating
system, the motherboard of global governance. The un performs
its own core functions and, at the same time, also enables myriad
sub-systems to work as well, both within the ambit of the un
organization (for example, unicef and the extraordinary work it
does for the world's poorest children) and outside it. The un
makes it possible for other organizations and groups, notably
nato, to function more effectively. The nato Treaty deliberately,

---

* Of which, 41 on the Middle East

and specifically, refers directly to Article 51 of the UN Charter as the legal basis of its collective defence commitment. Politically, NATO needs the approbation of the UN to bolster the legitimacy of its operations outside of Europe and North America. Otherwise, in the eyes of the world, NATO's presence in Afghanistan, for example, would be little more than an invasion.

The UN also makes it possible for ideas such as the Millennium Development Goals, designed to set targets and time frames for economic and social development in the UN's poorer countries, and the global fight against HIV/AIDS, to be subcontracted out efficiently. The reverse is also true. The decisions and views of other entities, notably the G8 and G20, can be imported into the UN for consideration by the entire membership. The members of such restricted groups can bind themselves by their decisions if they wish, but they can only commend such decisions to others, not command compliance with them. Without the UN and its universal membership and legal framework, smaller privileged groups, including the G8 and the G20, would be much more controversial than they already are, and their legitimacy even less accepted. They would also likely be correspondingly less effective.

Most fundamentally, the UN and its Charter provide the rule book for the conduct of international relations, which all states more or less respect. The cliché, for all its overuse, is true: if the UN did not exist, we would have to invent it. Whether this generation could muster the requisite vision and political will to do so, as the post-war generation did, fortunately is moot.

THE UN'S ACCOMPLISHMENTS

International news coverage of the UN tends to dwell on its failures, some of which have undoubtedly been tragic. The UN's successes are less newsworthy—the international governance equivalent of the 100,000 airplanes landing safely at Pearson Airport—but no less important. If the world is largely at peace, much of the credit goes to UN treaties, norms, and operations. Perhaps most consequential has been the Nuclear Non-Proliferation Treaty and the International Atomic Energy Agency, which have helped limit the spread of nuclear weapons.

As a former permanent ambassador, I know first-hand that the UN has all the internal contradictions, conflicts, rigidities, and frailties that might be expected of a sixty-something, quite human, institution composed of members with competing interests. I know, too, that it can be even more exasperating up close than it is at a distance. But I know, also from personal experience, that the world body remains far more innovative, effective, and important than politically motivated "UN-bashers" would have us believe— and even than most UN-apologists appreciate. People everywhere sense this, and view the UN more positively than negatively—and, in many cases, much more positively.[2] According to surveys published in 2009 by the Pew Global Attitudes project, 70 percent of Canadians and 61 percent of Americans have a favourable attitude towards the UN.

Stigmatizing Aggression

First and foremost, since the UN Charter was adopted in 1945, the UN has—that is, member states have—succeeded in stigmatizing aggression. Although the Cold War saw international law breached by both sides on occasion, and, more recently, although the American invasion of Iraq lacked the sanction of a Security Council mandate, the UN norm against aggression has become the standard by which international military action is judged. It was the standard by which the Iraqi invasion of Kuwait in 1990 was assessed to be aggression, and the standard by which the American-led, UN-approved response to it was condoned. It was, likewise, the standard by which the American invasion of Iraq in 2003 was condemned by a great majority of the membership.

According to a report of the independent UN High Level Panel on Threats, Challenges, and Change in 2005, there were fewer inter-state wars between countries large or small in the second half of the twentieth century than in the first half, despite a nearly fourfold increase in the number of states. The UN has served as midwife in the births of more than a hundred of these states since 1945, the great majority of which came into being peacefully. However bloody the world has been in the last sixty-five years, and it has been very bloody—over forty million have died as a result of conflicts, but "only" about one-fourth in wars between states[3]—it is fair to say our world would have been much worse without the UN.

Despite the impression of conflict that is produced almost daily, especially by our electronic media, including the Web-based media, the *Human Security Report* of 2005[4] found that, between 1992 and 2003, the number of armed conflicts around the world *dropped* by 40 percent. The number of battle deaths per year and per conflict have declined dramatically, albeit unevenly, since the 1950s. In 1950, for example, the average armed conflict killed 38,000 people; in 2002 the figure was 600, a 98 percent decline. Canadian losses in the Juno Beach landing in Normandy were greater on the first day—probably even in the first hour—than they have been in nine years in Afghanistan. Terrorism is the only form of political violence that appears to be getting worse, but the losses, while high profile and tragic—the equivalent of the plane crashing at Pearson Airport—pale in comparison to the losses suffered in armed conflict half a century ago. Even fatalities from the violence some states perpetrate on their own citizens, while horrific, have been in decline in the present decade, as compared to the 1990s.[5]

Intervention and Prevention

The *Human Security Report* argues that the single most compelling explanation for these declines is found in the unprecedented upsurge of international activism, spearheaded by the UN, which took place in the wake of the Cold War. (Ironically, these declines have occurred as Canada has largely abandoned UN military missions.) UN member countries have been much readier to authorize the use of force to stop internal conflicts than they were previously. From 1945 until 1989, there were thirteen UN military operations. Since then, there have been approximately forty-five such military interventions. One of the great ironies of the UN is that, whatever doubts the members profess to have about the organization as a whole, military operations are, literally and figuratively, booming. There are about seventeen UN military operations under way around the world as of February 2010, carried out by some 98,000 men and women from 119 countries, with a budget in excess of $7.8 billion.[6] Over the years, peacekeeping has evolved from essentially observing ceasefires and separating forces after inter-state wars, to complex interventions comprising the military, police, and civilians working together to help lay the foundations for sustainable peace. In fact, the term "peacekeeping" has become a misnomer. Missions are larger, more complex, more demanding, and more dangerous than peacekeeping missions traditionally were—although even the "classic" peacekeeping missions were more dangerous than most Canadians realized. (When I was ambassador to the UN, I accepted 107 medals awarded posthumously to Canadian military personnel who died over the course of nearly sixty years of UN military operations, the most losses, sadly, of any troop-contributing country.) UN missions deal increasingly with intra-state conflicts, sometimes where there are several protagonists at once and where some of them are still fighting. Since consent of all parties for the UN to intervene is sometimes unattainable, the UN forces can be seen as just another party to the fight. This is not to say that classic peacekeeping is dead—there are still occasions when it is possible—but "peace making" and "peace enforcement" are more accurate terms for UN military operations these days than "peacekeeping" is, at least in the deployment phase.

UN mission mandates include combat, the protection of civilians, the disarming of combatants and their re-integration into local societies, the re-establishment or actual creation of government institutions, the reform of the police and army, the fostering of the local economy, the administration of justice, the guaranteeing of human rights, and much more. According to James Dobbins of the Rand Corporation, and a very experienced former senior official in both the White House and US State Department, "the United Nations provides the most suitable institutional framework for most nation-building missions, one with a comparatively low cost structure, a comparatively high success rate, and the greatest degree of international legitimacy."[7]

In his memoirs, former Canadian chief of the defence staff General Rick Hillier disparaged the UN Security Council as "a dysfunctional committee" based in New York, which "could not respond to dynamic and rapidly changing situations, particularly on weekends and holidays." I am not sure what period he is alluding to, but my experience is very different than his. In my time on the council, we were in near-constant session, often returning to work in the middle of the night, and sometimes working right through the night. I watched more than one sunrise over the East River through the windows of the council chamber. As for the council being dysfunctional, I would concede it was sometimes conflicted, because member states disagreed with each other. The council reflects the world; it does not govern it and does not take orders from any one national capital.

The *Brahimi Report* on peacekeeping in the year 2000, named after the sage Lakhdar Brahimi, former Algerian foreign minister and respected UN trouble-shooter, triggered significant reforms in UN military operations. For Brahimi, the point was that any decision to *deploy* military force was also a decision to *employ* that force, and thus a serious decision, because people were going to be killed. The UN had to have the logistical capabilities, appropriate equipment, and the professional leadership needed to handle its responsibilities effectively. The report was largely adopted and, as a consequence, the UN now has a much more developed capacity at UN headquarters to manage military missions in the field, and a larger cadre of experienced staff. It is a far cry from the institution seen by General Hillier in Bosnia in the 1990s.

In perhaps his most important recommendations, Brahimi urged the secretary-general to refuse mandates from the Security Council that were accorded too few personnel and too little equipment to succeed, and to tell Security Council members not what they wanted to hear in drafting mission mandates, but what they needed to know. He also argued that neutrality could not be absolute, and sometimes the UN had to choose sides. UN peacekeepers had an implicit duty under the Charter to protect civilian victims of violence—to the extent they were able to do so.

The UN has also been placing increased emphasis on preventing conflicts. Sometimes, its work has been very high profile, as when former secretary general Kofi Annan brokered an agreement between factions in Kenya. Sometimes, it is much more low key, or at least meant to be much more low key, as was the case involving my friends and former colleagues Bob Fowler and Louis Guay, who were preventing future conflict in Niger and North Africa when they were kidnapped. Sometimes, it is very risky work.

Establishing Norms

As UN treaties and rules have progressively been absorbed into domestic legislation around the world, norms and standards of international behaviour have been established and upgraded. Since the UN General Assembly adopted the Universal Declaration of Human Rights in 1948, the United Nations has helped to enact dozens of treaties on political, civil, economic, social, and cultural rights, including, in particular, women's rights and children's rights. Over time, the provisions of these treaties have migrated into domestic law around the world.

Canada contributed actively to the creation of these norms, from the work of John Humphrey, the Canadian professor of law at McGill University who wrote the first draft of the Universal Declaration of Human Rights, to that of Louise Arbour, former UN high commissioner for Human Rights (and former chief prosecutor of both the International Criminal Tribunal for Yugoslavia and the International Criminal Tribunal for Rwanda, and former Supreme Court of Canada justice).

The same assimilation dynamic is at work on the environment, where a similar process of domestic integration of international standards has been taking place. The UN or its constituent bodies have concluded forty-five treaties on the environment, from the Kyoto Protocol to the Montreal Protocol on ozone depletion to treaties on migratory species and beyond.

Again, there has been a strong Canadian quotient. Maurice

Strong chaired the inaugural international conference on the environment in Stockholm in 1972, and its successor in Rio in 1992. Jim MacNeill, the noted Canadian environmentalist and former head of the OECD's environment division, served as secretary-general of the seminal Brundtland Commission, which conceived the idea of "sustainable development," reconciling the previously irreconcilable ideas of economic growth and environmental protection.

The assimilation dynamic is true also for counterterrorism. The UN General Assembly has passed thirteen counterterrorism treaties on issues as diverse as skyjacking and nuclear terrorism. Acting under Chapter VII of the UN Charter, the Security Council has "legislated" prohibitions against terrorism and terrorist financing, including the "no-fly" list, which has, regrettably, grounded some innocent Muslim-Canadians, among others.

All told, over 500 multilateral treaties have been concluded under UN auspices. In the process, the UN has helped member countries create an extensive body of international law and practice that makes it possible for increasing numbers of the world's people to live in dignity and freedom, as well as peace and prosperity. The diplomats and statesmen and women (there were a few women, including the Canadian diplomatic pioneer Elizabeth MacCallum) who drafted the UN Charter would likely be pleased by what their creativity and co-operation have yielded. In important respects, they succeeded in putting the UN at the heart of international relations.

Field Operations

A growing proportion of the world body's work these days is operational, far removed from the plush carpets and hushed discourse of the corridors and the delegates' lounge in UN headquarters in Manhattan. It is the gritty, but very necessary, work of helping the world to feed its hungry, shelter its dispossessed, minister to its sick, respond to its crises, and educate its children. It is a very big job, and a very dangerous one. The UN lost more than a hundred personnel in the January 2010 earthquake in Haiti, and many more in terrorist attacks in Bagdad, Algiers, and Kabul, among other places.

The results of the UN's field operations are impressive—and vital. In 2008, the UN High Commissioner for Refugees sheltered thirty-one million people—nearly the equivalent of the population of Canada—including refugees, the stateless, people displaced within their own countries by conflict, and asylum seekers. In 2008, the World Food Program (WFP), operating in seventy-eight countries, fed over 102 million people, more than three times the population of Canada. The World Health Organization (WHO), which in its earlier years led the successful program to eradicate smallpox, is now close to eliminating poliomyelitis. As a consequence of the work of the WHO and its private partners, including Rotary International, polio infections have fallen by 99 percent since 1988, and some five million people have been spared paralysis. With the assistance of the WHO and UNICEF, the immunization of children for the six major vaccine-preventable diseases—pertussis, childhood tuberculosis, tetanus, polio, measles, and diphtheria—has risen from 20 percent of the world's children in 1980 to an estimated 81 percent by the end of 2007;* at least 90 percent will be immunized by 2015. Meanwhile, the WHO has also been co-ordinating the world's response to SARS, the avian flu, and the H1N1 virus. This work has been belittled in some unenlightened quarters as mere international social work. It *is* social work, but social work that delivers very real human and national security benefits.

More mundanely, every time you take an international flight, post a letter abroad, or listen to an international broadcast, the UN has been involved through one or another of its seventeen specialized agencies. A whole "alphabet soup" of UN acronyms—ICAO, IPU, ITU, WMO, WLO, WIPO, among many others—stand for organizations helping the world to manage one aspect or another of international interchange.

---

* Deaths from measles, a major killer, declined by 74 percent worldwide and by 89 percent in sub-Saharan Africa between 2000 and 2007.

THE UN'S INNOVATIONS

An extensive international criminal justice system has developed under UN auspices, a major innovation foreseen nowhere in the original Charter. Four ad hoc courts have been established by the UN to prosecute major crimes: the International Criminal Tribunal for Yugoslavia, which tried the former president of Serbia, Slobodan Milosevic, and is prosecuting others implicated in Balkan atrocities, including Radovan Karadžić; the International Criminal Tribunal for Rwanda, which has placed the perpetrators of the Rwandan genocide on trial; the Cambodia hybrid (UN and Cambodian) court, which is bringing the remaining senior Khmer Rouge leaders to trial for crimes against humanity, among other crimes; and the Sierra Leone hybrid court, which is prosecuting Charles Taylor, the former president of Liberia, for war crimes and crimes against humanity, including murder, rape, sexual slavery, and mutilation of civilians.

During the Sierra Leone Civil War, the UN Security Council, on which I represented Canada, went on a field trip to West Africa to see for itself what was happening there. We met with the leaders of Sierra Leone, Guinea, Mali, Nigeria, and Liberia. It was evident that the last, Charles Taylor of Liberia, and his kleptomania were at the root of the war in Sierra Leone and its brutal bloodshed. Our delegation head was the British ambassador, then Jeremy, now Sir Jeremy, Greenstock, one of the UK's most able diplomats. The meeting took place around a boardroom table in the freshly painted foreign ministry, the only building in Monrovia with functioning lights besides the president's palace. Greenstock, in his element and drawing on his colonial instincts, leaned forward in his chair, pointed a finger straight at Taylor, and told him in no uncertain terms that we knew what he was doing and it must stop. Taylor's entourage gasped. Knowing Taylor's reputation, I started to make mental notes of the location of the exits, for whatever good that might have done. Fortunately, it was not necessary, as Taylor put on his best rogue act and tried to charm us, in vain.

At the heart of the UN's criminal system is the International

Criminal Court (the ICC), presided over initially by Philippe Kirsch, a Canadian. The ICC is independent of the UN, although linked to it, and represents another major step forward towards ending the impunity of the world's worst criminals. Since the ICC's inauguration in 2002, the world's monsters have not been able to sleep as soundly as they once could, confident that they are immune from prosecution. The ICC has indicted Joseph Kony, the head of the Lord's Resistance Army in northeast Africa, which comprises many current and former child soldiers; and a sitting head of state, Omar al-Bashir, president of Sudan. No one can count on getting away with major crimes anymore. Finally, the UN has also been investigating the assassination of former Lebanese prime minister Hariri, another innovation.

The Responsibility to Protect

The UN Charter treats national sovereignty and the prohibition of interference in the domestic affairs of states as absolute and immutable. Over time, however, a contradiction emerged between this cardinal tenet of sovereignty and the most basic purpose of the UN, "to save succeeding generations from the scourge of war," because most contemporary conflicts arise within the borders of existing states where governments are unable or unwilling to protect their own citizens, or are actually themselves perpetrating violence against them.

The worst single failure of the UN was its handling of the conscience-shocking Rwandan genocide. The small force that Canadian General Roméo Dallaire commanded had been stationed in Rwanda earlier to assist in the implementation of the Arusha Accords, signed in August 1993. The force was intended to aid the "peace process" between the Hutu-dominated Rwandan government and the Tutsi-dominated rebels. Dallaire's warnings of impending catastrophe fell on deaf UN ears, as did his requests for the reinforcements he needed in order to, at least, save more of the innocent. His troop strength was actually reduced in the course of the slaughter by some troop-contributing countries, and he was even ordered not to intervene militarily, because he lacked both the requisite resources and the mandate from the Security Council to do so. Canada, too, was of little help to him. To his eternal credit, he played the obscenely inadequate hand dealt him by the UN better than anyone had a right to expect, and saved those who could be saved.

In the fall of 2000, then secretary-general Kofi Annan asked, "if humanitarian intervention is, indeed, an unacceptable assault on sovereignty, how should [the world community] respond to a Rwanda, to a Srebrenica—to gross and systematic violations of human rights that offend every precept of our common humanity?"[8] In warp speed time for diplomacy, at the 2005 UN Summit, 150-plus heads of state and government endorsed the Responsibility to Protect, the Canadian-promoted answer. This new norm was one of the very few accomplishments of a summit that was largely sidetracked by a truculent, irresponsible Bush administration. That the Responsibility to Protect was passed in this unpropitious environment was thanks to two things. First, the idea was, and is, very compelling—some of the best foreign policy thinking in fifty years, according to Anne-Marie Slaughter, at the time the dean of the Woodrow Wilson School of Public and International Affairs at Princeton University and subsequently the director of policy planning for the Obama State Department. The second reason for its success was the astute management by Foreign Affairs over five years, including lobbying in the four corners of the earth and advocacy by leading lights from every region. This culminated in effective work in New York by my successor, Allan Rock, and last-ditch lobbying of recalcitrant leaders by then prime minister Martin. The strategy worked, and the Responsibility to Protect—or R2P as it has come to be known—was one of the few positive outcomes of the 2005 summit.

Representatives of many developing countries feared from the outset that R2P was a licence for the major powers to override the UN Charter, and that there would be too much military intervention as a consequence. Others, especially UN Secretariat staff, aware from bitter experience in Rwanda and elsewhere of the disposition of the richer countries to avoid entanglements, feared there would be too little intervention. Thus far, the latter have been right. Still, support for R2P has remained remarkably resilient.

Poverty Eradication

Potentially the most important innovation of the last decade in the economic and social agenda of the UN was the adoption by the 2000 world summit of the Millennium Development Goals (MDGS). The MDGS, as they are commonly referred to, comprise the world's vision, strategic objective, and central organizing concept in the collective effort to alleviate poverty. They lay out eight goals and specific timetables (culminating in 2015) for eradicating extreme poverty and hunger, including cutting in half the proportion of people living on less than $1 a day; achieving universal primary education; promoting gender equality and empowering women; reducing child mortality; improving maternal health; combating HIV/AIDS, malaria, and other diseases; ensuring environmental sustainability; and more generally developing a global partnership for development. Progress towards the goals has been uneven, with Brazil on track to achieve many of them, and China and India doing well, but the countries of sub-Saharan Africa are trailing and, in some cases, actually in retreat.

The UN has made other noteworthy innovations, perhaps the most visible the creation of the UN Office for the Co-ordination of Humanitarian Affairs (OCHA). It was OCHA that co-ordinated the massive international relief response to the 2004 tsunami in the Indian Ocean and the 2010 earthquake in Haiti. Another potentially major innovation has been "peacebuilding," the attempt to help countries avoid conflict or, having fallen over the abyss, to emerge from conflict successfully. Peacebuilding endeavours to integrate the UN's military efforts with civilian efforts to create sustainable peace, and to provide exit strategies for UN military missions. (Forty-six years after it was first deployed, there is still a UN peacekeeping force in Cyprus, in part because peacebuilding was not a priority in the past.)

The UN has supervised scores of elections and otherwise helped many member countries to make transitions to democracy.

According to the statistics and definitions of the American NGO Freedom House, over three-quarters of UN member countries are now full or partial democracies. It is worth bearing these numbers in mind the next time the UN is described as just a collection of tyrants and terrorists.

THE UN'S WEAKNESSES

While the UN has been more effective than many realize, its problems are real and significant. It has had its scandals, too, although arguably no more than most western governments. The institution has been plagued by divisions between rich countries and poor, between the Security Council and the General Assembly, between the nuclear powers and others, between the Israelis and Arabs and Muslims more generally, between the Indians and Pakistanis, between North Korea and its neighbours, and, during the Bush years, between a unilateralist Washington and a multilateralist New York. What is not always clear is whether the UN is divided because of the intractability of the problems it faces, or whether the divisions among its membership make its problems intractable. In either case, overcoming division does not come easily.

The UN's problems are worsened by Cold War relics, particularly the Non-Aligned Movement and the G77, groups of Third World countries united to resist the pressures of the major powers, but susceptible to destructive game-playing by spoilers among their membership, of whom there is a half-dozen ready and willing to oppose any northern or western idea. I fear I made few friends among the G77 one tiresome day in the UN's budget committee, when I told them that they were starring in an off-Broadway production that no one west of First Avenue in Manhattan was watching (the East River is the UN's other border). The UN General Assembly tends to be all politics, all the time.

Some, especially among the American neocon Right and their Canadian theocon cousins, have longed for the end of the UN, which they have seen as an obstacle to American power.

Richard Perle, until the spring of 2003 chairman of the US Defense Policy Board, probably spoke for many members of the Bush administration when he professed to see two benefits from the war in Iraq: first, the disappearance of Saddam Hussein; and, second, the end of the United Nations. "Thank God for the death of the UN," he wrote in the *Guardian*, in March 2003. Fortunately for Canada, reports of the UN's death were greatly exaggerated because, to paraphrase Joni Mitchell, we don't know what we've got till it's gone.

ALL THINGS CONSIDERED

The world's aspirations for the United Nations have often exceeded the organization's grasp; as a consequence, the UN is admired sometimes more for its ideals than for its accomplishments, more for what we want and need it to be than for what it has sometimes been and done. Still, with unforgivable and indelible exceptions, in particular the Rwandan genocide and Srebrenica, the world body has fulfilled its mandate acceptably well—in some respects, exceptionally well. It has adapted to rapidly changing times faster and better than most observers realize.

Quite evidently, the UN remains a major—indeed the central—factor in international governance and collective security. It is not the "basket case" it is sometimes portrayed as being, even if it does need constant reform, as most organizations do. From human development to human rights, to arms control, to environmental protection, to international justice, to democracy support, to disaster response, there has been considerable innovation in the ways the UN functions, much of it only partly visible to the non-expert eye.

The world is interconnected as never before, and we face threats that are global in nature and that will respond only to solutions that are global in character. No country, no matter how powerful, can solve these problems on its own as President Obama, the head of the most powerful country, has underlined. Further, in a world of powerful states, the continuing existence of a common set of rules by which all agree to live is greatly to be preferred to the law of the jungle, especially by Canada. The West is unlikely to dominate the next sixty-five years as it has done the last sixty-five, and has every interest, therefore, in continuing to inculcate a culture of law into the conduct of international relations, as the UN has done progressively over time. Moreover, the coming multi-centric world will continue to need its agora to negotiate new norms and rules of behaviour, and to settle its differences peacefully.

Few countries benefit more from a competent UN and its framework of international law than Canada does. And no country has more reason to help to make the UN more effective going forward.

6

AMERICAN NATIONAL SECURITY:
The Quest for Invulnerability

We don't want the smoking gun to be a mushroom cloud.
—National Security Adviser Condoleezza Rice

We believe he has, in fact, reconstituted nuclear weapons.
—Vice President Dick Cheney

These are not assertions. What we're giving you are facts and conclusions based on solid intelligence.
—Secretary of State Colin Powell

These three statements made in the lead-up to the Iraq War—the first of which was irresponsible hyperbole, the second of which was flat-out wrong, and the third a misleading sales job—constitute the strongest possible case for Canada to make its own judgments about international events and to conduct an independent foreign policy. They are testimony to how wrong things can go with American foreign policy, and should be framed and mounted on a wall in the minister's board room in the Pearson Building and in the cabinet room on Parliament Hill. They also constitute a potent argument for the necessity of understanding our giant neighbour, and an important reminder that we do not make Canadian foreign policy in a vacuum. For our own sakes, we need to understand the forces that drive American foreign policy.

THE AMERICAN FOREIGN POLICY GENOME

A genome carries the full complement of an organism's genetic information, which determines what that organism will be and do. It is a helpful way to think about underlying forces that shape American foreign policy. The US genome includes liberty and democracy, exceptionalism and righteousness, responsibility and leadership, and militarism and ambition. While some of the individual genes are readily identifiable and their presence constant, it is their combined effect that shapes American foreign policy. In that respect, they are relevant whichever US administration is in office—although, unlike human genes, they combine somewhat differently as a function of who is in office. The Republicans embody the militarism and righteousness genes rather more than the Democrats do.

Live Free or Die*

If multilateralism and good governance are in the DNA of Canadians, liberty and democracy are in the DNA of Americans. The US Declaration of Independence proceeds from the belief "that all men are created equal, that they are endowed by their Creator with certain unalienable rights, that among these are life, liberty, and the pursuit of happiness." The drafters of the Constitution set as its purpose, *inter alia*, "to ... secure the Blessings of Liberty to ourselves and our Posterity," a frequent reference in many an inauguration speech and State of the Union address over the last 200 years, not to mention high school valedictory. Thomas

---

* New Hampshire's licence plate slogan

Jefferson, in his last public act, extended the idea of liberty beyond the United States, writing that self-government would come "to some parts sooner, to others later, but finally to all."

Looking back from today's vantage point, American super power seems pre-ordained. But to those who lived the events of history, the outcomes were anything but certain. The declaration by a small handful of colonies of their independence from the most powerful state in the world with the most powerful navy to that point in history was a major, treasonous act that could well have failed, with perilous consequences for all concerned. Benjamin Franklin was not being facetious when he commented, when signing the Declaration of Independence, that "[we] must all hang together, or assuredly we shall all hang separately" (a quotation also attributed to Thomas Paine). "Give me liberty or give me death" was Patrick Henry's call in the lead-up to the Revolutionary War.

The very precariousness of the American act of independence, in which everything including life itself was risked, has become part of the frame of reference of Americans and is imprinted in their consciousness by the opening verses of the American National Anthem:

> *O, say can you see by the dawn's early light*
> *What so proudly we hailed at the twilight's last gleaming;*
> *Whose broad stripes and bright stars, through the perilous fight,*
> *O'er the ramparts we watched were so gallantly streaming?*
> *And the rocket's red glare, the bombs bursting in air,*
> *Gave proof through the night that our flag was still there:*
> *O, say! does that star-spangled banner yet wave*
> *O'er the land of the free and the home of the brave?*

Partly in light of this experience, Madison wrote in the Federalist papers that "the people of America may be said to have derived an hereditary impression of danger to liberty." The necessity to defend freedom, to ensure that democratic government should not perish from the earth, to paraphrase Lincoln's Gettysburg address, is perhaps the most frequently recurring theme in American political discourse. And in American foreign policy.

Liberty has, nevertheless, meant different things at different times in American history: liberty from the British and the predations of King George iii, liberty from European entanglements, liberty from the Nazis and the Communists, liberty from the state and from the encroachments of government and of each other, including from slavery, and liberty for everyone everywhere as a means of creating a world that would guarantee American freedoms.

President Kennedy, in his extraordinary inaugural address in 1961, set the bar high for preserving liberty and freedom, and for leadership, when he said,

> Let every nation know, whether it wishes us well or ill,
> that we shall pay any price, bear any burden, meet any
> hardship, support any friend, oppose any foe, in order to
> assure the survival and the success of liberty.

Over the generations, Americans have developed a strong sense of responsibility for world affairs on the commendable grounds, to paraphrase the Bible (Luke 12:48), that from those to whom much has been given, much is expected. The isolationist impulses of the founding fathers have gradually given way to responsibility and engagement. Willingness to embrace responsibility to lead seems equally strong on both sides of the political divide in Washington, even if the means employed and the style of doing so differ. In his 2004 State of the Union address to Congress, President Bush asserted "our special calling. This great republic will lead the cause of freedom." Responsibility in and for the world was also a theme of President Obama's inaugural address:

> What is required of us now is a new era of
> responsibility—a recognition, on the part of every
> American, that we have duties to ourselves, our nation
> and the world, duties that we do not grudgingly accept

but rather seize gladly, firm in the knowledge that there
is nothing so satisfying to the spirit, so defining of our
character than giving our all to a difficult task.

At the same time, Obama, faced with daunting challenges,
noticeably dialed back the leadership rhetoric, saying in his
inaugural address that "America is a friend of each nation and
every man, woman and child who seeks a future of peace and
dignity, and we are ready to lead once more." A far cry from
Kennedy, but much more realistic.

The idea of America as exceptional—exceptionalism—has
been another genomic determinant of foreign policy. Its origins
date from the Puritan migration in the seventeenth century, and it
was apparently first given written expression in John Winthrop's
sermon on the "City on the Hill," referring to how the Puritan
experiment would be seen by the rest of the world—or at least by
the rest of Christianity. "The City on the Hill" has morphed into a
metaphor for America itself. The idea has been expressed regularly
down through history, from Thomas Paine's *Common Sense* to de
Toqueville's *Democracy in America* to Woodrow Wilson's "Fourteen
Points" to Ronald Reagan, George Bush, Sarah Palin, and Barack
Obama in the modern age.

Exceptionalism evidently means different things to different
Americans at different times. According to Sarah Palin, speaking
in Nevada in September of the 2008 presidential campaign, "We
are an exceptional nation. . . . America is an exceptional country.
. . . You are all exceptional Americans." President Obama has a
more cosmopolitan "take" on exceptionalism, as he commented at
NATO shortly after assuming office in 2009:

I believe in American exceptionalism, just as I suspect
that the Brits believe in British exceptionalism and the
Greeks believe in Greek exceptionalism. I'm enormously
proud of my country and its role and history in the
world. . . . the enormous amount of resources that were
put into Europe postwar . . . our leadership in crafting

an Alliance that ultimately led to the unification of
Europe ... the largest economy in the world ...
unmatched military capability ... a core set of values
that are enshrined in our Constitution, in our body of
law, in our democratic practices, in our belief in free
speech and equality, that, though imperfect, are
exceptional.

Two dimensions of American exceptionalism stand out, one positive and one negative. Combined with a sense of responsibility and an instinct for leadership, exceptionalism has produced extraordinary American performance—the defeat of Nazism, the development of post-war institutions, the world's bulwark and bank against Communism, the promotion of human rights, and the development of international law. The US has also exercised an exceptional and judicious mix of power and diplomacy in preserving stability, not least among Japan, China, and Russia in Northeast Asia. Exceptional American vision and leadership largely shaped our modern world. No one else could have done these things; the debt of gratitude owed to the Americans is impossible to repay.

At the same time, it is the more self-serving expressions of exceptionalism and the double standards that they entail—from climate change to the invasion of Iraq to unilateral interpretations of international law generally—that have been problematic, distressing America's friends and, in some cases, prejudicing America's interests. Obama has dialed the exceptionalism rhetoric back as well, although it remains strong in the US Congress.

Margaret MacMillan, author of the seminal work *Paris 1919*, has observed that

"American exceptionalism has always had two sides: the one
eager to set the world to rights, the other ready to turn its
back with contempt if its message should be ignored.... Faith
in its own exceptionalism has sometimes led to a certain
obtuseness on the part of the Americans, a tendency to preach

at other nations rather than listen to them, a tendency as well to assume that American motives are pure where those of others are not..."[1]

Containing Communism, "X," and NSC 68

Since the Declaration of Independence and the Revolutionary War, through to the attack on Pearl Harbor and down to 9/11, two threads have run through America's foreign policy: a sense of insecurity and a quest for invulnerability.

Despite the extraordinary dominance the US enjoyed at the end of World War II, Washington and Europe alike feared that the Soviet Union would surpass American capabilities, including its nuclear capabilities. The US reacted to the twin spectres of Soviet power and Communist ideology with the policy of "containment," which, as outlined in a celebrated anonymous article in *Foreign Affairs* magazine by "X"—later revealed to be George Kennan of the US State Department and ambassador to Russia—aimed at both avoiding war with Moscow and blocking any further Soviet expansion. Kennan argued that

> the main element of any United States policy toward the Soviet Union must be that of a long-term, patient but firm and vigilant containment of Russian expansive tendencies. ... designed to confront the Russians with unalterable counterforce at every point where they show signs of encroaching upon the interest of a peaceful and stable world.

He also warned against an excessively militaristic response, because the competition was broader—about ideas as well as about military strength.

The policy of containment was given practical effect by the *National Security Council Report 68* (NSC 68) of 1950 on US Objectives and Programs for National Security. In this extra-ordinary document, which established the basic goal and framework of foreign policy for the next forty years, the observation was made that "the risk of war with the USSR is sufficient to warrant, in common prudence, timely and adequate preparation by the United States." NSC 68 went on to make truly sweeping recommendations, including that the United States

> develop a level of military readiness which can be maintained as long as necessary as a deterrent to Soviet aggression, as indispensable support to our political attitude toward the USSR, as a source of encouragement to nations resisting Soviet political aggression, and as an adequate basis for immediate military commitments and for rapid mobilization should war prove unavoidable.[2]

NSC 68 became dogma. In the ensuing years, the defence budget more than doubled in size[3] and the militarization of US foreign policy began in earnest. It has not ended yet, although the Obama administration embodies the possibility of greater balance.

Containing the Soviet Union

Containing the Soviet Union did not come cheap. In his famous farewell address on January 17, 1961, President Eisenhower, channeling an earlier general and president, George Washington, warned against the dynamic of the military-industrial complex, saying that

> the conjunction of an immense military establishment and a large arms industry is new in the American experience. The total influence—economic, political, even spiritual—is felt in every city, every Statehouse, every office of the Federal government. . . . In the councils of government, we must guard against the acquisition of unwarranted influence, whether sought or unsought, by the military-industrial complex. The potential for the disastrous rise of misplaced power exists and will persist. We must never let the weight of this combination endanger our liberties or democratic processes.

The United States has often been blessed by the quality of its leaders and the clarity of their insights. Regrettably, the insights have not always been acted on—and this one in particular has not. As a consequence, the US has seen fifty years of nearly uninterrupted military growth and concomitant political power. Rare is the Congressional district today that has no military facility or military-dependent industry. In these circumstances, sound management of foreign policy and the defence budget have become nearly impossible. For example, successive administrations have tried, but failed, to trim the costs of the F-22, an aircraft whose main rationale died with the collapse of the Soviet Union. Parts of the F-22 are made in forty-four states,[4] creating a powerful constituency for business as usual.

In the 1970s, the American Right came increasingly to see the world in apocalyptic terms, and American vulnerabilities were greatly exaggerated—as were Soviet capabilities. The Soviet invasion of Afghanistan in 1980 was taken as a shrewd Soviet strategic move at the time. It later came to be regarded as a very serious mistake, one that hastened the collapse of the Soviet Union. Throughout the Cold War, Soviet military strength was substantially, and very likely deliberately, overestimated.

By the 1980s, the Soviet Union's economic capacity to sustain the Cold War was crumbling. Thanks to globalization, particularly of communications, the ability of the Communists to persuade themselves that they were on the right side of history progressively eroded. On coming to office in 1985, General Secretary Mikael Gorbachev tried, too little, too late, with perestroika (restructuring) and glasnost (transparency) to revitalize Communism and the state. Five years later, the system collapsed, and the Berlin Wall was brought down. Chancellor Kohl was to tell Prime Minister Mulroney that this was accomplished by the appeal of German television commercials to the consumers on the other side, which revealed the disparity in the standards of living in the East and the West.

To his everlasting credit, Gorbachev did not use his still-formidable military force to try to preserve the Communist system, which he could have done—at the likely cost of enormous bloodshed.

The End of the Cold War and the Temptations of Empire

The end of the Cold War brought little respite from the national security obsessions of Washington, however. In 1992, as one of its last acts, the Pentagon of the George Bush Sr. administration under then Secretary of Defense Dick Cheney, drafted Defense Planning Guidance (DPG), the document that the Pentagon used in the preparation and planning of military budgets and forces. Though it was a classified document, it was, nevertheless, strategically leaked in the best Washington tradition and widely discussed. Among its principal authors were Paul Wolfowitz, then deputy undersecretary of defense for policy planning, "Scooter" Libby, principal deputy undersecretary for strategy and resources, and Zalmay Khalilzad, assistant undersecretary for policy planning at the Department of Defense, all three of whom were to play major roles in bringing about the Iraq War in 2003.

The 1992 DPG argued that US power was crucial to the functioning of the global order, that the US would be the undisputed power in every global region, and that the US would pre-empt any challengers, including allies. With its focus on benevolent domination by one power, the Pentagon document articulated a clear rejection of collective security, the centrality of the Charter of the United Nations, and the rule of law. It was a breathtaking shift. The document was aimed at keeping the United States the world's sole superpower. "We must maintain," it said, "the mechanisms for deterring potential competitors from even aspiring to a larger regional or global role."[5] The document embarrassed the George Bush Sr. White House, which ordered that it be toned down.

Meanwhile, slowly but surely from its nadir in Vietnam, the military rebuilt its capacity and its reputation with the American public. The first Gulf War and its demonstration of precision-guided munitions caught the temper of the electronic times. The war was also a resounding success; and it left Saddam Hussein in place and, thus, created no messy aftermath for the US to manage. Similarly, the rout of the Taliban and al Qaeda in Afghanistan in 2001 and the "shock and awe" of the Iraq campaign in 2003 demonstrated the dazzling technical advancement of the US military and the impressive skills of the American soldier. The Vietnam syndrome was vanquished. Rare is the US politician today who does not feel the need to salute, literally and figuratively, the US military.

The tendency to paranoia and threat exaggeration continued unabated. By 1998, the Commission to Assess the Ballistic Missile Threat to the US, chaired by Donald Rumsfeld, found that "a new strategic environment now gives emerging ballistic missile powers the capacity, through a combination of domestic development and foreign assistance, to acquire the means to strike the U.S. within about five years of a decision to acquire such a capability. ... Available alternative means of delivery can shorten the warning time of deployment nearly to zero."[6] The countries causing concern were Iran, Iraq, and North Korea, which President George W. Bush was to call the "axis of evil" after 9/11.

The US, accustomed to governing itself domestically by the checks and balances built into the US constitution by Madison, Jefferson, and the founding fathers, found that it faced few checks or balances abroad. There was, thus, little to brake US international ambitions and its growing appetite for empire, at least among some intellectuals and officials. Library shelves full of books on empire were written, including *Empire Lite* by Michael Ignatieff.[7] In an insight more accurate than he likely intended, the Conservative commentator Charles Krauthammer coined the phrase "the unipolar moment."

While the idea of empire certainly seems to have appealed to many soft-handed academics—and undoubtedly did to lots of hard-headed neocons—there is little evidence that the American people shared, or shares, that view. A poll done for the US Council on Foreign Relations and the Pew Research Centre for the People and the Press in late 2005, before the worst days of the Iraqi insurgency, found a revival of isolationist sentiment among the general public. Fully 42 percent of Americans said that the United States should "mind its own business internationally and let other countries get along the best they can on their own."

Very few American colleges or universities have offered programs in Middle Eastern languages or Islamic studies. According to the 9/11 Commission report of July 2004, the total number of undergraduate degrees granted in Arab-language studies in US colleges and universities in 2002 was six. Young Americans were evidently not preparing themselves for lives governing the dusty, far-flung outposts of empire. When Fareed Zakaria, interviewing US Secretary of Defense Robert Gates on CNN in May 2009, asked whether the US was repeating the "overstretch" mistake of the British Empire, Gates replied, "If we are an imperial power, we are a unique one in history, in that we are the only one in history that is always looking for an exit strategy."

9/11

Nous sommes tous Américains! (We Are All Americans!)
—Jean-Marie Colombani, *Le Monde*

It is difficult to exaggerate the impact of that infamous September day on the American national psyche. Nearly 3,000 innocent people were killed, more even than were lost in the Japanese attack on Pearl Harbor on December 7, 1941, another date that, as Roosevelt famously said, would "live in infamy." It transformed US politics and foreign policy, triggered righteous anger, and unleashed the dogs of war, creating a new enemy—al Qaeda, and for many Americans, Islam—that had to be fought beyond the constraints of law. Washington persuaded itself that US security could best, in fact, only, be assured by American military power. Neither treaties nor international law nor institutions, including the United Nations and NATO, were deemed either capable of protecting US interests or necessary to confer legitimacy on US action. War came no longer to be seen as a last resort, but rather as a ready instrument of American foreign policy.

There was little in the reaction of the international community to 9/11 to warrant such unilateralism, nor to justify the US's jeopardizing sixty years of development of international law, most of which previous US administrations had promoted (and all of which was significant to Canadian interests). On September 12, 2001, the UN General Assembly, which, as mentioned earlier, is not a decision-making body, issued a unanimous declaration of solidarity with the American people. Within days of September 11, the UN Security Council, whose decisions are binding, proscribed co-operation with terrorists, ordering member states to deny them both safe haven and the use of national banking systems to finance their operations. This was on top of the thirteen counter-terrorism treaties that the UN had negotiated previously—on such things as aircraft hijacking, hostage taking, and the making of chemical explosives. Many governments, including the Canadian government, sent troops to Afghanistan to fight the Taliban and al Qaeda alongside American forces. Nevertheless, the US, grievously wounded, deeply offended, and uniquely powerful, responded to the attack with a unilateral course of action that, regrettably, aggravated its injuries, gravely damaged its moral standing, and endangered the rest of us in the process.

I was Canadian ambassador to the UN in Manhattan when the al Qaeda attack on the Twin Towers took place, and I witnessed personally the shock and anger of Americans. Deeply engraved in my memory is the experience of threading my way southwards that morning towards my office near the UN through tens of thousands of New Yorkers streaming northward up the middle of New York's broad avenues, away from the Twin Towers, in mass and shocked silence. Equally indelible are the photographs of people leaping from windows; the buildings pancaking, one after the other; the small mountain of twisted steel and rubble where the towers had stood; and the smell of smoke. Rescuers came from as far away as British Columbia to find that the job had almost immediately become a search not for survivors, but for victims.

Few injured people escaped the buildings, and the flood of blood donations made that day went to serve other needs.

I also remember our urgent efforts to account for all of our own staff (seven young officers had had dinner at Windows on the World, the restaurant on top of the Twin Towers, the night before) and to help them notify their frantic relatives. That day, and in the days to come, the personnel of Canada's mission to the UN assisted their colleagues across town at the Canadian Consulate in responding to many thousands of calls from distraught Canadians, and tracking down their missing relatives. In the end, we accounted for the vast majority of the missing, but twenty-four Canadians died in the attacks. A perverse, unofficial tally of deaths among US allies was kept by the media as an indicator of solidarity with the United States.

I represented Canada at many memorial services at sites as diverse as St. Patrick's Cathedral and Yankee Stadium. In the process, I came to learn the words of "America the Beautiful," which for me, will always be a poignant hymn of loss and tragedy. For a long time after 9/11, I chose to walk the sunniest routes to the office through the shady canyons of New York as a kind of antidote to depression.

At Yankee Stadium, I was struck by the jumbotron clips of demonstrations of solidarity from Sydney and Ankara to Berlin and London. But not to Ottawa. The spontaneous gatherings across Canada were ignored, as was the semi-official gathering of 100,000 Canadians on Parliament Hill. If a demonstration of solidarity is not seen, does it count? In a further gesture of solidarity, Senator Jerry Grafstein led busloads of Canadians to New York City, and CTV, with host Pamela Wallin, broadcast the event live for hours. Regrettably, beyond one US radio report, I know of no other coverage in the US of this extraordinary gesture. Except for those New Yorkers who happened to be walking along 46th Street that day, no one saw the event. Another tree of solidarity fell unremarked in the forest. And when Bush thanked others publicly for their solidarity, he ignored Canada. Even in tragedy, when Americans were looking for friends, they couldn't see us, through no fault of our own. Our invisibility to Americans is one of the persistent challenges Canadian foreign policy faces.

It was not until November that the redoubtable *New York Times* reported the fact that on 9/11, Canada had welcomed all inbound transatlantic and transpacific flights and fed and sheltered 35,000 passengers, mostly Americans, for several days. Instead, immediately after and for several weeks the *Times* spent its time trying to prove the urban legend that the terrorists came via Canada, even replacing their reporter who was covering Canada and was apparently unwilling to tell the story the *Times* thought to be true. America's "paper of record" persisted for weeks more until then foreign minister John Manley told the editorial board personally, and bluntly, that they were wrong. The then New York senator Hillary Clinton went on repeating the story even after being told face to face that it was not true. Finally, I remember the outrage of many New Yorkers as the shock wore off, openly calling on Washington "to kill them all," whoever "they" were. It was mostly Arabs and Muslims who were the objects of their anger, but any tawny person would do. The *New Yorker* captured the American zeitgeist with a cover cartoon depicting a nervous, brown-skinned driver, whose yellow cab was festooned with dozens of American flags and plastered in red, white, and blue.

The US, which had spent, literally, trillions of dollars on high-cost, high-technology weapons in an effort to make itself invulnerable was mocked by the gods. It found itself attacked, out of the blue, by an enemy using low-cost, low-technology weapons, with horrific consequences. All the aircraft carrier battle groups, the high-priced missiles and precision munitions, the space-based gear, the advances in electronic weaponry and controls, and the fortune spent on the National Security Administration (which principally intercepts foreign communications), the CIA, and the FBI failed to deter, detect, or stop nineteen young fanatics with box cutters and airline tickets. Nevertheless, few Americans questioned, at the time, whether more national security spending would make the US anything other than more secure. In fact, 9/11 even became a rationale for pushing ahead with ballistic missile defence. The attack on 9/11, ultimately, facilitated the patriation of more power from Congress to the executive branch by the Bush-Cheney administration, making it easier for them to decide when to go to war in Iraq and on how to wage the war. It brought new life to the national security impulse.

In Afghanistan, the US and its allies, mostly Afghans, routed the Taliban and drove al Qaeda into the caves of Pakistan. But, following the initial success, Afghanistan was quasi-neglected, as Bush's national security team opted for attacking Iraq, thus beginning a decade-long, half-distracted battle for Afghanistan's future, during which the Taliban resistance grew steadily stronger. The Iraq decision prompted candidate Obama to accuse the administration of taking its eyes off the ball. It led Emmy-Award-winning TV satirist Jon Stewart to comment that the world should know that, when someone attacked the US, the US would not turn the other cheek. It would attack someone else.

"Why Do They Hate Us"?

In the immediate aftermath of the 9/11 attacks, President George W. Bush and many other Americans asked rhetorically: "Why do they hate us so much?" Regrettably, the Americans came rapidly to the wrong answer, concluding that the reason the US was hated was not what the US did, but what the US was. "They" hated the US for its modernity and success. It was a convenient answer. It meant that the world's opposition to US policies was simply a manifestation of anti-Americanism, something illegitimate that the US could not fix—and ought not, therefore, to be influenced by. But the right answer was precisely the opposite: it was what the US government did abroad, that is, US foreign policy, that created such animosity; and it was American success at home as a modern, prosperous democratic society that people everywhere admired.

Dr. Stephen Kull, editor of WorldPublicOpinion.org and director of the Program on International Policy Attitudes (PIPA) and the Center on Policy Attitudes (COPA) of the University of Maryland, testified in March 2007 to the US Congress that "the aspect of US behavior that [elicited] the strongest negative feeling

[was] how the US government [dealt] with other countries." On average, 75 percent of those that WorldPublicOpinion.org polled around the world disapproved of how the US was handing the Iraq War, 69 percent disapproved of US treatment of detainees in Guantanamo and other prisons, and 68 percent disapproved of how the US handled the war between Israel and Hezbollah in Lebanon. According to Dr. Kull, the US military presence in the Middle East was exceedingly unpopular in virtually all countries. On average, 69 percent of those polled believed the US military presence there "provoked more conflict than it prevented," while just 16 percent saw it as a stabilizing force.

Among all these negatives, there was also good news. There was, apparently, evidence that the unhappiness with US foreign policy was not a rejection of US values so much as a criticism of the US's departure from those values, notably in its behaviour in the Middle East and in its handling of detainees. This reality has had enormous significance for Canada. While there may be good tactical reasons for participating in American-led coalitions of the willing, such as cultural similarities and operational doctrines, there are strong strategic reasons for keeping a respectful distance when the objective rationale for joining up is not fully compelling.

TORTURE: PARAGON LOST

Perhaps nowhere did the Bush administration depart further from American values than on torture. Nor did anything else make co-operation by Canada and others with the American forces more fraught politically.

President George W. Bush told the American people and the world that "the United States does not torture. It's against our laws, and it's against our values. I have not authorized it and I will not authorize it."[8] He repeated the assurance numerous times. The International Committee of the Red Cross (ICRC), nevertheless, flatly contradicted him, albeit privately as per its rules (the document doing so was leaked, but almost certainly not by the ICRC). After interviewing "high value detainees" at Guantanamo, the ICRC reported that "the ill-treatment to which they were subjected while held in the CIA program, either singly or in combination, constituted torture. . . . other elements of the ill-treatment . . . constituted cruel, inhuman or degrading treatment."[9]

The ICRC's role includes monitoring compliance with the Geneva Conventions, which define the basic rights of those captured during a military conflict and establish protection for the wounded and for civilians. The Conventions have been ratified as is or with reservations by 194 countries, including the US and Afghanistan, and they apply to internal as well as international conflicts.

In 2002, Bush decided that the protections of the Geneva Conventions did not apply to members of the Taliban or al Qaeda, despite the fact the conflict took place in Afghanistan and that both the US and Afghanistan were, and are, parties to the Geneva Conventions. He had been advised by White House Counsel Alberto Gonzales that "the war on terror is a 'new kind of war.' . . . This new paradigm renders obsolete Geneva's strict limitations on questioning of enemy prisoners, and renders quaint some of its provisions."[10]

The Bush administration adopted "enhanced interrogation techniques" to be used by the CIA on high value detainees, and also sought and got legal advice from its own attorneys about their legality. The advice concluded that such techniques did not constitute torture, so long as the damage done did not rise "to the level of death, organ failure or the permanent impairment of a significant bodily function."[11] The US created its own unilateral definition of torture, with which the "enhanced interrogation techniques" complied. Hence, President Bush's claim that the US did not torture.

To be on the safe side, though, the legal advice effectively exempted practitioners of the enhanced interrogation techniques from prosecution, so long as they applied the techniques in a good-faith effort and not maliciously or sadistically. Secretary Rumsfeld authorized the use of the enhanced techniques by the US military at Guantanamo, and from there they migrated to Abu

Ghraib in Iraq and probably elsewhere. Up to that point, they had been used only by the CIA.

The practice of "rendering" foreign suspects to countries that would torture them was operational at the same time, and several Canadians of Arab descent, most egregiously Maher Arar, were tortured in Middle East prisons with US complicity. A few administration members, notably Secretary of State Colin Powell and state legal adviser William Taft IV raised objections, but to little avail. The view that the Geneva Conventions did not apply to al Qaeda and the Taliban was subsequently contradicted by the US Supreme Court. Some of the more questionable practices were eventually halted, but incalculably severe and long-lasting damage was done to the US's reputation internationally. The world lost its paragon of human rights. Canada's co-operation with the US was made more problematic.

THE NATIONAL SECURITY STRATEGY OF 2002

I will not wait on events, while dangers gather. I will not stand by, as peril draws closer and closer . . .
—President George W. Bush

For the Bush administration, the scale of destruction caused by the September 11 attacks raised the extremely urgent question of how to prevent another catastrophe; a terrorist attack with weapons of mass destruction would cost countless lives and transform international relations forever. It would be the ultimate paradigm changer. The administration concluded that it had to act before another threat could materialize. At West Point, in June of 2002, Bush declared that "the war on terror will not be won on the defensive. We must take the battle to the enemy, disrupt his plans, and confront the worst threats before they emerge . . . the only path to safety is the path of action. And this nation will act."

In September, the administration tabled the 2002 US National Security Strategy (NSS). The NSS owed much to the 1992 Defense

Planning Guidance, only this time no one was embarrassed by it—and no one toned it down. Much of the new NSS was, in fact, unobjectionable, even laudable. It was, moreover, blessedly brief, dramatically shorter than all recent Canadian foreign policy reviews. Its main problems lay, first, in its unilateralist, preventive posture, and second, in the determination it expressed to preserve US dominance perpetually.

At West Point, President Bush had told graduating students that "America has and intends to keep military strengths beyond challenge, thereby making the destabilizing arms races of other eras pointless, and limiting rivalries to trade and other pursuits of peace." Bush was announcing a Pax Americana without end. Fareed Zakaria, writing later in *Newsweek*, observed that the danger of American idealism was not that American ideals were wrong, but that American policy makers had lost sight of practical realities and opened a chasm between rhetoric and reality.

While the NSS talked of pre-emption, which is permitted under customary international law and the UN Charter, subsequent US actions amounted to prevention, which is not. The difference is not just a matter of legalistic hairsplitting. Under international law, to be declared pre-emptive, an act must meet rigorous tests regarding the capability and intent of an adversary to do harm and the urgency of the need for self-defence (for instance, the attack must be imminent, and there must not be effective alternatives to immediate military action). It also presumes the availability of highly credible intelligence.

The Bush administration clearly thought that *preventive* military force would have to be at the core of its strategy, because it believed that terrorists, unlike states, could neither be deterred nor contained, the policy strategies that had worked against the Soviet Union in the Cold War. "Deterrence," Bush explained at West Point, "means nothing against shadowy terrorist networks with no nation or citizens to defend. Containment is not possible when unbalanced dictators with weapons of mass destruction can deliver those weapons on missiles or secretly provide them to terrorist allies."

Whatever the costs of lowering the barrier to using force preventively, the administration argued, they were outweighed by the dangers of waiting too long to act. As the NSS put it, "the greater the threat, the greater is the risk of inaction—and the more compelling the case for taking anticipatory action to defend ourselves, even if the uncertainty remains as to the time and place of the enemies' attack."

The Iraq War was the first test of the US policy of prevention, even though it was presented as pre-emptive—to stop a tyrant already possessing weapons of mass destruction and preparing to use them imminently. The UK's dossier on Iraq, later to be called the "Dodgy Dossier" for its inaccuracies and misinterpretations, added to the argument for pre-emption, claiming that some Iraqi weapons of mass destruction were deployable within forty-five minutes of an order to use them, a claim that misled people into believing that such missiles put the UK, and even the US, in jeopardy. The war was soon to illustrate the wisdom of those who framed UN Charter, who had made the declaration of war a UN Security Council prerogative.

THE IRAQ WAR

The Bush administration made the decision to go to war before even approaching the UN Security Council, confected the *casus belli* of Iraqi weapons of mass destruction, failed to attract even majority support for war in the UN Security Council, let alone the 60 percent (including the votes of the other P5) needed to pass a resolution, and attacked Iraq anyway, severely damaging the US's reputation in doing so, strengthening the appeal of Islamist extremists, and costing the lives of literally uncounted Iraqis, the total reaching very conservatively into the many scores of thousands and, in some estimates, ranging as high as a million.

The Bush administration had plenty of help around Washington, London, and beyond. The credulous US media, including icons like the *New York Times* and the *Washington Post*, to say nothing of the conservative media, including the *Wall Street Journal* and the bellicose Fox News, acted more like "homers" than professional journalists, cheerleading for the war and failing in their fundamental duty of providing the public with critical judgment and circumspection as a psychosis of war developed. As Elizabeth Palmer, a Canadian reporter employed by CBS, told the audience at a 2005 Couchiching Conference outside Orillia, Ontario, the White House bullied the American media, at least those that needed coercing, into patriotic coverage of the story. Nor was the professional US military immune to war fever. Already in the spring of 2002, I was told by a then retired, former high-ranking US Army general that support for an attack on Iraq had become a litmus test for the US military. Those who doubted its necessity or its likely efficacy either kept their own counsel or found their careers side tracked. As for politicians, "soft on security" was a label few thought they could risk wearing, and few opposed the evidently increasing militarization of American foreign policy. In the US Congress in the fall of 2002, even congressmen and congresswomen who knew better—or ought to have, like Hillary Clinton—did not dare to vote against the resolution authorizing the Bush administration to attack Iraq.

Not least responsible for the attack on Iraq was the government of Tony Blair, and Blair himself, who put the close UK relationship with Washington ahead of every other consideration, including the many thousands of lives that would inevitably be lost. The British could possibly have stopped the march to war if they had had the courage to part company with Washington. Instead, they fell in and marched along behind their patron for whatever vicarious power they could derive from doing so.

The Case *Against* War: The View from New York

In the fall of 2002, I participated in two separate briefings by UN ambassadors for American lawmakers, including the late senator Ted Kennedy and Senator John Kerry. We unanimously told the senators that there was little support at the UN for the war, that the US rationale for war was flawed and dangerous, that the weapons inspectors should be allowed to do their jobs, and that Iraq was sufficiently contained by the international sanctions and the efforts of the inspectors to minimize whatever threat it represented.

The ambassador of Jordan, Prince Zeid Ra'ad Zeid Al-Hussein, told the senators, presciently and graphically, that attacking Iraq would be like swallowing a razor blade. Extracting it afterwards could only be painful and bloody. Another told the senators, also presciently, that the Americans might win the military campaign in Iraq in sixty days, but the situation would not stabilize there again in sixty years, and it would not be forgotten by Arabs for six hundred years, a sentiment I heard him express directly to Secretary Powell on the floor of the Security Council on the eve of the war. Nor was it only the Arabs who were reacting negatively; opposition to the war was widespread. For example, Sergei Lavrov, then Russian Permanent Representative and now Russian foreign minister, commented that the United States would "burn its fingers on Iraq."

On the congressional resolution to go to war, the late Senator Kennedy voted against. In his own words: "My vote against this misbegotten war is the best vote I have cast in the United States Senate since I was elected in 1962."[12] Senator Kerry, against what I presume was his better judgment, voted for the resolution, a vote that possibly cost him the presidency in 2004. His vote was relentlessly exploited by the Republican Party in the electoral campaign as decisive evidence of an indecisive character, one prone to flip-flopping on major national security issues. Similarly, in the 2008 primary campaign, Hillary Clinton could not escape her vote authorizing the war. Barack Obama had no similar baggage to carry.

Bush, the father, had a solid case for war in 1990, made it well, and got ample international support; Bush, the son, had a flimsy case in 2003, made it badly, and could not get Security Council support, let alone avoid the three vetoes (French, Russian, and Chinese) that almost certainly would have been exercised. As I reported to Prime Minister Chrétien at the time, there was no prospect of attracting majority support among the rest of the membership.[13] In fact, the contrary was true. The diplomacy of Bush Senior's administration had been deft, that of Bush Junior's over-confident, ham-handed, and ineffectual. The cost for Americans would be enormous.

The CIA's Own "Dodgy Dossier": The Worst Moment of a General's Career

The early months of 2003 were a time of high drama at the UN in New York, as the British, especially, and the Americans sought a UN Security Council resolution authorizing the invasion of Iraq that they were determined to carry out—and as most of the rest of the membership resisted giving it to them. Drawn to conflict, news networks from around the world converged on UN headquarters in New York. Scores of mobile TV trucks lined First Avenue and TV reporters did endless "stand-ups" against the backdrop of the iconic UN building. I remember having to take a mission car and driver just three blocks to the UN from my office so I could enter the UN building through its garage and evade press scrums at the entrances, especially on those days I had little I wanted to say.

At the World Economic Forum conference on "Building Trust" in Davos, Switzerland, at the end of January 2003, Secretary of State Colin Powell got into a highly publicized and emotional debate with the former archbishop of Canterbury, George Carey, about the wisdom of the looming war. Pursuant to the theme of the conference, Powell said America could be trusted. He pointed to recent American involvement in Afghanistan, Kosovo, and Kuwait as examples to prove that people "can trust us to do our jobs and then leave." All the US asked for, he said, was a little bit of earth in which to bury its soldiers.[14]

A week later, Powell came to New York and misled, to use a very generous descriptor, the UN Security Council and the world. With the director of the CIA, George Tenet, sitting behind him in the Security Council chamber (there is only one seat per country at the horseshoe-shaped table), he made a long, detailed case for the invasion of Iraq and for regime change. Little or nothing of what he said has ever been corroborated. Much of it has been categorically proven wrong. Notoriously, he insisted that "every statement I make today is backed up by sources, solid sources. These are not assertions. What we're giving you are facts and conclusions based on solid intelligence."[15]

He discussed everything from stockpiles of chemical weapons ("100 to 500 tons, enough to fill 16,000 battlefield rockets") to aluminum tubes for gas centrifuges (to enrich uranium for nuclear weapons) to mobile biological weapons laboratories. He held up an empty vial of botulinum toxin for dramatic effect (prompting Maureen Dowd of the *New York Times* to observe that there was likely more botox—the cosmetic industry's name for the same material—in the wealthy Upper East Side of New York than there was in Iraq). For anyone used to dealing with intelligence, the weaknesses of the case were all too apparent. It was hard to escape the conclusion that either Secretary Powell had been misled himself, although someone of his experience should not have been so misled, or that the secretary of state of the United States was using a formal session of the UN Security Council to dupe the world on a matter of war and peace. Reactions in the room, including mine, ranged from incredulity to anger to intense disappointment.

For many among the US public, the speech sealed the deal, and Americans, for the most part, supported the war in good faith. I sat in the Council, listening to the presentation, and heard the most dramatic possible interpretations by Powell of what struck me, at the time, as the flimsiest of evidence. As Hans Blix, head of the UN weapons inspectors, later said, where others would put a question mark on an issue, the Bush administration had put an exclamation point.

Following the active combat phase of the war, despite the intense efforts of literally 1,400 weapons inspectors in the US's Iraq Survey Group, the Americans could not substantiate any of these allegations. The Survey Group acknowledged, subsequently, that they had found no weapons of mass destruction (WMD), but they also made a thinly supported claim that the Iraq regime had had the intention of building such weapons—eventually. Even that dubious assertion undermined the case for legitimate preemptive war, which, as mentioned earlier, requires imminent danger, among other things. It also gave the lie to the idea that, in the 1990s, the Iraqis had not substantially complied with UN Security Council resolutions, which had required them to get rid of whatever weapons of mass destruction they had.

The Bottom Line

The jury is *not* still out on the war on Iraq, as some American conservatives hope and claim. In fact, it is in. The verdict of the international community is that the attack was possibly the worst foreign policy mistake in American history (though the war in Vietnam is a strong contender).

It has often been said since then that, though the intelligence was faulty, everyone believed it at the time. That contention, too, is just more self-serving spin. In fact, many did not believe it. I, and many other ambassadors and officials in capitals, who had ready access to the freely available UN inspectors' reports, did not believe the American case. I spent hours before Powell briefed the Security Council poring over the reports to be sure I understood them. I did the same check again after his testimony to see whether I had missed anything. I talked to Hans Blix, the head UN weapons inspector, who told me that he had asked the Americans and British to give him their best information. But when they did so, he found nothing, which apparently resulted in White House threats to discredit him. Nevertheless, on March 30, 2003, Defense Secretary Rumsfeld told ABC, "We know where they [the WMD] are. They're in the area around Tikrit and Bagdad and east, west, south and north somewhat." A very helpful insight.

In fact, the UN weapons inspectors' reports told a different story than Washington's. The inspectors were much closer to a complete accounting of Scud missiles, nuclear materials, and chemical weapons precursors (the materials from which chemical weapons are made) than Powell's presentation suggested. The outstanding doubt was mostly about biological weapons, because of the relative ease of their production and the normal difficulty of proving a negative (that is, proving that there were none). Those UN reports were available to the US, as they were to me and to everyone else.

The problem was that, at no time in the lead-up to the Iraq War in the winter–spring of 2002–03, did it seem to give Washington officials any pause that a very large majority of UN member states did not agree that war in Iraq was necessary and urgent. It did not seem to occur to the war's advocates that these objections were anything other than the usual unavoidable and small-minded reaction to far-sighted American leadership that would have to be endured until the policy vindicated itself. Washington could not see that profound disagreement really mattered, that it could mean that the US assessment of the situation was wrong, and that it could undermine US prospects for success in Iraq beyond the war itself.

ALL THINGS CONSIDERED

During the Bush administration, stimulated by the al Qaeda attack of 9/11 and the Iraq War, the by-then-reflexive American national security mindset grew stronger. In an age of international terrorist threats, Washington convinced itself that US power alone could protect American interests. The ready recourse to military force and covert operations, the renewed standing of the US military in American self-perceptions, as well as the colossal scale of military resources, the disdain for multilateral co-operation and for treaty commitments, and the influence of fundamentalist religious voters, all imbued American foreign policy with a certitude that left little room for the input of its allies, let alone for their dissent from a particular course of action. Sycophancy was treated as friendship and dissent as anti-Americanism. Together, these factors made the US a difficult partner to work with.

The distance between delusion and hubris is short, and the Bush administration covered it at a gallop. The administration's actions had an air of Greek tragedy about them, a subject worthy of the pen of a Shakespeare. Nevertheless, the American people are the ultimate check on any administration's policies and the balancer of US behaviour. American voters, to paraphrase Churchill, showed in the election of Barack Obama (albeit after re-electing Bush in 2004) that they can be counted on to do the right thing, if only after exhausting the alternatives.

Lessons Learned?

There are many "take-away" lessons from the Iraq War, but five seem particularly relevant, four of general application and one of particular significance for Canada.

First, power corrupts; it especially corrupts judgment. Whatever the reasons adduced for invading Iraq, when the "spin cycle" stopped, it became clear that the US had done so because it could (that is, it had the capability to do so), and because it wanted to do so, for all manner of reasons, not because it had to. The administration thought the "demonstration effect" of destroying Saddam Hussein would serve American interests. The administration wanted to rid itself of a psychopath and to demonstrate to other psychopaths that it could, and would, do the same to them if it wished. There were secondary reasons for the war, from safeguarding oil, to protecting allies (Israel), even possibly to protecting the Iraqi people. But without power, there would have been no war. The British, for example, even if they fully shared American motivations, which is doubtful, would never on their own have tried to invade Iraq. Too much military power is a liability.

Without overwhelming military capability, decision-makers in Washington would likely never have acted in Iraq on the confection of rationales they cobbled together in the winter of 2002–03. Washington even thought that attacking Iraq would be easy (a "cake walk" in the immortal words of Ken Adelman, former director of the U.S. Arms Control and Disarmament Agency during the Reagan administration, and friend of Dick Cheney) and that it would be cheap (it would pay for itself, in the equally enduring Congressional testimony of Paul Wolfowitz, the Bush administration's deputy secretary of defense).

The second lesson is that empire is not what it used to be; the

US could not create a graveyard in Iraq and call it peace. Americans, to say nothing of the rest of the world, would not accept the carnage. The greatest military power in the world was unable—in significant part because of its own decent values—to subdue a Third World country with a population of twenty-five million that had, in the span of one generation, fought two earlier, costly wars, endured a decade of military embargoes and economic sanctions, and suffered five years of attacks on its air defences. The irony of the US action was that it demonstrated US limits as well as US strength.

Third, reputations are more easily destroyed than constructed. In flouting the UN Charter and in perpetrating war crimes, notably transgressing the Torture Convention and the Geneva Protocols, the US sacrificed, possibly forever, its standing in the eyes of the world as the paragon of democracy, human rights, and the law. Opposition to US policy at the UN and around the world, especially the Muslim world, became widespread and deeply held. In defying the international community, the Bush administration dug the US into a hole of distrust that will take it a long time to climb back out of.

Fourth, the world is governable, but only co-operatively. Today's most intractable and consequential problems, from nuclear security to climate change to public health to terrorism, are global in their essence and require global solutions. The idea of benevolent hegemony, the neocon fantasy of the Bush era, is best confined to international relations theory, not to practical governance. As the late George Kennan observed, "I can say without hesitation that this planet is never going to be ruled from any single political center, whatever its military power."[16]

The world, as we know it, let alone the world as it is becoming, does not respond to unilateral decision-making and ultimatums. Giving others the choice to be with America or with the terrorists, as President Bush did in the fall of 2001, is unavailing in a world in which many countries have the desire and the option to be neither.

Fifth and finally, the lesson for Canada is that in matters of war and peace, we cannot just rely on assessments made in

Washington or London or wherever. We should not shrink from disagreeing with the Americans when we think they are wrong. Likewise, we should not hesitate to agree with them when we think they are right. But in all cases, it is vital to the well-being of Canadians that we retain, indeed enhance, our capability to understand the world and to make our own decisions.

7

THE US UNDER NEW MANAGEMENT:
Paragon Regained?

At times, American foreign policy has been far-sighted simultaneously serving our national interests, our ideals and the interests of other nations. At other times, American policies have been misguided, based on false assumptions that ignore the legitimate aspirations of other peoples, undermine our own credibility and make for a more dangerous world. . . . In other words, [the US] record is mixed.
—Barack Obama, *The Audacity of Hope*

P eople around the world wanted a clean break from the Bush years. With the election of Barack Obama, probably the most worldly president ever elected in the United States, they got it. Obama is a man of penetrating intellect and truly extraordinary communications skills; what remains to be determined is whether he has the strength of character and reserves of conviction to escape the inertia of national security obsessions at home, and to bend the arc of American foreign policy abroad. His health care victory was a *sine qua non*, for international reasons as much as domestic ones. Had he lost, the world would have taken him much less seriously. Indeed, a Russian friend of mine had already begun to call him Barack Hussein Gorbachev.

Barack Obama is a very different kind of American leader, with very different foreign policy ideas. His orientations towards the world are much more North-South than East-West. Famously born of a Kenyan father and an American mother, he still has family in Kenya, some of whom are Muslims. His mother worked with NGOs in Third World countries. His early childhood years were spent in Indonesia, where he attended a local, not an international, school with Indonesian Muslim children. In his own words in his book *The Audacity of Hope*, he "ran the streets with the children of farmers, servants, sailors and clerks." He went to high school in offshore Hawaii, the most multicultural state in the US, one that is neither mainland nor mainstream. Born in 1961, he was twelve when conscription was abolished and has no direct military experience. The Cold War ended before he was thirty and had little direct impact on his life or his thinking. As an American leader, he really is "something new under the sun."

It is instructive to compare President Obama's background to that of Senator McCain's. The Republican candidate for the presidency in 2008 is the son and grandson of admirals. He is a graduate of Annapolis Naval Academy (graduating infamously 894th out of 899 in his class—there is hope for everyone) and a naval veteran. He has served as chairman of the Senate Armed Services Committee and is currently its Ranking Member. McCain's world view is heavily one of allies and enemies, of threats and dangers, and of power projection. In important respects, McCain is the embodiment of the militarization of American foreign policy that has progressed since Truman and Eisenhower. He has admirable qualities, not least his capacity for straight talk and his willingness to stand apart from his party—especially, but not exclusively, on the issue of torture. But, had he been elected, he would have been perhaps more commander-in-chief than president. The election of McCain would have meant continuity with the national-security-dominated policy launched after the Second World War.

Seeing the United States as Others See It

The gap between the perception others have of the US and the self-perception of Americans has grown perilously wide. In March 23, 1983, in an address to the nation on national security, President Reagan asserted that "the defense policy of the United States is based on a simple premise: The United States does not start fights. We will never be an aggressor." President George W. Bush told a Memorial Day audience in 2004 that "it is not in our nature to seek out wars and conflicts. We only get involved when adversaries have left us no alternative." Nor is this historic amnesia a uniquely Republican affliction. At the 2004 Democratic convention, Senator Kerry said: "The USA never goes to war because it wants to. We only go to war because we have to."

To put it most charitably, neither history nor recent practice validates these self-perceptions. They are true with respect to the Second World War and Afghanistan. They are *not* true for most of the scores of conflicts in US history, from Mexico, Cuba, the Dominican Republic, Grenada, Panama, and Nicaragua to the Philippines, Vietnam, and Iraq—not to mention CIA interventions in Iran, the Congo, Chile, and beyond.*

American aggression and interference are enduring elements of the national narratives in the countries in which they occurred.

---

* Canada fared better. "Manifest Destiny" in Canada's case turned out to be neither manifest nor destiny, although various Americans, notably the Fenian terrorists in the east and President James K. Polk in the west, sought to include Canada in whole or in part in the US federation. In the 1844 election, Polk ran on the campaign slogan of "Fifty-four Forty or Fight!" (after 54°40′ of latitude, the line he saw as the appropriate northern boundary of Oregon—the southern boundary was the 42nd parallel). In the event, Polk and the British/Canadians agreed that the border would be the 49th parallel. Splitting the difference at the 48th parallel would have been fairer. The Mexicans were not so lucky. In 1845, the United States annexed Texas, and in 1846 declared war on Mexico. In the subsequent Treaty of Guadalupe Hidalgo, the US took possession of California, New Mexico, and adjacent lands; the Rio Grande was recognized as the southern border of the US.

Iran is the most obvious case in point, where the US intervened with the British to overthrow the democratically elected government of Mohammad Mossadegh in 1953, because of British unhappiness with the nationalization of the Anglo-Iranian Oil Company. For most Americans, US-Iranian history begins with the Iranian takeover of the US embassy in 1979; for Iranians, it started twenty-five years earlier. The reality is that the US is one of the most conflict-prone of states, third after the UK and France since 1945.[1]

President Obama is that rare American—and especially rare American leader—who can see the United States as others see it. His upbringing has left him clear-eyed about American foreign policy. As he observed in *The Audacity of Hope*, American engagement in Indonesia provides, in broad outline, a record of US foreign policy over the past fifty years, including the US's role in

> liberating former colonies and creating international institutions to help manage the post-World War II order; our tendency to view nations and conflicts through the prism of the Cold War; our tireless promotion of American-style capitalism and multinational corporations; the tolerance and occasional encouragement of tyranny, corruption and environmental degradation when it served [US] interests . . . the growing economic power of Asia and the growing resentment of the United States as the sole superpower; the realization that, in the short term at least, democratization might lay bare, rather than alleviate, ethnic hatreds and religious divisions.

President Obama's unusually worldly upbringing has direct relevance to his foreign policy. As he told Agence France Press on November 19, 2007,

> If you don't understand [foreign] cultures then it's very hard for you to make good foreign policy decisions. Foreign policy is all about judgment . . . The benefit of my life of having both

lived overseas and traveled overseas ... is, I have a better sense of how [people] are thinking and what their society is really like. [My] knowledge about foreign affairs isn't just what I studied in school—I studied international relations when I was in college—it's not just the work I [did] on the Senate foreign relations committee. It's actually having the knowledge of how ordinary people in these other countries live.

It has been Obama's foreign policy judgment and his personification of the change away from the exceptionalist, unilateralist-minded, national-security-obsessed Bush administration that explains the resurgence of the US's image in many countries. The confidence that President Obama will "do the right thing in world affairs" is now much stronger in Western countries than it was in the Bush era.[2]

President Obama has proven more popular abroad than at home, and has enjoyed higher favorability ratings in Germany and France, for example, than Chancellor Merkel and President Sarkozy. In Canada, he has proved more popular than Prime Minister Harper and opposition leader Ignatieff combined. In a poll conducted by WorldPublicOpinion.org in the spring of 2009, support for the new president from allies was in the 80–90 percent range, although judgments were more mixed on whether the US was "playing a mainly positive role in the world." A poll by the German Marshall Fund, published in mid-summer 2009, confirmed that Obama had nearly reversed the collapse in public support for the United States witnessed across much of Europe under his predecessor, George W. Bush. According to the Swedish Nation Brands Index,[3] a survey conducted in twenty developed and developing countries around the world, "Brand America" leapt ahead seven places in 2009 to rank first in the world. (Canada fell from fourth to seventh.) At the same time, the populations in Bulgaria, Poland, Romania, Slovakia, Turkey, and Russia have been markedly less enthusiastic about President Obama and the United States than their West European counterparts. Attitudes towards the US in the Muslim world have also been shifting, albeit cautiously, especially as regards the Israeli-Palestinian conflict, where the expectations of fairness that Obama's electoral rhetoric and his speech at Cairo University raised have not been matched with results, and Congress has remained reflexively and uncritically committed to Israel.

On October 9, 2009, the Norwegian Nobel Committee awarded its most prestigious prize to Obama "for his extraordinary efforts to strengthen international diplomacy and co-operation between peoples . . . [for his] vision of and work for a world without nuclear weapons." In a sense, the prize was awarded to the American people for having elected someone who personified the better angels of the American character, and who represented hope for a future that transcended nationalism and power politics. The Nobel committee praised him for having created a new climate in international politics.

THE FOREIGN POLICY PHILOSOPHY OF PRESIDENT OBAMA

In April and May 2010, President Obama issued two key documents, . his National Security Strategy (NSS) and his Nuclear Posture Review (NPR). Together they lay out the Obama administration's approach to global affairs. The NSS tone differs markedly from that of Obama's predecessor, stressing national renewal and global leadership to rebuild American strength, and the role of diplomacy and development assistance as well as military capability in serving American interests. Although "clear-eyed" about the shortfalls of the international system, the US promises to work within the currents of international co-operation, not to step outside them. Gone is the disposition to preventive war and unilateral action, although that prospect is not ruled out. Back are co-operation, strengthening alliances, and creating new partnerships. In another rejection of the policies of this president's predecessor, the Obama National Security Strategy argues that US "security will not come from [the US's] ability to instill fear in other peoples, but through [its] capacity to speak to their hopes." The NPR commits the

United States to maintaining a strong nuclear arsenal, while making modest reductions in nuclear weapons. The US intends to work for nuclear non-proliferation, and enshrines the goal of the elimination of nuclear weapons in US policy, undertaking to reduce the role of nuclear weapons in US defence strategies. While not promising not to be the first to use nuclear weapons, the document undertakes not to use or threaten to use nuclear weapons against states without nuclear weapons that are party to the Nuclear Non-Proliferation Treaty and that are in compliance with their nuclear non-proliferation obligations. The promise is much less qualified than that of the previous administration, but the latter clauses do exclude Iran.

The NSS and the NPR are a condensation of foreign policy ideas that Obama began to develop shortly after inauguration day in 2009. In Prague, Strasbourg, Ankara, Cairo, Moscow, Accra, and the United Nations, as well as at home in Washington, Obama launched a series of extraordinarily eloquent, insightful, and well-gauged speeches, expressing a world view of co-operation and partnership. Secretary of State Clinton, in an interview with Fareed Zakaria on CNN, confirmed that she and the president "have a world view that says America should be leading by example." The Bush administration often seemed to expect to lead by exemption.

The Bush administration's approach to international relations was unilateralist when it could be, and multilateralist when it had to be, notably when it embraced the idea of the G20 when the financial sky was falling, or when it needed the UN to pick up some of the pieces in Iraq. The Clinton administration's impulse had been the reverse—multilateralist when it could be and unilateralist when it had to be. The Obama administration has indicated that it intends to think and act outside this box. The US faces enormous, costly problems at home and abroad, and cannot afford to deal with them all on its own. Health, education, and green technology are all domestic priorities that cost vast amounts of money. If they are to be affordable, more effective international burden-sharing and multilateral co-operation are essential, not elective. A breath of fresh air, this thinking should be very welcome in Ottawa.

In his first speech at the UN in September 2009, it was evident how little President Obama's attitude towards the world body had in common with that of his unilateralist, UN-bashing, multilateralism-hating predecessor. He announced "a new era of engagement based on mutual interest and mutual respect." He acknowledged the UN's failings, but maintained that they were not a reason to abandon the institution. The same month, at a Brookings conference in Washington, Secretary of State Hillary Clinton amplified Obama's sentiments when she argued that "the US [had] to have effective global institutions. That is not a choice. That is an imperative. It is up to [the Obama administration] to determine how to make them effective." She went on to say that, in her view, "the US would ignore the UN and walk away from it at [its] peril, especially in the twenty-first century, where interconnectiveness gives voice and prominence to views that could have easily been either ignored or marginalized in the past"—notably the views of the emerging powers, especially China and India. In her confirmation hearing in Congress in January 2009, she had made a complementary point, saying,

> We must build a world with more partners and fewer
> adversaries. America cannot solve the most pressing
> problems on our own, and the world cannot solve them
> without America. The best way to advance America's
> interests in reducing global threats and seizing global
> opportunities is to design and implement global solutions.
> That isn't a philosophical point. This is our reality.

It is also Canada's reality. And it is a major departure from the world view of the Bush administration.

Since Obama came to office, the US has paid its arrears to the UN, or at least most of them, joined the Human Rights Council, signed the Convention of the Rights of Persons with Disabilities, and embraced the Millennium Development Goals designed to set targets and time frames for economic and social development in the UN's poorer countries. The same co-operative policy principles apply in the Obama administration's approach to other multilateral organizations, both the old—the IMF, the World Bank, and NATO— and the new, such as the G20 and the Financial Stability Forum. NATO, which has long been dominated by the US, is central to managing two major files, Afghanistan and Russia, and significant on others, including arms control and disarmament.

To a considerable extent, the Obama administration has staked its reputation on inducing co-operation by others. Speaking to the Clinton Global Initiative in September 2009, former president Clinton's international foundation, Obama stressed that isolation was impossible in the modern age, and that no one nation, no matter how large and powerful, could meet contemporary challenges alone. Nor could governments do so. New partnerships across sectors and across societies were essential. In short, what was needed, according to President Obama, was "a new spirit of global partnership."

The Obama administration has been at pains to persuade the international community that the US means it when it says it seeks the co-operation of others. Still, after years of growing American unilateralism and imperial flirtations, Washington's emphasis on working with others to meet common ends is met with understandable caution. The words have been very welcome, but judgments remain suspended pending actions.

Terrorism and Torture

With the Obama administration's heavy emphasis on co-operation and the rule of law, it is evident that he has abandoned the policy of unilateral preventive war. This does not mean that the new administration imagines that it is time for the lamb to lie down with the lion. The US is conducting two wars, in Iraq and Afghanistan, and a third "war" against international terrorists. In his first national security speech as president, Obama made clear that the US is indeed at war with al Qaeda and its affiliates (but not with terrorism in the abstract). He acknowledged that the US needed to update its institutions and methods to deal with this threat.

President Obama most emphatically parted company with

his predecessor on the legal dimensions of fighting terrorists, stressing "an abiding confidence in the rule of law and due process; in checks and balances and accountability." Decisions made over the previous eight years, in his view, had established an ad hoc legal approach for fighting terrorism that was neither effective nor sustainable, that departed from legal traditions and time-tested institutions, and that failed to use American values as their compass.

The Bush administration had taken the view that what the CIA did was not torture, but, even if it was torture, it was necessary and saved the US from further attack. According to Vice-President Cheney, coddling terrorists and reading them their Miranda rights would not have worked in the dirty world the terrorists inhabited. Referring specifically to Cheney, Obama responded that "that philosophy has done incredible damage to our image around the world."[4] He said the US should never turn its back on the Constitution's enduring principles for expedience's sake, because it was those same principles that strengthened the country and kept it safe, a sentiment echoed in the 2010 National Security Strategy. Values had been the best national security asset, in war and peace. Obama's first decision as president was to ban the use of the "enhanced interrogation techniques" that had been approved by the Bush administration. His second decision was to order the closing of the prison camp at Guantanamo Bay. The latter has proved easier said than done.

FOREIGN POLICY GOALS OF THE OBAMA ADMINISTRATION

At the outset of his presidency, President Obama established four overarching goals:

1. to stop the spread of nuclear weapons, and work for a world without nuclear weapons;
2. to pursue peace, specifically in Afghanistan and Pakistan; Darfur; and Israel, Palestine, and their Arab neighbours;

3. to preserve the planet, specifically to address the
   challenges of climate change; and
4. to rebuild the global economy.

It is a very large agenda—in fact, the agenda of a superpower. He has made an impressive start in implementing this agenda, particularly in eliciting international co-operation to restore the functioning of the global financial system and restart economic growth. He has also made encouraging progress on arms control and disarmament, where he has concluded a nuclear weapons reduction treaty with Moscow, and secured a new agreement among the leaders of forty-four countries with nuclear facilities to control nuclear material.

What remains to be seen is whether the administration has the political determination, even tenacity, to persevere in the face of entrenched interests at home and difficult challenges abroad. The financial meltdown cum "great recession" has forced its way to the top of his agenda, and raised questions about the US's global standing. The situation in Afghanistan has worsened, and the Europeans remain reluctant to send more troops to Afghanistan to help with the heavy lifting against an insurgent Taliban. Stability in Pakistan remains precarious. China is wary of sanctions on Iran, as is Turkey, and the Iranians have reacted dismissively to Obama's offer of dialogue. The Israelis press for military action against Iran, but have resisted President Obama's pressure to stop building settlements on Palestinian land and to relent on Jerusalem as their exclusive national capital, just as they have resisted similar pressures by previous US administrations. They have complicated Obama's task by attacking a Turkish-flagged ship in international waters attempting to force its way through the Israeli blockade of Gaza, which many regard as excessive. Muslims, moved by the sincerity and comprehension evident in Obama's Cairo speech, are, nevertheless, well aware of the power of the pro-Israel lobbies in the US and are reserving judgment on Obama's promise. If Obama's Cairo speech results in no change on the ground for Palestinians, including Gazans, his credibility and America's reputation among Arabs and Muslims will not recover for a long time to come.

In deciding which issues the US will take up internationally, and how, the new administration has options—some controversial. One[5] holds that in order to be more secure, the US should *reduce* its military power and gear back its foreign policy accordingly, because the US's vast capacity results in pressures to do too much; and that other countries should assume greater responsibility for affairs that affect their interests. Former army officer and current respected academic Andrew Bacevich has argued that "America doesn't need a bigger army. It needs a smaller—that is, more modest—foreign policy."[6]

Time will tell whether such minority views gain traction among US policy makers in the Obama administration. Certainly, the affordability of unrestrained American foreign policy is becoming an issue. According to the *2009 Yearbook* of the Stockholm International Peace Research Institute (SIPRI), US defence expenditures in 2008, in current dollars, were US$607 billion, just over 40 percent of total global defence expenditures, and that is a relative decline attributable in part to currency volatility (it has approached 50 percent). The US outspends the next ten countries combined, five of which are allies. That kind of expenditure buys a stupendous capability. According to various public sources, the US has more than 280 warships, including eleven aircraft carrier groups, as many carriers as the rest of the world combined; 8,000 military aircraft (Canada has about 250); vast numbers of tanks and armoured personnel carriers; 5,113 nuclear warheads deployed and in storage; and 1.4 million men and women under arms. Estimates of the number of US bases abroad vary widely and range as high as 700–800 (secrecy precludes an accurate public count). In an interview with Fareed Zakaria on CNN on May 3, 2009, Secretary of Defense Robert Gates said:

> The reality is the United States has global interests. Our
> defense budget is about the same as the defense budgets
> or military budgets of every other country in the world

put together. . . . the defense budget is still less than 4
percent of our gross domestic product. During the
Korean War, it was as high as 9 percent, [and] much
higher, obviously, during World War II. And it was 7 or
8 percent during Vietnam. So . . . the size of military we
have is not a burden on our economy.

In fact, it is a burden. At a time when no other major country
is spending such vast amounts of money on its military, absolutely
or relatively, 4 percent of the economy's production represents a
great deal of money; it also represents significant opportunity
costs, as Eisenhower warned it would. Defence spending has
contributed to consecutive budget deficits. At a time of a soaring
$1 trillion budget deficit, with health costs burgeoning and
spending cuts necessary, there is ample reason to reduce the
defence budget appreciably.

A more modest foreign policy would deliver benefits abroad—
in diminishing American responsibility and inducing others to do
their parts—and at home. A reduction of military spending to 3
percent of the nation's economic output (the level during the
Clinton administration) would have more or less covered the costs
of buying health care ($155 billion) for the notorious forty-seven
million uninsured Americans who lacked it. The average insurance
costs for a family of four is about $13,000 a year.[7] The US defence
budget would still be about $450 billion, five times greater than
the second leading spender, China. But the US system of governance
does not lend itself to such rational decision-making. As the
American Pulitzer Prize–winning author, journalist, and historian
Gary Wills has observed,

> The monopoly on use of nuclear weaponry, the cult of the
> commander in chief, the worldwide network of military
> bases to maintain nuclear alert and supremacy, the secret
> intelligence agencies, the entire national security state, the
> classification and clearance systems, the expansion of state
> secrets, the withholding of evidence and information, the

*permanent emergency that has melded World War II with
the cold war and the cold war with the "war on terror"—
all these make a vast and intricate structure that may not
yield to effort at dismantling it.* [8]

As Eisenhower had warned.

LOOKING AHEAD

President Obama's more nuanced, more open-to-discussion,
and less immediately muscular approach to foreign policy will
require significant adjustments by an American foreign policy
establishment, Democratic as well as Republican, that cut its
teeth on the national security paradigm of the past sixty years.
The global peripheral vision of President Obama—and, indeed,
of Secretary of State Clinton—is welcome, but their ability to
carry the entrenched Beltway class along in the execution of a
more complex, more flexible diplomacy is no foregone conclusion.
Obama has surrounded himself with veterans of the Clinton
administration, dismissed by one critic[9] "as ancient satraps . . .
stepping forward to tell us what is off the table." It is a criticism
with some validity, especially as regards Obama's various special
envoys and White House and NSC advisers, re-treads from the
1990s, some of whom had a direct hand in creating the problems
he now faces, though to be fair, it is not evident where he was to
find experienced people untainted by previous public service.
Congress will be even more difficult. The electoral horizon for
members of the House of Representatives is considerably more
immediate than Obama's. In a deeply and culturally divided
Washington, getting Republicans to co-operate with him will be
difficult.

The question now—and it is almost as important for Canadians
as it is for Americans—is whether the Obama administration will
be able to begin to reverse the hold that national security
"imperatives" have on the America national psyche. Will the

Obama administration come to be seen as the first break from this way of thinking, or will it be seen as an aberration? Will the American foreign policy establishment, deeply invested in power politics, and the Congress, deeply beholden to a variety of lobbies, work with President Obama or against him? Will other countries take him at his word and co-operate with him? He has made progress. To paraphrase former national security adviser Zbigniew Brzezinski,[10] Obama has succeeded in re-conceptualizing US foreign policy, notably with respect to Islam, Russia, China, Afghanistan, nuclear disarmament, international finance, and, to a lesser extent, climate change.

Perhaps the most difficult challenge Obama faces is transforming the poetry of his extraordinary rhetoric into the prose of political accomplishment—at home and abroad. The "old politics" that he decried in his campaign cannot easily be bypassed. He will need exceptional resolve if his pragmatism is to yield more than simple surrender, and if he is not to become a prisoner of the presidency. The health care victory is a positive omen. The oil spill in the Gulf of Mexico, believed to be the worst in American history, is a further huge challenge to a man who already had more than enough challenges.

Americans and foreigners alike are hugely invested, almost certainly over-invested, in Obama's prospective success. The Obama White House needs to marry his oratory for the ages with hard accomplishments for the here and now. Almost equally important, others—Canada above all—will need to support his efforts to return to the law-abiding, treaty-respecting, international-law-developing America of old.

To rebuild the partnerships bruised and broken by the Bush administration, co-operation will have to be elicited—it cannot be commanded. The US will have to privilege co-operation over domination, multilateralism over unilateralism, the effective over the merely efficient, and the legal over the expedient. Partnership will need to mean not just hearing others before deciding and acting, but rather developing shared assessments and taking co-operative action. It will require fewer sermons and less certitude from Mount Washington and more openness to the perspectives of others.

President Obama's two great gifts, his worldly judgment and his ability to inspire new confidence in the United States, will be severely tested, not least in the Middle East and Afghanistan. While Obama is a man of his times, the world earnestly hopes that he is a man *for* his times.

Those times are changing fast.

8

A MULTI-CENTRIC WORLD?

*Nations, even ones as large and powerful as the USA, are affected
profoundly by world events; and not affected in time or at the
margins but at breakneck speed and fundamentally.*
—Tony Blair

Whether security-centric, as US administrations have been for a half-century and more, or cosmopolitan, as is the case with Obama now, the enormous US presence in world affairs is the first reality that Canadian foreign policy must confront as we make our way in the world. The second reality is that times they are a-changing, to paraphrase Bob Dylan, and are doing so very fast. Most of the change is being driven by "the newly emerging economies," the BRIC (Brazil, Russia, India, and China), as Goldman Sachs famously described them. They, too, are creating realities for the rest of us. For our foreign policy to succeed, we need to update our understanding of our rapidly evolving world.

THE US, LEADING BUT NOT DETERMINING

In the words of the 2002 US National Security Strategy, "The United States possesses unprecedented—and unequaled—strength and influence in the world. Sustained by faith in the principles of liberty, and the value of a free society, this position comes with unparalleled responsibilities, obligations, and opportunity." Read "power." It was obviously not an idle boast; in fact, it was probably an understatement. Nevertheless, if history is a reliable guide to the future, power is a "zero-sum" game and, unlike diamonds, it is not forever.

If power is transitory over the long run, capacity is decisive in the interim. Capacity, unlike power, is not a relative concept and, in any meaningful, calculable future for Canadian foreign policy, American capacity will remain unmatched. American culture will remain pervasive. American science, especially medical science, will lead the world. The US, which has won the lion's share of Nobel prizes, 320, will likely continue to do so. (The US won more prizes in 2009—nine—than the Chinese have won in the history of the prize.)[1] American universities will continue to set international standards for excellence, even as others gain on them. Of the top two hundred universities in the world, according to a Times Higher Education 2009 report, fully fifty-four are American (thirteen of the top twenty), twice the number of universities as the UK, the runner-up. China has six in the top two hundred—eleven if Hong Kong is counted as part of China—but none in the top twenty. The American economy, more than triple the size of runner-up Japan's, according to the IMF, will continue to generate enormous wealth. The US military is, and will remain, without peer in terms of sheer firepower for a very long time to come. Beyond these tangibles, American values will continue to attract respect and admiration, if not always imitation.

According to the World Economic Forum, the US remains the second-most-competitive economy in the world (after Switzerland, because of the weakening of the financial market); China ranks twenty-ninth. The US is first in innovation, first in brain retention, first in industry-university collaboration in R&D, second in the quality of its research institutions, second in company spending for research and technology, third in labour-market efficiency, fourth in the quality of its management schools, fifth in the availability of scientists and engineers, fifth in the intensity of local competition, sixth in personal computers, sixth in college and university education enrolment, seventh in venture capital availability, and thirteenth in technological readiness. China does not come within twenty countries in any one of these categories.[2] In virtually every sector, US firms lead the world in productivity and profits. With one-fourth the population of China, the US has triple the economic production.

While the very large budget, trade, and current-account deficits that Washington is racking up in response to the recession cannot be sustained for long with impunity, even by a superpower, American debts are denominated in the world's main reserve currency, the US dollar. That allows Washington to evade some of the discipline of having to pay debts in a foreign currency, a benefit most of the rest of the world does not enjoy. That also allows the US to print dollars to pay its bills, an advantage that some foreigners have long lamented. Former French President Charles de Gaulle called it "an exorbitant privilege." Nixon treasury secretary John Connally famously told a delegation of Europeans who were worried about exchange rate fluctuations that "the American dollar is our currency, but your problem."

A further US advantage is the enormous depth and liquidity of US financial markets. No other financial system has been large enough and reliable enough to absorb the huge quantities of money that foreign pension funds and other large entities have to invest. In fact, after an initial slide, the US dollar actually appreciated in value during the 2007–08 financial crisis, as some investors and governments suddenly sought safe-haven investments (and US Treasury bills were still seen as comparatively safe) and others scrambled for liquidity to pay off debts. China has enormous reserves in US dollars, over $2 trillion by some estimates, which means that it has some leverage over US policy making—

but also a great deal to lose if the dollar weakens. In the short run, China and the US are Siamese financial twins, joined at the wallet. Precipitate separation would cost each plenty.

Those who anticipate a steep decline in the United States are near certain to be disappointed, as others have been in the past. Our neighbour's resilience and capacity for re-invention should never be underestimated, and ought to come as no surprise to Canadians. In the late 1980s, Yale professor Paul Kennedy, in his work *The Rise and Fall of the Great Powers*, which spawned "the American decline school," predicted that Japan would overtake the US. That thesis was promoted by some in Canada as grounds for not concluding a free trade agreement with an eclipsed United States. In the two decades that followed, Japan faltered, the US surged, and Canadian prosperity soared. It is likely that, sooner or later, Kennedy will be proven right, but in prophecy, as in comedy, timing is everything.

Current US capacity means that it is safe to conclude that the US will be the global leader for a long time to come, happily for Canada. There are caveats to this optimistic, but probably realistic, assessment of the prospects of contemporary America—and of Canada. The "great recession" of 2007–09 has damaged the US economy, the foundation of American power in the world. How much it has done so is not yet knowable—although probably less than some detractors hope, but possibly more than many Americans realize. Today's enormous budget deficits, created by the economic recession and the responsive stimulus programs, are tomorrow's taxes and/or public-policy budget cuts. The US public education systems—already under financial pressure—will likely be hit hard by depressed public spending and diminished endowment funds. The US banking and financial system has suffered a major blow to its credibility. The reckless policies of the banks and other financial institutions and the lax oversight of the regulators created trouble across the planet. The economic policies that Washington is pursuing to get out of the crisis—deficit spending, low interest rates, the bailing out and outright purchase of banks and other industries—are precisely the opposite of the

austerity regimes the Americans imposed on other governments
in the past, notably during the Asian financial crisis. As a
consequence of both financial recklessness and policy inadequacies
and inconsistencies, confidence in the quality and reliability of
American international leadership is diminished. According to
Nobel Prize winner Joe Stiglitz writing in *Vanity Fair* (July 2009),
"While there may be no winners in the current economic crisis,
there are losers, and among the big losers is support for American-
style capitalism." The differential impacts of the financial crisis
internationally and the recession seem certain to accelerate the
advent of a multi-centric world.

Any calculation of American standing must also factor in
the damage done by American national-security obsessions
generally, and the excessive, unilateralist behaviour of the Bush
administration that those obsessions drove. The disregard of the
Bush administration for international law, which previous
administrations had helped to create, and its unilateral reinterpretation of the law as regards torture, were especially
corrosive. Leading Singaporean diplomat and scholar Kishore
Mahbubani described the US as being exemplary in implementing
the rule of law at home, but "a leading international outlaw in its
refusal to recognize the constraints of international law."[3]

The election of new leadership in the US, while very welcome
in most countries around the world—even acclaimed—was not,
in itself, sufficient to compensate for eight years of lawlessness by
Washington. The actions of the Obama administration will need
to speak louder than its words, welcome as those words are as
indicators of change.

A final caveat is the growing question of whether the US is still
able to govern itself effectively. Democracy is notoriously messy
and recalcitrant, and here too the Americans are setting standards.
But in this case, they are damaging ones. In the wake of the US
election of the first black president, which gave expression to the
inherent values the US has long espoused and reconfirmed its
enormous potential, it is sobering to behold the state of US
governance. The Obama administration's attempt at improving

health care coverage was met with hostility and ignorance. The knowledge deficit about the ways that other countries approach health care was profound. The distrust of government was appalling. Participants indulged in preposterous stereotyping, portraying Obama at once as a communist, a fascist, a grandma killer, etc. All this was coupled with a callous indifference to the well-being, or otherwise, of the nearly 17 percent of their fellow citizens without health-insurance coverage, and in the middle of a recession when jobs and attendant medical insurance benefits were being lost.

There has been, as well, the inchoate anger channeled by Sarah Palin, the prospective know-nothing Republican Party candidate for president in 2012, and the nativist xenophobia, even animosity, evident in the deepening culture wars encouraged by cable news networks and talk radio. On top of that has been the US Supreme Court decision removing electoral spending limits on corporate and other major donors, a decision that President Obama said would "open the floodgates for special interests." He called it "a major victory for big oil, Wall Street banks, health insurance companies and the other powerful interests that marshal their power every day in Washington to drown out the voices of everyday Americans."[4] Limits have been lifted on an electoral system already corrupted by money. For foreigners, who cannot buy influence in the US Congress legally, relations with the US seem bound to become more difficult. No country will be more affected than Canada.

CHINA, EMERGING

Among the BRICS, China is streets ahead of the rest, its economy larger than those of the three other BRIC countries combined.[5] China, Japan, and India currently rank second, third, and fourth in the world in economic production as measured by purchasing power parity (a measurement of what people can buy using their own currency).[6] Japan is second after the United States in absolute

terms. Mexico, South Korea, and Turkey, as well as the countries of
the Association of South East Asian Nations, notably Singapore,
are also making strong progress.[7] By 2050, which seems a long way
off, but is actually about as long as the average working life, the
order will be China, the US, India, Brazil, and Mexico. Only two
EU members will make the top ten. Canada will be sixteenth.[8]

We in the West forget all too easily, if we ever really knew,
that China or India *not* being major powers is the *exception* in
history, not the rule. As observed by Kishore Mahbubani, the
West has long regarded Asians as just consumers of world history,
reacting tactically and—with the obvious exception of Japan—
defensively to the surges of Western commerce, power, and
thought. Now, the Asians are again producing history—and
economics—as they did for sixteen centuries before the rise of
the West. In that sense, it is more accurate now to speak not of the
"rise" of Asia, but of the renaissance of Asia, although "Asia" is
not a unity culturally, religiously, or geographically, as Europe is,
or even the Americas are. But the fulcrum of world affairs is
shifting eastward, and the countries of Asia are certain to become
ever more consequential in world affairs. The pace of change in
Asia has been nothing less than astonishing. At current growth
rates in Asia, standards of living may rise a hundredfold, 10,000
percent within a human lifespan.[9]

China spent a jaw-dropping $43 billion on the Beijing
Olympics, according to various reports, perhaps twenty times what
the 2010 winter games cost Canada.[10] The sheer scale of the
expenditure, the magnificence of the opening and closing
ceremonies, the quantity of medals the Chinese harvested, and the
quality of the venues were meant to show the rest of the world that
China was back as a major power. And it did, burying for good any
residual belief that China was still the Communist backwater of
Chairman Mao. With a population of 1.3 billion, China has been
enjoying a pace of economic development never before seen by
humanity. In the intervening thirty years since Deng Xiaoping
launched the till-then-backward peasant kingdom on its
modernization course in 1978, the country has accomplished

almost as much as the West did in the previous three hundred years, since the beginning of the Industrial Revolution. According to the Goldman Sachs BRICS study, China will overtake the US as the world's largest economy in 2041. China overtook Germany in 2009 as the world's top exporting nation, although it did so because Germany's exports fell more steeply than China's did in the "great recession." [11] China is the largest foreign holder of US money and financial instruments.[12] By World Bank estimates, 500 million Chinese have escaped poverty in a generation.[13] On adult literacy, an indicator of national achievement and an important factor in economic potential, 91 percent of Chinese are literate by UNESCO standards.

While contemplating all the superlatives, it is worth reminding ourselves that China ranks well down the UN's Human Development Index (ninety-second; Canada is fourth).[14] China's economic production per capita is still just one-sixth of Canada's (India's is one-twelfth of Canada's). Further, China's explosive economic growth has come at a considerable cost. It has become the world's largest emitter of greenhouse gases. Perhaps more immediately consequential to the Chinese, at least, only *1 percent* of China's 560-million urban residents breathes air considered safe by international standards. Ambient air pollution alone is blamed for hundreds of thousands of premature deaths each year. China's rivers are notoriously polluted; nearly 500 million people lack access to safe drinking water. Pollution has made cancer the country's leading cause of death.[15] At the same time, China has begun to invest aggressively in green technology development, and will be a formidable competitor to Western industry in this field.

The Communist Party remains firmly in charge, its legitimacy a product not of the voice of the people but of the success of its own policies. Human rights continue to have only selective application. The Chinese system of government remains opaque, and China's long-term goals remain obscure. Corruption is a significant problem.[16] China's increasing economic significance in the world is having an impact on China's own foreign policy, as its economic interests take it to places it has rarely been before, notably Africa and Latin America, and even Canada. By most measurements, China is the second-most-powerful country on earth, and has the second-largest military budget, albeit spending only about one-seventh as much as the US does. Strategists on all sides are pondering what China's long-term impact will be. Some worry that China's sheer size will, ultimately, create friction as it rubs up against others in the quest for resources to feed itself and the maw of its industry, crowding others out. Others fear an active conflict with China is inevitable, despite the many built-in impediments to war in the twenty-first century. Still others, like former US secretary of state James Baker, do not think conflict is pre-ordained at all, and worry the idea could become a self-fulfilling prophecy. I agree with Baker.

Neither the US nor China has an interest in conflict; indeed the reverse is true. China still has the problem of uneven development among different regions, and between China's urban and rural areas. Its priority for some time to come will be to improve the lives of its 800 million farmers in rural areas and its millions of very poor urban citizens. To paraphrase Premier Wen, China remains a developing country, a powerful one, but not a superpower. The Chinese leadership seems very much focused on China's internal problems, rather than on its international ambitions. According to Premier Wen, "China's democracy will continue to grow. In twenty to thirty years' time, the whole Chinese society will be more democratic and fairer, and the legal system in China will further be improved. Socialism, as we see it, will further mature and improve."[17]

China has shown no interest in evading or upsetting the multilateral system of international governance. On the contrary. Ever-greater economic integration into the global economy with the US, Japan, and others is crucial for China to meet its primordial development objectives. Conflict would be prohibitively expensive, indeed irrational. If events conspired malevolently, however, it would not be impossible. To quote former US defense secretary Donald Rumsfeld, "Stuff happens."

Deng Xiaoping advocated that China hide its light under a

bushel,[18] and not attempt to lead the world. The Chinese say they favour dialogue over confrontation, co-operation over containment, and partnership over rivalry.[19] The administration of President Obama, the first modern American leader who grew up partly in Asia, has likewise stressed dialogue, as has US Defense Secretary Robert Gates, speaking at the International Institute for Strategic Studies conference in Singapore, in order to build military leaders' confidence in each other's intentions. At the same time each side is wary. There is little doubt that the India-US strategic co-operation agreement is intended by both India and the US as a hedge against Chinese power, as is the Japanese-American alliance.

Beyond the US-China relationship lie Chinese relations with its major neighbours—Japan, Russia, the Koreas, and India—each of whom has much at stake in a peaceful future for China. The world has to come to grips with the fact that China is united and increasingly powerful. At the same time, China needs to see itself as a stakeholder in world order; to come to terms with its responsibilities for helping to run the planet, not just reaping the benefits of global trade; and to accept the burdens and constraints of leadership, notably as regards climate change and international economics. As Ramesh Thakur of the University of Waterloo has observed, China's "Middle Kingdom" mental legacy does not prepare it to be a great power in a system of other great powers, or for leadership in the modern multi-centric world. Still, as the last twenty-five years show, and as the Olympics underlined, China is capable of enormous change.

INDIA, DAWNING

China apart, few countries are making the transition from poverty to prosperity as dramatically as India. In a few short years, India has become one of the richest countries in the world, ranking twelfth in economic production worldwide.[20] (Canada ranks ninth.) In terms of purchasing power, India has become the world's fourth-largest economy, growing at 6 to 8 percent annually, including an estimated 4.5 percent for 2009, a year of painful economic performance in the West (and even more so in Japan). Within the next fifteen years, India will be just shy of the top ten worldwide in economic production and tenth in international trade. It is expected to reach developed-nation status (often regarded as $20,000 per capita income) in 2028, well within the working life of most readers of this book. This is quite an accomplishment for a country that literally could not feed itself when I was a child.

Since the Indian government released its ideological grip on the economy in the early 1990s, the wider world has been wowed by India's extraordinary economic development. The migration to a market-based economy engineered by Prime Minister (then finance minister) Manmohan Singh, India's Deng Xiaoping, has been truly transformative, if not fully complete. Not the least achievement has been the growing presence of homegrown Indian entrepreneurs in world markets, such as Intelsys, Reliance Industries, Mittal Steel, Tata Motors, the Mahindra Group, and the Jindal Group, among many others. If China's diaspora has helped to make China the world's factory, India's indigenous talent and overseas Indians, especially including many talented Indo-Canadians, are making India the world's technology laboratory.

The breathtaking progress notwithstanding, however, India remains a developing country, home to hundreds of millions of people who are living on the equivalent of a dollar or two a day.[21] Corruption remains a problem.[22] Average literacy rates are low, especially for women, placing India 147th in the world. Health and disease remain important issues, especially HIV/AIDS, and the caste system persists. According to the United Nations University, a UN think tank, in 2008 nearly half of India's population had access to mobile phones, but only about a third of the population had access to proper sanitation. These numbers are reminders that, for all the talk about Indian progress, the country has a long way to go.

There is more to India than economics, obviously. India is a vibrant democracy, the world's most populous, with strong state institutions, a vigilant civil society, an irreverently free press, a respected judiciary, and vigorous opposition parties. The country has one national language, Hindi, fourteen other official languages, and numerous dialects; English is widely spoken. Indian diversity makes Canada look Swedish in our homogeneity.

Much is not clear about India's future. How much will India's internal constraints, notably its ethnic and religious divisions, its family-based politics, and its low level of educational attainment hinder the country's rapid pace of economic growth? How will Indian foreign policy evolve? India's interests are outgrowing the comfortable ideological confines of the non-aligned movement and the G77 group of developing economies, of which it is still part. An original member of the G20, India is seeking a permanent seat on the UN Security Council. The nuclear agreement India concluded with the Bush administration has delivered the recognition of major-power standing that India has long craved. The Indian nuclear weapons program is an insurance policy and a deterrence factor vis-à-vis both Chinese power and Pakistani intransigence over Kashmir. Still, as is the case with China, India's accession to the status of a major power, prepared to assume responsibilities as well as rights for world affairs, is a work in progress.

JAPAN, FLATLINING

With all of the emphasis on China and India these days, and in light of the renewed weakness of the Japanese economy caused by the "great recession," it is easy to forget that Japan remains an economic powerhouse, the second- or third-richest country in the world, the fourth-largest trader, and the home of much technological innovation. Japan ranks seventh in military spending, limited by its post–Second World War constitution in its ability to spend, but still very capable.

In the 1990s, Japan went from world-beater to world-beaten, descending into stagnation and deflation. Cheap capital was followed by the burst of a property bubble. (I had the occasion myself to see the effects at the 2000 G8 foreign ministers' meeting in Miyazaki Prefecture. The Japanese hosts put all delegations up at the magnificent Sea Gaia Hotel, which had been constructed for the princely sum of $2.2 billion. We were told by the staff that the resort had no other customers than us, and was to close after we left, which it did. It was subsequently acquired for a tenth of the original price, and is back in business.) When, over a decade later, Japan seemed to have regained its footing, the "great recession," the most severe for Japan since the Second World War, set it back again. The Japanese fiscal stimulus package has sent government debt further skyward,[23] at 170 percent of gross domestic product, far higher than the OECD average of 44 percent. For the longer term, Japan's population is both aging and shrinking. Given Japanese discomfort with the idea of immigration, it is hard to see how these problems can be surmounted without a retreat in Japan's standard of living and standing in the world. Still, it would be unwise to write off such an industrious, well-educated, technologically advanced, and resourceful people.[24]

The destiny of Asia in this century will be determined by Japan, China, and India, and their interactions with the US and Russia. The three Asian giants could lead an Asia-wide effort to construct architecture of a regional order that fosters peace and promotes prosperity across Asia and the world. On the other hand, rivalry and competition among them could roil the world.

RUSSIA, NOSTALGIC

Russia remains significant militarily and economically, despite having had the worst century of any major country, with the possible exception of China. The Russian people suffered through the Russo-Japanese War, the First World War, the Communist Revolution, the Second World War, almost seventy-five years of Communist rule with its numerous controls, gulags, and purges, forty-five years of Cold War competition with the West, and the collapse of the Soviet Union. As the late George Kennan, the noted American diplomat, remarked in an interview in the *New York Review of Books*, "the [largely self-destructive] process took place over most of an entire century. . . . such enormous losses and abuses are not to be put to rights in a single decade, perhaps not even in a single generation."[25] Remarkably, though, under Vladimir Putin and thanks to its own blend of elected autocracy, Russia remains a factor in international affairs. No longer the world's other superpower, Russia is not a Third World mendicant either. Economically, Russia ranks tenth or eleventh in the world, just behind Canada, and its economic production per capita is $15,200,[26] which puts Russians in the top third of the international ranking. In terms of human development, the UN Development Program ranks Russia seventy-first; adult literacy is 99.5 percent.

Following the 1998 Russian financial crisis, rampaging commodity prices, especially of oil and gas, and a growing economic relationship with Europe, restored lost strength to the Russian economy. Russian growth averaged 7 percent per year until 2008, resulting in a doubling of real disposable incomes and the emergence of a significant middle class. In 2009, Russia became the world's largest exporter of both oil and natural gas, and also the third-largest exporter of steel and primary aluminum.[27] But the "great recession" of 2007 hit Russia particularly hard, knocking almost 10 percent off its economic production, as international oil prices plummeted and the foreign credits on which Russian banks and firms relied dried up. Still, as the world recovers, Russia is well positioned to benefit because of its world-leading stores of natural resources and its well-educated population.

Russia has yet to find a comfortable relationship with the post–Cold War modern world, and there is a truculent, legalistic quality to its foreign policy. The nineteenth century undertones, especially its tendency to see neighbouring states as part of its "near abroad" and a "zone of privileged interests,"[28] is incompatible with modern concepts of international order. The fact that Russia turned the tap of its gas pipeline to Europe on and off in its dispute with Ukraine has not reinforced anyone's confidence in Moscow.

Militarily, Russia remains the second-most-powerful country in the world, with a military budget that is the fifth highest in the world[29] and stockpiles of nuclear warheads of all kinds in excess of 16,000. As is the case with other countries that possess nuclear weapons, however, the nuclear dimension is beneficial only as deterrence, because using such weapons aggressively would, almost certainly, be suicidal. Under the 2010 agreement to reduce nuclear weapons, the Russians (and the Americans) will reduce their deployed strategic (long-range) warheads to 1,550 each, and their delivery vehicles (missiles and airplanes) to 800, a significant down payment on deeper cuts to come eventually. The agreement with the US does not change Russia's strategic ranking. Further, as its strong opposition to NATO's expansion into Ukraine and as its own intervention in Georgia showed, Russia intends neither to be taken for granted nor dominated. It craves equality again with the US, although it seems very unlikely to achieve it.

BRAZIL, DANCING

Few things more graphically convey Brazil's rapidly rising fortunes than the twin mega-awards—the right to host the 2014 World Cup of Soccer and the 2016 Summer Olympics. That the latter was won over Chicago and the personal lobbying of the extraordinarily popular (abroad) President Barack Obama is a barometer of Brazil's standing.

Brazil, with its maturing democracy, diversified industrial sector, and strong financial industry, has benefited from more than a decade of sound political stewardship, steady economic growth, and diminished unemployment. In recognition of Brazil's success under his leadership, President Luiz Inácio Lula da Silva was named the 2010 World Statesman by the World Economic Forum, the organization that runs the prestigious gathering of business and political leaders at Davos, Switzerland, every winter.

Brazil's strong economic fundamentals helped the country survive the financial crisis with comparative ease. In a food- and resources-hungry world, Brazil is in a position to supply both. Brazil is a world leader in biofuels, specifically ethanol from sugar cane, and will soon be a major oil exporter, thanks to the potentially huge deposits off its coast. Its aerospace sector, specifically Embraer, is a strong competitor to Canada's Bombardier. Recognizing its vibrant domestic market, investors are beating a path to Brazil's door. And, as the *Economist* pointed out, "Unlike China, [Brazil] is a democracy; unlike India, it has no insurgents, or ethnic and religious conflicts or hostile neighbors; unlike Russia, it exports more oil than arms and treats foreign investors with respect." On the down side, income disparity is still very significant, and crime and insecurity are widespread.

Brazil's economic production of nearly $1.5 trillion (in nominal dollars) is the eighth largest in the world, ranking just ahead of Spain, Canada, Russia, India, and Mexico. On the other hand, Brazil's economic production per capita is $7,737, which places Brazil in sixtieth place worldwide, well behind Canada's $39,217.[30] Brazil ranks seventy-fifth on the 2009 UN Development Program Human Development Index; to put that number into perspective, Canada ranks fourth.

Brazil's growing economic strength is underwriting an increasingly influential foreign policy. In particular, Brazil has won seats at key negotiating tables, not least at the "Doha Round" of trade negotiations and at the Copenhagen climate change negotiations, where it was part of the very small group, including China and the US, that cut the final deal. (There was a time—not long ago—when Canada would have had seats at both tables, as well.) Together with South Africa, Brazil has been playing a key constructive role in keeping the complex-but-crucial climate-change process moving forward. Brazil, a member of the G20, has growing influence at the United Nations, where it is a strong candidate for a permanent seat on the UN Security Council. Brazil is aware of its own significance in world affairs, and is charting an appropriately constructive and quite independent course, notably in its nuclear relations with Iran and Turkey, despite Washington's druthers.

EUROPE, STILL UNITING?

The European Union is the world's most interesting attempt to pool national sovereignty in order to raise standards of living, bury ultra-nationalist impulses, and regain standing in the world. It is also the most complex. As British historian and author Timothy Garton Ash has observed in an essay in the *Guardian*, in Europe, "behind the monetary lurks the fiscal; behind the fiscal, the economic; behind the economic, the political; and behind the political, the historical."[31]

With a combined economic output of almost $17 trillion, the very wealthy EU is the world's largest economic entity, and is correspondingly capable of making enormously constructive contributions to world affairs. It is a huge spender on engineering and technological innovation, and a leader in environmental research and development. Europe dominates the tables of world competitiveness, with six countries—Switzerland, Sweden, Denmark, Finland, Germany, and the Netherlands—in the top ten.[32] Six of the ten leading exporters and importers in world merchandise trade in 2006 were European.[33] The EU is cumulatively the world's largest aid donor and is projected to account for an estimated 76% of global aid increases between 2008 and 2010.[34]

Europe is a work in progress. Its stability and prosperity had been taken for granted, but the major failings of the Greek economy, which were there for all to see, though few wanted to, have revealed major structural problems in the European financial system. The countries that embraced the euro lack the tools for emergency response possessed by their non-Europe counterparts, notably the ability to devalue the currency. This requires a painful solidarity of the sound European economies with the unsound ones, if the entire financial enterprise is to remain intact.

The EU accounts for $209 billion of military spending, cumulatively second only to the US.[35] But its ability to project power is fractionated, and its interest in doing so is lacking, as the conflict in Afghanistan underlines. As Henry Kissinger, in a penetrating insight, told *Der Spiegel* in 2009, people are less prepared to risk their lives and make sacrifices for Europe than they are for their own nation-states.

The EU has become an exceedingly complicated structure that only EU officials fully understand, an entity more akin to the Holy Roman Empire* of ten centuries ago, with its migrating authority and complex governance structures, than to a modern nation-state. "Who do I call if I want to call Europe?" Henry Kissinger once dismissively asked. To answer that question, belatedly, and to reinforce the idea of a single foreign and defence policy for Europe, the EU adopted the seminal Lisbon Treaty, among other things, creating the post of president of the European Council. In principle, the president speaks for Europe internationally, and he is the person Obama (and Harper) should call. Still, there are grey areas and overlaps, and the EU will either have to get its act together properly or go on punching well below its weight. Personally, I doubt that a single, common EU foreign and defence policy will ever be possible as long as Europe has two permanent members of the UN Security Council, each with its own nuclear arsenal.

AFRICA, SURVIVING

Largely because of its enduring, pernicious twin legacies of slavery and colonialism, which so fractured the continent and divided and combined diverse ethnic groups, and partly because of widespread misgovernment, Africa, especially sub-Saharan Africa, trails most of the rest of the Third World in economic and social development. It nonetheless merits being taken seriously in the evolving world, both because it too holds promise of graduation to better times, and because its troubles can migrate across borders.

---

* Which Voltaire famously described as neither holy nor Roman nor an empire.

If current demographic trends continue, in 2050, Africa will have a population equal to that of China or India. This will be one of the largest agglomerations of people, and the highest proportion of young people, anywhere in the world. The more Africa succeeds, the more this young population will be beneficial; the more Africa fails, the greater the risk they will present to themselves and the rest of us, especially to Europe.

Africa's troubles are extensive. Thirty of the thirty-two poorest countries listed on the UN Human Development Index are in Africa (Afghanistan and Haiti are the two non-Africans on the list). Gabon is the best-ranking African country on the index at only 103rd. Checkered progress has been made in sub-Saharan Africa in achieving the UN's Millennium Development Goals, notably regarding reducing extreme poverty. A woman's risk of dying from treatable or preventable complications of pregnancy and childbirth over the course of her lifetime is 1 in 22 in sub-Saharan Africa, compared to 1 in 7,300 in the economically advanced world.

Not all the news about Africa is discouraging; it does have its bright spots. At a time when the population of Africa is growing rapidly, infant mortality rates are nevertheless dropping, deaths from measles are down spectacularly, deaths from malaria are down appreciably and appear to be on the way to elimination. Literacy levels and primary-school enrolment are rising, and more girls are attending school than ever before, even if around 38 million children of primary-school age in this region are not attending school at all, according to UN statistics. The economic production of Africa as a whole grew less strongly in 2009, although in the previous two years it grew by 5.9 percent and 5.2 percent; in 2010 and 2011, growth is projected to be 4.3 and 5.3 percent.[36] It is noteworthy that China is investing strongly in Africa and that India is beginning to do so as well. Increasingly, in Washington and other major capitals, Africa is seen not as a perpetual basket case, but as a land where the scope for economic growth is large, as African economies converge with others over the long term. In addition, it seems likely that Obama's African heritage, together with concerns about international terrorism, will keep the continent on the US radar. Perhaps all of this will be enough to put Africa back on Canada's foreign-policy agenda after the Harper government's initial downgrading of it.

PART IV

CANADIAN FOREIGN POLICY IN A NEW WORLD

In recent years, there has been a tendency to look back to the Golden Age as the pinnacle of Canadian diplomacy and to regard the years since as a secular decline from glory. There is a tendency to exaggerate in our minds how golden the Golden Age was, and to diminish what we have done since. It is easy to forget that Canada was excluded from meetings in the 1940s (and in Quebec at that) on world affairs, and that even our figurative peek through the windows at Dumbarton Oaks where the UN was created was scarcely tolerated. By dint of brains and grit, Pearson and his talented colleagues helped lay the foundation of a multilateral world order. Trudeau, Mulroney, Chrétien, and Martin, in turn, racked up achievements that Pearson would have respected. Now we are members of the two most important, most exclusive, clubs in the world—the G8 and the G20. And despite our all-too-typical self-deprecation, we deserve to be in both. It is not delusional to believe that Canada matters.

Meanwhile, as we saw in the previous chapters, the international context is changing, and the US is led by the most internationally aware president ever, who is bringing new style and substance to American foreign policy and renewed interest in multilateral global governance. New powers are emerging that will progressively change the world order. In the integrating multi-centric world before us, sound foreign policy will be decisive to national well-being, and effective diplomacy will be vital in advancing and protecting our interests.

To succeed in this changing world, it is important that we remind ourselves of the principles and purposes of our foreign policy, and take stock of where we stand. Not all the news is good.

9

CANADIAN FOREIGN POLICY AND DIPLOMACY

Foreign policy is, after all, merely domestic policy with its hat on.
—Prime Minister Lester B. Pearson

In essence, foreign policy is the product of the government's
progressive definition of and pursuit of national aims
and interests in the international environment. It is the
extension abroad of national policies.
—"Foreign Policy for Canadians," Government of Canada
(foreign policy review of the Trudeau government, 1970)

Prime Minister Trudeau, who at that time fancied himself a more hard-nosed realist than his predecessor, might have been surprised at how nearly identical, if considerably more prosaic, his foreign policy definition was to Pearson's. Although it is presumptuous for me to disagree with either—and who could not admire the wit and brevity of the Pearson version—I do not believe that either leader actually quite captured the full meaning of the term in these quotations. Foreign policy is, or ought to be, more than the sum or even the "product" of domestic policies, although those policies are certainly part of it. It is, or ought to be, the manifestation of what Canada *qua* Canada stands for in the world, and what our government seeks to achieve on our behalf. Canadian foreign policy is an expression of what we, as a polity, believe, and what we wish to achieve. It is an amalgam of the values we hold, the principles we personify, the will we exhibit, the objectives we set, the decisions we make, and the interests we intend to serve. It is the expression of our national purpose to the rest of the world, and how we mean to achieve that purpose.

PRINCIPLES AND PURPOSES

What are—or what should be—the purposes or principles that guide our foreign policy? They have changed somewhat since Prime Minister St. Laurent first articulated them in his Gray Memorial Lecture in 1947, because the times have changed. The imperial connection with London, still important in St. Laurent's time, is now history. The world was a lot smaller then and a lot more colonial; there are more than three times as many states now. The world was locked in a struggle between East and West then; the Soviet Union has since disappeared and Communism has retreated. India and China were of mainly humanitarian interest; now, few problems can be solved without their active participation. We are a lot more integrated with the US now than we were then. Finally, globalization was in its infancy in St. Laurent's day; now, it extends to the furthest, poorest, corners of the world. The principles St. Laurent enunciated in 1947 have had to change with the times, although he would recognize his own thinking in them.

In these circumstances, then, Canadian foreign policy should,

1. protect the security of Canadians and advance their economic and social interests;
2. serve Canadian unity, respect the diversity of our population, and privilege neither founding nation nor

any province, ethnic group, economic interest, or religion;

3. respect the Charter of Rights and Freedoms and promote and defend liberty, democracy, and human rights in the world;

4. defend our sovereign independence, while fostering and respecting international law and developing the treaty-based system of global governance; and

5. for both moral and self-interest reasons, assume our share of the responsibilities for the management of international affairs, including preserving peace and security, safeguarding the natural environment, and alleviating the poverty of people less fortunate than we are.

VALUES AND INTERESTS

Like most other foreign policies, including American foreign policy (see especially the US National Security Strategy of 2002), ours is both values-based and interests-oriented. The foreign policy decisions the government makes derive from the Canadian ethos—from the values and interests of Canadians. Many of those values are universal, such as the satisfaction of basic human needs, the primacy of family, and the protection of children, among others. People everywhere want a decent life for themselves and a better life for their children.

Mature democracies, in addition, share the more advanced values—liberty, equal justice, human rights, free enterprise, free speech, and the rule of law. Female equality and women's rights are manifestly a value in Canada, as they are in Scandinavia, for example, and, to a greater or lesser extent, in all liberal democracies; they are not a value in Saudi Arabia, Afghanistan, and many Islamic countries.

There are also some values that are particularly Canadian, notably solidarity and diversity. Solidarity is an underlying value of our social system, manifested through our aid programs abroad and the interprovincial transfers of funds at home that allow all Canadians to have decent health care and educational opportunities. Our respect for diversity is derived from our historical experience of reconciling English and French communities, and their religions and cultures, since the seventeenth century. This accommodation ultimately carried over to welcoming and integrating immigrants from virtually everywhere, with their manifold religions and cultures. Diversity is not a value, for instance, in Germany or Japan, where the native-born are uncomfortable with foreigners living in their midst, and not good at all at integrating them into society. But we welcome immigrants because we believe they ultimately strengthen and enrich us. These values manifest themselves in our attitudes towards the world, and, therefore, in our foreign policy decision-making.

Our values create the framework within which we pursue our interests abroad and determine the manner in which we pursue them. For example, we do not sell arms to terrorists, even though it would be profitable to do so, and could be said by some to be in our mercantile interests.

I have always thought that the debate that arises from time to time in Canada about whether we should have a values-based or interests-based foreign policy—which in reality is often a proxy for the extent to which we should agree with Washington or not, for example on the Iraq War—misses the essential point. Values and interests are not contradictory; they are complementary, indeed integral to each other. How do you know what is in your interest if you don't know what you value?

Foreign policy is, or should be, an expression of both values and interests, of principles and pragmatism. We send our soldiers abroad to keep the peace or to enforce it, because we believe we are our brother's keeper and we feel a responsibility to shoulder our share of the burden of maintaining peace and security. We also have an interest in the preservation of peace and the maintenance of order, because we know that they are preconditions to our enjoying untroubled security in Canada.

We favour trade and investment liberalization, because we understand that free enterprise is integral to democracy and modernity. We also realize that liberalization generates prosperity and that the more prosperous the world is, the better off we, as a major trading nation, will be, and the more we will be able to afford twenty-first-century health care and a world-class education system, and the more we will be able to lift Canadian families out of poverty.

We provide development assistance and humanitarian relief to the poor abroad out of a sense of solidarity with those less fortunate, especially the billions caught in poverty. We also help because we know that successful societies abroad generate peace and prosperity for their peoples, and eliminate the conditions that incubate extremism and disease and that generate refugee flows, all of which could come here to afflict us.

We negotiate international environmental agreements (or we did), because we believe that we hold our natural heritage in trust for our children and that its protection is a duty of global citizenship. We also know that the decisions we make at home to meet the challenges that our own environment faces—notably from global phenomena like climate change—and to protect our own health from pandemics will be undermined without the co-operation of other governments.

We promote the rule of law abroad (through such things as the creation of the International Criminal Court), because we believe all people should enjoy the same rights and protections as we do. We also know that the wider the ambit of the law, the more our own rights and protections are safeguarded and the more secure life will be for our own citizens, including the millions of Canadians working and travelling abroad.

Those who advocate hard-headed, narrow self-interest in foreign policy would do well to reflect on the case of Japan, the major country that has had arguably the most interests-first foreign policy of all modern states. In his book *Getting It Done*, Derek Burney,[1] a distinguished former Canadian ambassador, senior official, chief of staff of Prime Minister Mulroney, and once a senior diplomat in Japan, described Japan as "easy to respect [but] ... very much alone in the world and [with] little stature of consequence in any international association other than the G8." The image of Japan has improved in recent years, but the Japanese still do not get much mileage out of soft power.

At the same time, our national character is not immutable. Events abroad and our reactions to them help drive decisions at home and, over time, shape our national identity and values. The battle of Vimy Ridge is one such event, Dieppe another. Climate change is a more current example.

Beyond principles and purposes, and values and interests, an effective foreign policy requires assets, instruments, vision, and will. Canada has assets in abundance. It needs to muster the leadership to employ them, and seize the opportunities of the multi-centric world that are emerging all around us. To decide where we want to go, we need to take stock of where we are.

10

THE HARPER GOVERNMENT:
Not "Back" Yet

When something happens in the world, the Americans ask,
"What should we do?" whereas when something happens in the
world, we ask, "What should the Americans do?"
—The possibly apocryphal answer of a British diplomat,
completing an exchange assignment with the US State Department,
when asked the major difference between working at State and in
the British Foreign Office

In Canada, we ask, "What should we say?"
—Anonymous

In its 2007 Speech from the Throne, the Harper government claimed that "Canada [was] back as a credible player on the international stage." The speech went on to say that "focus and action, rather than rhetoric and posturing, are restoring [Canada's] influence in global affairs . . . our government will continue Canada's international leadership through concrete actions that bring results." Ironically, after four years of Conservative rule, and the pre-programmed G8 and G20 meetings notwithstanding, there have been ample rhetoric and posturing, but the results have been scarce. A lot has been said, but less has been done.

A balance sheet on where we stand is helpful in deciding what we need to do to get back into the worldly game. Where do we stand? What have been the Harper government's hits and misses on foreign policy since coming to office, in terms of both style and substance, and what is their significance?

FOREIGN POLICY: STYLE

On coming to office, the Harper government had little experience in international affairs and less trust in the foreign policy bureaucracy. It has tended to compensate for inexperience with ideology, to subordinate substance to communications, and to privilege partisan advantage over national interests. To be fair, Canadians had not demanded more. During the televised electoral debates, candidates were not asked a single question about foreign policy.

Prime Minister Harper's front bench lacked experience in governing in general and in international affairs in particular—not surprising for a party largely comprising former Progressive Conservatives who had spent the previous thirteen years in Opposition, and Reform/Alliance party members who had had no experience in governing at all. The government's minority standing in parliament added to the problem of inexperience, keeping ministers tethered to Ottawa more than might otherwise have been the case, at least in the early years. Travel and participation in international summits, meetings, and conferences are invaluable to political leaders for the opportunities they provide to expand their intellectual horizons and to check their instincts and theories against reality. And, as the prime minister and ministers have felt it safe politically to absent themselves from Ottawa to meet their counterparts abroad, they have gone up the learning curve. Hosting the G8 and G20 has increased the government's international sophistication and perhaps its interest in the world, although its ideological proclivities and political calculus remain intact.

Neither the number of foreign ministers Harper has appointed—four in as many years—nor the paucity of the international experience most of them brought to the job (David Emerson was an exception), nor in some cases their aptitude for the work, suggests that he wanted much from them. None had enough time to learn the portfolio and to interact effectively with his foreign counterparts. Foreign policy is not rocket science, but neither can it be mastered in one year in office, especially by people with little or no salient experience or previous interest. The revolving door to the minister's office on the top floor of Ottawa's Pearson Building guaranteed the muting of Canada's voice and the diminution of Canada in international consciousness.

"Light-switch diplomacy" diminished Canada's impact further. "Light-switch diplomacy" is the term coined in the 1980s by then US secretary of state George Shultz to describe a tendency in American foreign policy to change directions and priorities with each change of incumbent. The Harper government came to office determined to differentiate itself from the Liberals. That, plus the party's social conservative ideology, led them to try to disown the human security agenda the Liberals had conducted under the leadership of Lloyd Axworthy and Bill Graham, and for which, the Conservatives' wishes notwithstanding, Canada is still widely respected. The desire to be different and distinct also appeared to be a factor in the Conservatives' preference for Latin America over Africa. The reasoning process did not appear to be much more complicated than a determination that, if the Liberals "did" Africa, the Conservatives would "do" Latin America. In its inexperience, the government seemed oblivious to the damage being done to our international relationships and interests by these judgments. NGOs were encouraged to toe the government's ideological line, particularly on abortion and Israel, or see their funding cut.

Tight control of communications, centralized decision-making, and policies designed to appeal to the Conservative Party base and potential recruits have constituted the basic *modus operandi* of the Harper government. That has been the case across the foreign policy board, but particularly regarding the mission in Afghanistan, which the government apparently wanted to keep as far off the front pages of the papers as possible. Canadians seemed, in the main, prepared to support this elective war as long as the expected benefits were worth the effort, the anticipated costs were commensurate with Canadian interests, the prospects of success— however narrowly defined—were reasonable, and the government generally appeared to know what it was doing. For Canadians to be able to reach these conclusions, however, they needed their government to communicate with them about what was happening. Initially, the government, obsessed with message control, tightly limited official communications. Meanwhile, ramp ceremonies for Canada's fallen soldiers and civilians, coverage of which the Harper government tried initially to prohibit, broadcast the costs of the conflict loud and clear. It is ironic that a technologically savvy government, preoccupied with political messaging, was losing the strategic communications war with the Taliban who, thanks to TV, the Internet, and the twenty-four-hour news cycle, could create uncontrollable bad news for the government almost at will. To succeed in the communications contest, the Taliban simply had to get news coverage, not even win any fights. Following the report of the bipartisan commission on Afghanistan, headed by John Manley, the government made a greater effort to level with Canadians, including producing quarterly reports on the situation in Afghanistan, but a lot of public support had already been lost.

On the allegation that Canadian soldiers turned detainees over to the Afghan authorities without appropriate safeguards to prevent their torture, the government seemed more concerned to spin a narrative of competence and support for our troops than to assure itself that it was right on substance. As questioning persisted, Harper prorogued parliament, stopping investigation for several months. The Harper government was not the first to put the communications cart before the substance horse on foreign policy, and it will not be the last. But, to an unprecedented degree, communications imperatives have trumped policy considerations in this administration, ironically very often with negative effects for the government itself.

A further marked characteristic of the Harper government's foreign policy has been the extent to which it has attempted to exploit international affairs for partisan political purposes. The Trudeau definition of foreign policy as the extension abroad of national policies has been stood on its head. Under Harper, foreign policy has become the importation of international issues for domestic political advantage.

The government appeared to consciously take positions on international issues that it could not adopt on domestic issues, notably on abortion, capital punishment, and women's and gay rights. As host of the G8, the government promoted an otherwise welcome initiative on maternal health but that excluded abortion funding, at least by Canada, earning a rare, strong public expression of disagreement from Secretary of State Hillary Clinton. She rightly saw it as a replay of the Bush administration policy that had been severely criticized by groups working in the field. The government was also rebuked by the prestigious international medical journal the *Lancet*, which labelled Canadian policy "hypocritical and unjust," because the government was depriving women in poorer countries abroad access to contraception and safe abortions, while both were available to women living in Canada. The *Lancet* called on Ottawa to adopt policy "based on sound scientific evidence, and not prejudice."[1] Still, at the G8 summit, the government did commit itself to spend $1.1 billion in this field, and persuaded others to pony up $6.2 billion more.

In the context of UN human rights negotiations, the government discouraged Canada's diplomats from using some standard terminology (such as "gender equality" and "international humanitarian law") derived from international treaties that Canada had ratified previously, apparently because the words offended the sensibilities of the party's social conservative base.

On capital punishment, the government abruptly reversed Canada's long-standing policy of supporting clemency for

Canadians convicted in capital cases abroad, thereby prejudicing the appeal of Ronald Smith, a Canadian on death row in Montana. In doing so, the government effectively sent the message that, while the execution of Canadians (and anyone else) was prohibited in Canada, it could be acceptable if done elsewhere. The Federal Court of Canada intervened, ordering the government to support Smith's efforts to avoid execution. The same year, the Harper government also failed to co-sponsor the annual UN resolution against capital punishment, after previous Canadian governments had done so repeatedly over the years—in the company of most democracies (it did vote in favour of the resolution eventually).

The government systematically courted interest groups, making concessions to, for example, Quebec nationalists on their aspirations for diplomatic representation abroad, notably at UNESCO headquarters in Paris as a first step, and tailoring foreign policy to suit the desires of diasporas. Previous governments, the Liberals especially, had scarcely been indifferent to the international interests of Canada's many ethnic groups—the Tamils were an especially dubious case in point—but the Conservatives transformed courtship into pandering, undermining some of the basic tenets of our foreign policy in the process and damaging our international reputation for fairness that had been earned over generations. While claiming principle as its motive, the Harper government played politics with disputes between the Palestinians and the Israelis, the Macedonians and the Greeks, the Armenians and the Turks, and China, Taiwan, and Tibet, actually turning some conflicts into wedge electoral issues and manifesting little concern about the potential impact that doing so might have on the public peace in Canada.

The sharpest policy change the Harper government made on assuming office was with respect to Israel and Palestine. While it maintained the basics, notably support for the two-state solution, the government changed the tone, style, and fulcrum point of Canada's policy, making it very clear that it was solidly pro-Israel and wished to be seen as such[2]. It manifested little interest in Palestinian rights or suffering. Largely reactive to events on the rest of the foreign policy agenda, the government was pro-active in supporting Israel. The Harper government was the first to suspend ties with, and assistance to, Hamas, when the latter was elected to office in Gaza (Israel, the US, and other countries followed suit). Ottawa announced a boycott of the 2009 human rights conference in Durban, South Africa, fifteen months before it was held, because of concerns about how Israel would eventually be treated, and it walked out of the UN General Debate in 2009 before Iranian leader Ahmadinejad spoke, for the same reason.[3] At the UN General Assembly, the Harper government shifted Canadian positions in Israel's direction on half the votes held each fall on Middle East issues.* The government has remained largely silent on the ongoing building of illegal settlements on Palestinian land, the appropriation and demolition of Palestinian homes in Jerusalem, the location of the Israeli security barrier inside Palestinian territory, and the ongoing siege of Gaza, all of which violate the Geneva Conventions that Canada has signed and ratified, and customary international law. In publically giving the Israelis the benefit of the doubt on their attack on a Turkish ship attempting to force the very restrictive blockade of Gaza, an incident that cost nine lives and many injured, Harper seemed indifferent to the fact that Turkey is a NATO ally.

The prime minister took us into uncharted territory when he suggested the existence of a Canadian alliance with Israel. In his words, "those who threaten Israel also threaten Canada.... Canada stands side-by-side with the State of Israel, our friend and ally in the democratic family of nations."[4] In fact, while Canada's relations with Israel have always been friendly and supportive, legally there

---

* These votes are part of the means by which the Palestinians ensure that their issues are not forgotten, and are regarded as acid tests for attitudes on the Middle East. They have been taking place for many years, and successive Canadian governments voted the same way year after year unless the resolutions changed or the situation changed, making what they described as "fair-minded and principled" assessments.

is no formal alliance; Canada is allied only with its NATO partners and is committed to treating an attack on any of them as an attack on itself. Calling Israel an ally was either rhetorical hyperbole or linguistic inexactitude or cynicism, or all three, but in any case, potentially dangerous. By using the term "ally," Harper implied stronger support for Israel in a crisis than the government could likely have delivered. It also suggested a willingness to put Canadian soldiers in harm's way on behalf of Israel in its ongoing conflict with its neighbours, without any say on the tactics or strategies the government of Israel was employing.

The Harper government's defence of human rights has been decidedly selective. Initially openly critical of China, it was less demanding in the Middle East. In 2006, the government gave scant voice, for example, to the very heavy human and infrastructure costs caused by the Israeli bombing of Lebanon, which had been roundly criticized by reputable international human rights organizations. The immediate cause of the war had been the illegal attacks on, and killings and kidnappings of, Israeli soldiers by Hezbollah extremists. Under international law, Israel enjoys the right of self-defence, but in exercising that right Israel is obliged itself to respect international humanitarian law, particularly as regards the protection of civilians in conflict, distinctions between combatants and non-combatants, and the proportionate use of force. Harper characterized the Israeli bombardment of Lebanon at the time as "measured," a judgment that few shared. When the Israeli Defence Force killed a Canadian peacekeeper, Major Paeta Hess von Kruedner, by dropping a five-hundred kilogram GPS-guided bomb on an unarmed UN observation post whose location had been known to the Israelis literally for decades, Harper even appeared to blame the UN. The UN had contacted Israeli military and political leaders a dozen times that day, urging them to stop targetting the post. Harper uttered no word of criticism of Israel.

In Gaza in 2009, the Harper government remained largely silent in the face of allegations by the Israeli human rights NGO, B'Tselem; Human Rights Watch; Amnesty International; and others of possible war crimes by Israel against Palestinian civilians as well as war crimes by Hamas against Israel. According to research by B'Tselem[5] into the 2009 Gaza War, Israeli security forces killed 1,387 Palestinians, of whom 330 were combatants; 248 were police officers who died, for the most part, in aerial attacks on police stations on the first day; and 773 were people who did not take part in the hostilities, including 320 minors and 109 women over the age of eighteen. The extensive harm to the civilian population and the enormous damage to property did not indicate, in and of themselves, that the Israeli military breached international humanitarian law, but according to B'Tselem there was a well-founded suspicion that the harm to civilians resulted from breaches of the principles of international humanitarian law, especially the obligation to distinguish between combatants and non-combatants. The Harper government also voted against the UN decision to follow up on a report, by Justice Richard Goldstone,* which alleged war crimes by both sides, and called on each party to the conflict to conduct its own investigations, and for the international community to do so if they did not.

The Harper government has been relatively silent about the enormous hardships imposed on Gazans by several years of Israeli blockade, including the draconian control of imports (Peter Beinart, writing for the *Daily Beast*, has reported that beyond munitions, the Israelis were blocking the transfer to Gaza of cilantro, sage, jam, chocolate, French fries, dried fruit, fabrics, notebooks, empty flowerpots, and toys, as well as cement and steel) and the extinguishment of Gazan *exports*. The blockade was intended in part to prevent the transfer of munitions into Gaza

---

* Justice Goldstone served as a justice of the Constitutional Court of South Africa and chief prosecutor of the United Nations International Criminal Tribunals for the former Yugoslavia and Rwanda. He was a member of the International Panel of the Commission of Enquiry into the Activities of Nazism in Argentina (CEANA), the chairperson of the Independent International Commission on Kosovo, a member of the Independent Inquiry Committee, chaired by Paul Volcker, to investigate the Iraq Oil for Food program, and the recipient of many prominent awards and distinctions.

and in part to undermine Gazan support for Hamas. According to a UN report in 2009,[6] the blockade has prevented the re-building of 3,700 homes destroyed in war. Secretary of State Clinton and President Obama called the blockade unsustainable and unacceptable. Meanwhile, Canada tightened its controls on aid transfers to Gaza. The opposition in Parliament was largely tongue-tied.

During the Harper tenure, Canadian courts have become involved, to an unprecedented degree, in foreign policy through cases brought by Muslim Canadians against the government. The Federal Court (three times) and the Supreme Court (twice) found against the government regarding Omar Khadr, the child soldier accused of murdering an American soldier during a firefight in Afghanistan. Nonetheless, the Harper government remained steadfast in its refusal to repatriate him and try him in Canada, making Canada the only Western country prepared to allow much-criticized US military commissions to try their citizens. The Federal Court ordered the government to repatriate Abousfian Abdelrazik, a Sudanese-born Canadian citizen whom the government had prevented from returning to Canada for national security reasons, while paradoxically allowing him to live for about eighteen months in the Canadian embassy in Khartoum among Canadian diplomats whose security did not seem to be an issue for the government.

FOREIGN POLICY SUBSTANCE: HITS, MISSES, AND SUSPENDED JUDGMENTS

When the Harper government came to office, it received ample unsolicited advice from old foreign policy hands not to conduct a foreign policy review, something that almost all of its predecessors had done, including the Martin government only three years earlier. Given its "minority" status, the feeling was that launching such a review might have seemed presumptuous. In retrospect, it would have been a very good idea. The Conservatives' instincts were to distance themselves from what they considered failed and ineffective Liberal Party policies, but it was not evident that they knew what to put in the place of those policies, beyond populist rhetoric and ideology. Had the Conservatives conducted a foreign policy review, it would likely have helped them sort out what they believed and created a framework for what they wanted to achieve. It would also have helped them respond effectively to the inevitable surprises and shocks that new governments get. If you don't know where you are going, said Lewis Carroll, any road will take you there, and Harper's foreign policy has lacked coherence and strategic direction. Perhaps as a consequence, the Harper government has done relatively better in responding to events than in leading them, staking out only limited new ground as it proceeds up the learning curve. The G8 and G20 summits in Canada accelerated that climb, as Harper as the host was required to develop the agenda, in co-operation with other governments, and conducted the proceedings. At the same time, the government seemed to lose control of the preparations for the meetings in Huntsville and Toronto, and found itself stuck with an unprecedented, budget-busting price tag of over $1 billion, giving Canadians collective sticker shock, and undermining the government's claims of managerial competence.

On the positive side of the ledger has been the Harper government's handling of the international financial crisis. As a G7 and G20 member, the government had a hand in resolving a potentially major issue in a field that is not always considered to be foreign policy at all. This occurred when the G7* finance ministers and G20† leaders (Canada is a member of both)

---

*The G7 comprises the finance ministers of the US, Canada, the UK, France, Germany, Italy, and Japan.

† The G20 comprises the leaders of the seven, plus Russia, China, India, Brazil, Mexico, Argentina, Turkey, Korea, Indonesia, South Africa, Australia, and Saudi Arabia, as well as the EU.

probably *saved*—not too strong a word—the international financial system from collapse at the nadir of the financial crisis on the weekend of October 10, 2008. The lack of trust among financial entities at the time was such that there was a very real risk that markets would simply not open on the following Monday and that there would be a "run" on British banks, with the "contagion" spreading elsewhere. G7 finance ministers laid out co-operative policies to prevent the failure of major institutions, to unfreeze credit, and to re-establish confidence. G20 leaders then met in London, Pittsburgh, and Toronto to take steps to lay the groundwork for actions they would take in Seoul to try to ensure that a crisis like the financial near-collapse would never happen again, and also to stimulate global growth to escape the recession the financial crisis had caused. Canada's financial strength, derived from many years of sound policy making and regulatory enforcement by successive Canadian governments, gave the Harper government a strong hand to play. The government also used that hand to turn aside an effort by some major G20 countries to establish a levy on banks in order to create a fund to reduce taxpayer liability for future financial crises, on the reasonable grounds that the Canadian banks had not been part of the problem, and the existence of a new fund would encourage reckless behaviour. At Toronto, Harper also persuaded the advanced members among the G20 to commit themselves publically to cut their budget deficits in half by 2013 and to stabilize their debt-to-GDP ratios by 2016, thus sending a signal of intended financial probity to international markets. Some participants, notably US President Obama, acquiesced despite concerns that it was too soon to end stimulus spending and that doing so could lead to the much-feared "double-dip" recession.

The management of the Canada-US relationship, which transcends foreign policy and embraces virtually every area of public policy and every level of government, is a challenge to every federal government. Shortly after coming to office in 2006, the Harper government concluded an agreement with the US regulating Canadian exports of softwood lumber to the US, thus ending, for the time being, squabbling over an issue that had triggered successive legal attacks by US interests over years. (Softwood lumber was one of my key files when I was director of the US Relations Division in Foreign Affairs twenty-five years ago.) Less positive was the fact that the government recovered only $4 billion of the $5 billion the US had illegally collected from Canadian softwood exporters. More recently, the government reached agreement with Washington on removing "Buy America" barriers to Canadian eligibility to participate in state and municipality procurement programs under the US stimulus program. Ottawa and Washington reached agreement on new common standards on automobile emissions, and both contributed to the bailout of General Motors and Chrysler. Ottawa also imaginatively offered a cash-strapped Michigan government a loan—up to US $550 million, to be repaid over time from tolls—in a project to build a second bridge between Windsor and Detroit.

A good deal of the Canada-US relationship plays out through multilateral summits, where Canada and the US often have interests in common. At the Nuclear Security Summit in Washington in April 2010, for example, Ottawa responded to a major US priority when it undertook to return to the United States a large amount of highly enriched uranium (HEU) fuel from medical isotope production. Ottawa also agreed to work together with the US, Mexico, and the International Atomic Energy Agency (IAEA) to convert Mexico's research reactor from the more dangerous highly enriched uranium fuel, which can be used for bomb-making, to low-enriched uranium fuel. Also important to the Obama administration has been Ottawa's championing of the extension of the G8 Global Partnership Against the Spread of Weapons and Materials of Mass Destruction, which had initially been launched at the Kananaskis summit of 2002. Further, as host of the G8 summit, the government inscribed Iran's suspect nuclear program on the agenda, another major US, as well as Canadian, interest.

Also on the positive side of the ledger have been the free trade agreements negotiated with Jordan, Colombia, Peru, and the European Free Trade Association (including Norway and

Switzerland). Negotiations are under way for a trade agreement with the EU, long a Canadian objective, which could potentially be very positive, if the provincial governments co-operate.

The government responded to the Haiti earthquake quickly and competently, using the refurbished military to good effect, and taking a leadership role in the longer-term effort to rebuild that country. Positive, as well, has been Harper's promoting Canadian sovereignty in the Arctic. The government is working with the other Arctic coastal states to map the underwater topography to determine the extent and location of the continental shelves and other physical features. This data will be necessary in establishing the extent of each country's economic zones and the legitimacy of its claims over the waters and the land beneath. Given the small number of coastal states directly involved, five, and the principles enshrined in the Law of the Sea, a diplomatic solution should be quite achievable, although the government's propensity for Cold War–era discourse has been discordant.

Less satisfactory has been the Harper government's management of Afghanistan, the dominant foreign policy issue of its tenure—so far. Harper came to office saying we would never "cut and run" from Afghanistan while he was leader, but he and the Liberal opposition concluded an agreement to terminate the mission in 2011, a position he has stuck to firmly. Setting a deadline for departure, without regard to the circumstances prevailing on the ground when the time arrives to leave, is not serious policy making. If the mission is not worth the sacrifice, we should not wait for 2011 to leave. If it is worthwhile, Canada should not be leaving on an arbitrarily chosen date. Nor is the disproportionate size of our contribution reason enough to do so. It is not disproportionate to the contributions of the Americans and British, our two principal allies in Afghanistan.

Inadequate thought appears to have been given to the impact Canada's military withdrawal from the conflict will have on our NATO allies, particularly Washington. After an extensive review, the Obama administration added forces to the mission in Afghanistan, because Obama concluded that US security was at stake there and in Pakistan, the epicentre of violent international extremism, and that the US needed to deal with it. Canada's departure in 2011 means either that we do not share that assessment or that we do share it, but are leaving the Americans to carry on a necessary fight without us.

Secretary of State Clinton has made it very clear, publicly, in Canada that the US would welcome Canada's keeping some of its troops in Afghanistan after 2011, even if it were in a non-combat capacity, both for the political support doing so manifests, and because the experience and capability of the Canadian troops are highly valued. It is important to engage with Washington in international affairs where our interests dovetail, and Canada's participation in the Afghan conflict has been a major point of co-operation. Leaving prematurely could drain the political capital we have banked from our Afghanistan efforts.

The government's decision to commit itself to playing a larger role in the Americas, for the longer term, has been positive, although the fallout from the decision has been negative in Africa. Latin America is a region of considerable, albeit not transcendent, importance to Canada. Canadian firms have been prominent investors there for many years—more so than they have been, for example, in Asia—and Canada also has significant security interests in the region, especially those arising from the illegal drugs trade and gang violence. Upgrading relations with Latin America is self-evidently a good thing. The Latin Americans are pleased, but, having also been named a priority by each of the Trudeau, Mulroney, and Chrétien governments with few results to show for it, are withholding judgment. John Graham, a former Canadian ambassador and chair emeritus of the Canadian Foundation for the Americas, welcomed the new policy, but commented that "a vision without resources is a hallucination."[7] In the meantime, at the suggestion of Mexican President Felipe Calderón, Latin American leaders have agreed to create a Community of Latin American and Caribbean States that excludes the US and Canada.

The Harper decision to shift our foreign assistance focus towards Latin America and away from Africa, which comprises almost all of the poorest countries in the world, was received with dismay by the Africans. Five relatively less-poor countries from Latin American and the Caribbean region were added to Canada's list of principal aid-receiving countries while seven relatively poorer countries from Africa were dropped. Ottawa has been at pains to downplay the significance of the decision, but it nevertheless signaled a retreat from a relationship that we have developed over fifty years. Embassies in Africa have been closed. Kwesi Botchwey of the Fletcher School at Tufts University, and chairman of the African Development Policy Ownership Initiative, writing in *Canada Among Nations, 2009–10: As Others See Us*, asserted that there is "a widely shared perception that Canada's relations with Africa have been somewhat on the wane in recent years." He added that "there is a noticeable general lessening of Canada's visibility in the global arena." In the same volume, John Schram, former Canadian ambassador to half a dozen African countries, quoted a respected Ghanaian politician as asking, "Where has Canada gone?"

Managing relationships has not been a strong point of the Harper government, which, for example, appeared only belatedly to recognize the significance of India and China to Canada. The government initially downgraded relations with China partly for human rights reasons but largely out of ideological antipathy. The prime minister famously skipped the Beijing Olympics, one of the few significant foreign leaders to so, and drew considerable anger from the Chinese. Former Chinese ambassador to Canada Mei Ping[8] writing in *Canada Among Nations* before Prime Minister Harper's tardy visit to China, and President Hu Jintao's visit to Ottawa prior to the Toronto G20 summit, reflected Chinese displeasure when he described the Harper government's approach as "short-sighted and out-of-date." The Canadian government, he said, "lacked a strategic view in its dealings with China," and Canadian policy makers had "overestimated Canada's influence and seem to believe that Canada matters a lot for China." Ottawa subsequently reversed course, but considerable damage had been done by the neocon tone of Harper's policy and the evident sympathies of many in the government's ranks for Taiwan, Tibet, and the Falun Gong. With the visit of President Hu to Ottawa, the Chinese indicated they were ready for relations to return to normal.

After some delay, Ottawa made India a priority in its emerging-markets strategy. Followoing the Toronto G20, the Harper government also concluded a nuclear-co-operation agreement with India, to the applause of the Indian diaspora in Canada—and to the chagrin of the advocates of nuclear weapons control. The agreement puts an end to the three-decade-long Canadian-imposed restrictions on nuclear relations with India. These restrictions dated from the 1974 Indian nuclear weapon test, in which Canadian technology was covertly used, and they were reinvigorated after the 1998 series of nuclear weapons tests by India. The Harper agreement also signalled the possibility of uranium sales (Australia, in contrast, refuses to sell uranium to India), downplaying Canada's obligations under the Non-Proliferation Treaty (NPT).

Relations with other countries in Asia have also been largely neglected. In *Canada Among Nations,* Paul Evans of the Liu Institute at UBC quoted Asian diplomats as saying that "Canada used to have an influence and role in Asia-Pacific comparable to Australia's. Now it ranks with Spain or Poland." Kishore Mahbubani, writing in the same volume as a self-proclaimed "loving critic of Canada" ("tough-loving critic" was more like it) asked, "Will Canada be the next Argentina?" According to Mahbubani, "Canada is . . . one of the few countries that is an underperformer in the international arena," "Canadian thinking on international affairs [has] functioned on auto-pilot," and "if Canada were to withdraw its presence completely from East Asia today, few Asians would notice." So much for Asian inscrutability. Sadaaki Numata, former Japanese ambassador to Ottawa, was more indirect and diplomatic in that same volume, writing that "many internationally conscious Japanese would be disappointed to see Canada waiver in its pursuit of [an] active multilateral role in the world." He also suggested that "Canada should pay more attention to the dynamism of East

Asia." Don Campbell, former deputy minister of foreign affairs and international trade and former Canadian ambassador to Japan, was more direct, saying that Canada was "increasingly self-absorbed and uncertain . . . [Canada] no longer plays the role on the international scene that it once did," and lacks "any coherent strategy in Asia."

Relations with Mexico were damaged significantly by the Harper government's clumsily imposed visa requirements on Mexicans in 2009, to stop an inflow of unsubstantiated refugees. According to Statistics Canada, the number of visitors from Mexico in the third quarter of 2009 (after the visa imposition) dropped more than 50 percent from the same period the year before, costing the Canadian economy hundreds of millions of dollars. Andrés Rozental, a former deputy minister of foreign affairs in Mexico and currently associated with the Centre for International Governance Innovation in Waterloo, as well as Brookings, has said that the Harper government's sudden decision to impose visas on all Mexicans visiting Canada is a clear indication of the low priority relations with Mexico are given in Ottawa.[9]

Also on the negative side of the Harper ledger has been what former United Nations deputy secretary-general Louise Fréchette has described as "a distinct reticence toward the organization." As observed by Mme Fréchette, "the UN comes across in many official [Canadian] pronouncements as a distant organization about which we sit in judgment rather than a club for which we are jointly responsible."[10] Beyond invoking UN endorsement of the mission in Afghanistan, for whatever political cover that affords, the Harper government has manifested only intermittent interest in UN affairs. Harper's commitment to Canada's campaign for a two-year seat on the Security Council, a seat that Canada has won once a decade since the late 1940s, has seemed to be more motivated by a fear of being the first government to fail to do so, with the political costs that that might entail domestically, than by either the benefits a victory would bring to Canadian foreign policy or by the opportunity it would provide for making a mark on the world. In Harper's tenure, Canadian participation in UN peacekeeping missions remained at a low ebb—we stood fifty-third among troop contributors as of January 2010.[11] Even counting our significant deployment to Afghanistan, we did not rank in the top ten troop contributors to UN-sanctioned or UN-led military operations. Moreover, the Muskoka G8 summit is the first one in ten years to which the UN secretary-general did not receive an invitation.

Also very much in the negative column for Harper is climate change, the most pervasive, complex, and difficult of international governance challenges. The file has languished under three consecutive Canadian prime ministers, including Harper. Partly out of the fear of alienating Albertans, successive Liberal governments did much beating around the bush without ever dealing directly and effectively with the issue. On coming to office, the Conservatives abandoned the commitments made at Kyoto a decade earlier by their predecessors, in part because they could no longer be met in the time frame the treaty specified. The Harper government then unilaterally established its own, less demanding, target and time frame for reducing greenhouse gas emissions, but did not, however, put a program in place to achieve it. The Harper government has subsequently decided to align its policies with those of Washington—as, and when, those policies materialize. It has made no apparent effort to establish its own position first, in order to establish its *bona fides* and induce the Americans to act, as the Mulroney government did on acid rain in the 1980s. At the major international climate change negotiation in Copenhagen, the Harper government contented itself with obscurity and a modest outcome, earning Canada the dubious Fossil of the Year award.

ALL THINGS CONSIDERED

Not all the responsibility for Canada's slipping reputation can fairly be laid at the Harper government's door. The interest of Canadian governments in the world has been flagging since the budget cuts and national unity crises of the 1990s. But it is the Harper government that claims that, under its "leadership," "Canada is back." The claim is more aspirational than factual. Domestic tactics have trumped international strategy.

For whatever reason—ideology, inexperience, indifference, political risk avoidance, a lack of confidence that Canada matters in the world, perhaps all of the above—foreign policy has simply not yet been a major priority for the Harper government. Perhaps hosting the G8 and G20 summits will have kindled an interest.

The government deserves credit for strengthening the weakened armed forces, contributing to international financial stability, making the Arctic a priority, and responding effectively to the disaster in Haiti. Some will see its frank support for Israel as an accomplishment; many others will see in that support the sacrifice of Canada's long-standing reputation for fairness. Likewise, some welcome the shift of priority to Latin America from Africa; others deplore it. The government underestimated the significance of China, insulted Mexico with its ham-handed visa policy, ignored the suffering of Palestinians, mishandled the cases of Canadian Muslims, decided to walk away from our mission in Afghanistan without even a debate, and dragged its feet on climate change.

The government's foreign policy has, initially at least, lacked ambition for the country, and its light-switch character has lowered Canada's profile in world affairs. Unless he makes some significant adjustments in the meantime, when Prime Minister Harper leaves office, Canada will still be on the international sidelines, largely alone. It is not too late to get back on the field, but the game-clock is ticking.

PART V

GETTING BACK IN THE GAME:
A Foreign Policy Playbook

To get back into the game, we have to do two things: first, get our own house in order; and, second, determine which issues we wish particularly to address—and how. With some leadership, smarts, and ambition, we can accomplish a lot, as we have done in the past. Our problems are largely man-made; with the right policies and leadership, they can be man-unmade. We have the talent and the resources to play the diplomatic game effectively, and no one is stopping us from doing so.

The following pages lay out a playbook for how we can re-take our position in the world. It is advice that assumes neither a change in government nor a continuation of the status quo. The advice is premised on the recognition that the world is changing around us, and based on a belief that Canada can itself change constructively. It proceeds from the assumption that Canadians want their country to be responsible, respected, and effective. Here's how it can be done.

11

GETTING OUR HOUSE IN ORDER:
The Need for Policy Coherence

There is no security without development, no development without
security and no security or development without human rights.
—Former UN Secretary-General Kofi Annan

T he Government of Canada, like many others, has not yet fully assimilated former Secretary-General Kofi Annan's insight that security, development, and human rights are integrally related, nor fully endorsed "Kofi's corollary," that multilateral co-operation is essential to the achievement of all three. In fact, very few—if any—Western countries fully recognize the reciprocal quality and interconnectedness of budgets for overseas aid and the military, and therefore strive for overall policy coherence. Instead, aid is seen as the instrument for doing nice things and the military as the one for doing nasty things, not as the complementary instruments of international policy that they actually are. Equally unrecognized is the symbiotic relationship between diplomacy and the military and aid policies.

In Canada, the military budget is growing, the aid budget is flatlining, and the diplomacy budget is shrinking; the 2010 budget is making the distortions worse. Policy coherence among departments and ministers is not the priority it needs to be in Ottawa in the multi-centric, integrated world of the twenty-first century, in which actions have immediate consequences. If Canada is to profit from the changing world order, it cannot afford to have multiple foreign policies; competing priorities have to be reconciled.

FOREIGN AFFAIRS AND POLICY LEADERSHIP

Canadians need Ottawa to develop and lead a foreign policy agenda that advances the country's interests, reflects its values, integrates its efforts, generates fresh ideas, negotiates new treaties, and promotes required reforms and innovations in international governance. This is an agenda that has to be much more than the sum of departmental interests, provincial ambitions, and diasporas' aspirations. To pull it off, Canada needs a highly competent Department of Foreign Affairs and International Trade,* with strong policy staff in Ottawa and effective embassies and consulates abroad. Fortunately, it has one. Unfortunately, it is the department that Ottawa loves to hate.

Since 1973, Foreign Affairs has been located in the Pearson Building at 125 Sussex Drive, on Ottawa's "Ceremonial Route," at the junction of the Ottawa and Rideau rivers, across the street and down a couple of blocks from the prime minister's residence at 24 Sussex Drive, and looking north to the Gatineau Hills. It is a splendid site, especially when the fall colours are resplendent (the best moments of many a day in my eighth-floor Foreign Affairs office were spent looking out of the window over the Ottawa River

---

* For the sake of convenience, and with no disrespect intended to the Trade Commissioner Service or the minister of international trade, I refer to the Department of Foreign Affairs and International Trade simply as "Foreign Affairs."

to the forests of the Gatineau. I got a kick out of showing the magnificent view to foreign visitors and telling that the next city in the direction they were looking was Ulan Bator.) The Pearson Building is remote from the intrigues going on "downtown" and at "the Centre."* Partly because of its location and the international mindset of its personnel, Foreign Affairs has been disparaged over the years for being out of touch with "the town," ironically at the same time as "the town" was being found by others beyond the Queensway to be out of touch with reality.[1]

Tensions across Sussex Drive

Effective foreign policy requires a symbiotic relationship between an engaged prime minister and a competent Foreign Affairs department whose domestic personnel and foreign service can translate his political vision into policy accomplishment. Unfortunately, relations between Prime Minister Harper and Foreign Affairs did not begin smoothly, and they retain all the warmth of a January day in Ottawa.

To some extent, conflict is programmed into the relationship between new prime ministers and Foreign Affairs. New brooms want to sweep clean, and some corners don't think they are dusty. Brian Mulroney observed in his memoirs that Foreign Affairs had a culture that said only they understood the world, and they did not want "a pesky politician—particularly a newly-elected prime minister that they hadn't yet trained—poking around in their files."[2]

New prime ministers, on the other hand, sometimes see international relations as a field in which they can make some relatively cost-free gestures that produce good political returns at home. This is particularly the case for diaspora pressures and for Quebec's international ambitions. Foreign Affairs, steeped in a

---

* "The Centre" is usually the PCO and the PMO. "Downtown" is usually the PCO, the PMO, Finance, and Treasury Board. But the terms are used interchangeably, without affection.

long tradition of constructive international engagement, counts the international costs as serious, and considers that it has a duty to apprise prime ministers of what those costs will be, whether they want to know them or not.

Prime ministers, in turn, sometimes see the advice as mere bureaucratic resistance to the change mandated by an election— or, at least, permitted by one. Sometimes they are right, but sometimes they are not. In either case, prime ministers, especially those who do not value expert advice, can make life difficult for Foreign Affairs. "Downtown"—where the Treasury Board and Finance reside and conspire, often with the complicity of the Privy Council Office and the Prime Minister's Office—has been only too happy to pile on. Foreign Affairs ministers with sufficient standing in the party in power can restore some balance, but in recent years few have been in office long enough to be much help.

In most cases, things improved between prime ministers and diplomats over time. Mackenzie King feared that Lester Pearson's activism at External Affairs would lead to entanglements that could be dangerous for Canada—or, at least, for his electoral prospects—but he relied heavily on Pearson and, ultimately, encouraged him to enter politics. St. Laurent's relations with Pearson were symbiotic in the Golden Age, and when Pearson himself became prime minister, relations with his old External Affairs Department were strong. In 1957, John Diefenbaker came to office after twenty-two years of Liberal government and was suspicious of the motives of the "Pearsonalities," whose entire careers had consisted of serving Liberal governments. The suspicions never fully dissipated.

When Pierre Trudeau was first elected, he made a show of preferring the New York Times to the reports of Canada's diplomats, and relied on the advice of his own confidants, especially Ivan Head, who was the architect of Trudeau's North-South policy. Trudeau came eventually to rely on Foreign Affairs to backstop his major international activities, including his North-South work and his peace initiative, and even conceded that the department was talent-rich.[3] As prime minister, Joe Clark found resistance at

External Affairs to his electoral promise to move Canada's embassy in Israel from Tel Aviv to Jerusalem, notably from his two most senior officials, Allan Gotlieb and Klaus Goldschlag, who were convinced that the move would be a mistake. Clark is remembered at Foreign Affairs, nevertheless, as one of Canada's most thoughtful foreign ministers.

Brian Mulroney was the first Tory elected to a majority in twenty-five years, and he, like Diefenbaker, initially distrusted public servants whose entire careers to that point had been spent serving Liberal governments. Mulroney first threatened pink slips, and actually issued one or two (although not to diplomats). Over time, nevertheless, he staffed the Prime Minister's Office with seven foreign service officers (disclaimer: including the author), who helped deliver the Free Trade Agreement and other elements of his active foreign policy agenda. In retirement, with the sour relations between Foreign Affairs and Prime Minister Harper obviously in mind, Mulroney praised the department publicly, saying that any government that did not take full advantage of "the brilliance and innovation of the Department of Foreign Affairs and International Trade" was making a mistake.[4]

Stephen Harper, like Diefenbaker and Mulroney, came to office after a lengthy period of Liberal rule and evinced distrust of the department, mixed with ideological disagreement. The distrust apparently persists. Both sides need to get over it. The government needs Foreign Affairs to generate fresh ideas, negotiate new treaties, and promote required reforms and innovations in international governance. Successive prime ministers have found that they cannot fully succeed on their own.

THE IMPORTANCE OF MANAGING FOREIGN RELATIONSHIPS

The foreign minister is, in theory, responsible for managing all of Canada's international relations. In practice, he or she necessarily plays second fiddle to the prime minister at "summit" meetings and on major files, and on some less major, but politically sensitive, issues as well. (Strong foreign ministers have managed, nonetheless, to carry out major agendas, notably Joe Clark on apartheid, Lloyd Axworthy on human security, and John Manley vis-à-vis the US post-9/11.) There are also several other violinists in the cabinet orchestra, some with significant parts to play, notably the international trade minister and the Canadian International Development Agencey (CIDA) minister. The minister of national defence is the chairman of the Cabinet Committee on Foreign Affairs and Security, while the foreign minister is chairman of the Afghanistan committee and a member of the powerful Planning and Priorities Cabinet Committee. Many other departments and agencies have international interests and responsibilities, including primarily CIDA, National Defence, Finance, Citizenship and Immigration, Environment Canada, Health, and Fisheries and Oceans.

It is half true that in the modern age, the distinction between domestic and international affairs has become so blurred that every government department must conduct its own international relations. And that the monopoly of diplomats on overseas experience and expertise is a thing of the past. The supposed corollary is that the role of Foreign Affairs is shrinking, and that the department should concentrate on core programs and support other departments in their efforts abroad. Like all half-truths, these are at least half wrong and, in some respects, quite counterproductive. "Outsourcing" foreign policy and diplomacy responsibility to "line" departments can create as many problems as it solves. Most fundamentally, such dispersal undermines the relationship management function that only Foreign Affairs is in a position to provide. Further, NGOs and business tend to be concerned with single issues and special interests. With its network of missions abroad, and with the depth of judgment its foreign service has accumulated over time, Foreign Affairs is the only institution and only department with an overview of all the relations between Canada and a given country, and the only one in a position to manage the flow of issues and make judgments about what the traffic will bear, and how best to advance Canadian interests.

The Mexican visa fiasco provides an illustration of why relationship management is important, though there are many other less-known examples of "line" departments inadvertently harming Canadian relations with a given country or organization. In mid-July 2009, the immigration department decided to impose visa requirements on all visiting Mexicans, estimated at 250,000 per year.[5] What triggered the decision was a spike in unsubstantiated refugee claims by Mexicans. Coming, as the visa decision did, at the height of the travel season, and without appropriate notice to either the Mexicans or the Canadian tourism industry, without adequate arrangements having been put in place to process visa applicants in Mexico—on the eve of a trilateral meeting of foreign ministers and in the lead-up to the trilateral leaders summit in Guadalajara—it amounted to gross incompetence, and it cost Canadian business hundreds of millions of dollars. The case provides abundant evidence, if any were needed, of the folly of allowing each department in Ottawa the independence to run its programs without reference to Foreign Affairs. It is manifestly in Canadians' interests, and in the government's interests, that Foreign Affairs be accorded the authority and the resources to manage relationships between Canada and other countries.

The second problem with the half-truth is that it makes a virtue of a financial necessity. The tighter the Foreign Affairs' budget has become, the more the department has been forced to shrink what was once considered its core business. Cutting its program suit to fit its (shrinking) financial cloth has forced the department to abandon functions to other departments that are better funded but worse placed to do the job.

None of this is to say that the line or technical departments do not have international avocations. Obviously, regulators on either side of the Canada-US border, for example, need to consult and work together to be effective—the public safety department needs to work closely with the US Department of Homeland Security, and our respective health authorities need to be in direct touch with each other to manage cross-border pandemics. What *is* the case, though, is that when that co-operation engages the national interest in a major or precedent-setting way, or when treaties need to be negotiated, then Canada needs Foreign Affairs to lead and to carry out its oversight, relationship management, legal advisory, and treaty negotiations functions to ensure coherence and avoid unintended harm to Canadian interests, including those beyond the one at issue.

THE IMPORTANCE OF STRATEGIC AND COHERENT BUDGETING

Over the space of a decade or two, government spending on diplomacy, defence, and development assistance (foreign aid), the "Three Ds" of foreign policy, has become disproportionate to the needs. Under the Harper government, the process has continued, and ideology has magnified the problem, short-changing diplomacy in particular.

In 2004, the UN's High Level Panel on Threats, Challenges and Change argued that economic development is the indispensable foundation of a collective security system that takes prevention seriously. The panel, whose blue-ribbon international membership included American General Brent Scowcroft, former US national security adviser, saw economic development as a security strategy that is complementary to military capacity. More recently, US Defense Secretary Robert Gates made a similar point when he observed that direct military force would remain important against terrorists, but that the US "cannot kill or capture its way to victory" and "kinetic [military] operations should be *subordinated* [emphasis added] to measures aimed at promoting good governance and economic development."[6]

Whether you agree with these perspectives or not—and I do agree with them—they have the virtue of aligning the interests of rich and poor alike. Development saves lives in the poorer countries as it lowers infant mortality rates, increases education levels, and raises employment levels. It also reduces commerce in illicit small arms, reduces intrastate conflict, increases stability, and diminishes the lawless havens in which international terrorism is incubated. Witness Afghanistan, Pakistan, Yemen, and Somalia.

The Military

Defending Canada and Canadians is perhaps the most fundamental responsibility of any Canadian government, and one of the few absolutes of governance. The capacity to project military force abroad is, at the same time, integral to Canadian foreign policy. Whether in a national security or human security role, in combat or peacekeeping, the ability to put our muscle where our mouth is in those relatively rare instances when coercive military force might be needed is fundamental to the credibility of our foreign policy. The government has begun to implement a twenty-year strategic investment plan to provide what is hoped to be predictable funding increases. It has built strongly on the start that Paul Martin made in reinvesting in the Canadian Forces, following the budget-deficit-driven disinvestment of the 1990s. The military budget of about $19.2 billion annually has grown dramatically under the Conservatives; it stood at about $13.5 billion when Harper came to office in 2006.[7] Since then, the government announced a series of equipment purchase decisions to stretch over twenty years, totalling over $60 billion.[8] Budget 2010 promised to slow this growth, but not to reverse it. Over the next twenty years, National Defence's annual budget is planned to increase to over $30 billion. In total, the government plans to invest close to $490 billion in defence over this period.[9]

This increased funding for the military is a welcome change, following, as it does, a decade and a half of drip-feed funding, as first the Mulroney government and then the Chrétien government cut defence spending to help reverse the deterioration of government finances. It does, nevertheless, raise questions about the other foreign policy budgets.

The Aid Budget

Unlike the military budget, the aid budget, at about $5 billion, is to be capped at 2011 levels, far short of the target of 0.7 percent of

GDP established by Mike Pearson's World Bank report of 1968, which remains the international target. Parliament has called on successive governments to propose a realistic timetable for achieving that goal; the Harper government is only the latest *not* to do so. In 2008, Canada spent 0.32% of GDP in aid to poorer countries, ranking us fourteenth among twenty-seven OECD countries. The ratio figure somewhat understates the increases in actual Canadian spending in recent years, because of Canada's strong economic growth—the larger the economy, the more funding a given percentage of it yields. We nevertheless trail the OECD country average of 0.47%, which we had pledged to attain. With our aid capped, our relative standing will retreat further. How Canada's fixed budget is going to pay for new commitments to poorer countries, not least regarding the climate change assistance promised at Copenhagen and the maternal health program promised in Muskoka, is not obvious.

Perhaps with no irony intended, the Auditor General has found that while CIDA is well regarded in the field, the complex and lengthy processes required to obtain corporate approval for project funding in Ottawa are a problem. Few Canadians, including CIDA officials themselves are completely happy with the results achieved, but spending money responsibly and effectively is more difficult than it looks. The complexities of operating in the Third World make this area of public policy more susceptible than most others to the laws of unintended consequences.

Few policy subjects have been more studied and written about to less conclusive effect than foreign aid. Notable recent studies have included Dambisa Moyo's *Dead Aid* and Paul Collier's *The Bottom Billion*. The consensus seems to be that aid works, that aid is necessary, but not sufficient. The same is true, not incidentally, of markets. Claims that aid does not work because the ills of the world are still with us underestimate the complexity and magnitude of the challenge. Aid cannot do the whole job alone; enlightened trade and finance policies are also necessary, as is the resolve to stand up to corruption and tyranny.[10]

The Foreign Affairs Budget

At just over $2 billion, the Foreign Affairs budget is obviously not trivial; it takes money to recruit people, teach them languages, transfer them and their families abroad and back, safeguard their security, and provide them with the modest resources they need to do their jobs effectively. Despite this, however, the Foreign Affairs budget is still only equivalent to a rounding error in the government's $259 billion public accounts. Further, funds for the core business of Foreign Affairs and International Trade, the smallest component of our foreign policy, have been reduced year after year and are projected to continue to decline. The cumulative impact on Foreign Affairs's 2009–2010 core business budget of successive cuts every year since 2004 is $188 million; by 2012–13 the shortfall will rise to $214 million. In other words, Foreign Affairs has about $200 million less to spend on core business than it had in 2004.*

The 2010 budget indicates that things will get worse before they get better, with the result that Canada will be increasingly handicapped diplomatically, precisely at the time when diplomacy will be of unprecedented importance in a multi-centric world. Many of our allies, including Washington, are gearing up their diplomacy, or have already done so. Ottawa should take note that US Secretary of State Clinton, describing "diplomacy and development as core pillars of American power," has sought an additional 600 foreign service positions for the US State Department, even after 2,000 additions the year before. The State Department budget is set to grow by almost 10 percent.[11] Secretary of Defense Robert Gates has made the extraordinary gesture of advocating greater emphasis on diplomacy, and even urging the

---

* These reductions come on top of a decade of government-wide cuts beginning in 1988–89 to end the budget deficit created in the 1970s and 1980s (see the Department of Foreign Affairs website, January 2010).

provision of greater resources for the US Department of State.*
According to the 2010 US National Security Strategy, "diplomacy
is as fundamental to ... national security as ... defense capability.
Our diplomats are the first line of engagement, listening to our
partners, learning from them, building respect for one another,
and seeking common ground." Unlike Ottawa, Washington is
preparing for the next war or, at least, a world where diplomacy
will be vital.

One area where Ottawa's budget cutting has been particularly
destructive is public diplomacy, which has been all but gutted.
Public diplomacy is the deliberate effort to "sell" Canada to the
wider world, to publicize Canada's strengths, and to persuade key
foreigners that engaging with Canada is worth their time and
effort. Public diplomacy, including cultural programs, permits
diplomats to convey an image of Canada as culturally sophisticated,
economically successful, and technologically savvy, and is a helpful
complement to the "Mounties, mountains, and molsons" image
foreigners have of us. It is also a necessary antidote to the bad
publicity that arises from the seal hunt or the tar sands or forestry
practices or climate change deficiencies or shortsighted visa
requirements or whatever negative news we generate about
ourselves. Cultural funding is also very helpful in developing
contact networks abroad that extend well beyond the arts. Public
diplomacy abroad is particularly important for Canada because of
the near-total absence in Canada of foreign news bureaus that
could transmit our stories to the wider world.

Other countries aggressively promote themselves abroad. The
US budget for public diplomacy is $1.3 billion; the budgets of the
British, Germans, and French exceed a billion dollars each. The

---

* In a speech delivered in July of 2008 entitled "US Global Leadership
Campaign," Gates noted that "our diplomatic leaders—be they in
ambassadors' suites or on the State Department's seventh floor—must have
the resources and political support needed to fully exercise their statutory
responsibilities in leading American foreign policy."

Canadian budget is approximately $22 million. The US outspends us 28:1. When I was ambassador in Germany, the Italian government had a larger budget for public diplomacy programming in the city of Bonn alone than Canada had for the entire world. We are G8 in economics and politics, but we are decidedly Third World in public diplomacy, which is all the more surprising considering the role that communications has played in our history.

WHAT WE SHOULD DO

Canada needs a foreign policy that is conceived and executed in the national interest and that reflects national values. This requires, first, that the prime minister view foreign policy as the important policy field it is, and lead the development and implementation of that policy, personally. The prime minister's personal leadership is essential to ensure coherence across the range of Canadian interests in a multi-centric world. It is also necessary in recognition of the fact that leaders' summitry has become a key vehicle of diplomacy. The number of multilateral summits has multiplied over the years, and the issues addressed at those gatherings have become more encompassing, more numerous, and more politically important.

Second, it should be automatic that the prime minister appoint as the foreign minister a senior colleague who both commands respect in the party and has an aptitude for the job. Further, barring political crises, the prime minister should leave that colleague in the job for the several years it takes to become familiar with the myriad of issues involved and comfortable in his or her relationships with the foreign ministers of other countries.

Third, the government needs Foreign Affairs to be the senior manager of relationships between Canada and our international partners, both other capitals and multilateral institutions. Relationship management is necessary if Canada is to profit from opportunities and to avoid mishaps. Currently, it sometimes seems as though Canada has multiple foreign policies under the leadership of the Finance Department, Citizenship and

Immigration, CSIS, and Environment Canada, as well as CIDA, National Defence, and Foreign Affairs. Formally and informally, the prime minister needs to make it clear that Foreign Affairs is in charge of managing relationships on his behalf and in his interest. Canada is not big enough to afford incoherence. Foreign Affairs should particularly develop strategies for managing Canada's relations with all of the G20 countries, where coherence is likely to be most important.

Fourth, to bring greater unity and symbiosis to aid and foreign policy, the president of CIDA should report to the parliament through the foreign minister, who would issue CIDA policy guidelines. CIDA would be better off with the part-time attention of a senior minister than with the full-time attention of a junior minister. The CIDA program is crucial to Canada's capacity to contribute effectively to international development. It also goes to the heart of Canadian foreign policy values and interests. In fact, aid is central to Canada's image in much of the world, and is the main content of Canada's relationship with the twenty countries on which CIDA is concentrating its official development assistance. It is also central to the relationship with several other countries besides, as well as with the World Bank, the UN Development Program, and other multilateral agencies.

Fifth, the budget of Foreign Affairs should be reset in order to reverse the downward trend. The current track of diminishing funding for core diplomacy and increasing money for the military is programming a foreign policy of the "Gold Rules" ("he who has the gold, rules"), which would be rooted in national security issues, because that's where the money is. There is a lot more to foreign policy than the projection of military power. More adequate funding is necessary in order that our missions abroad have the resources to do their jobs effectively, that we can increase the ratio of Canadian staff posted to the field, that we can carry out effective programs of public diplomacy and representation, that we can conduct student-exchange programs with countries that may be of major future interest to us, that we have the staff to manage relationships in Ottawa, and much more.

Finally, when budget allocation decisions are being made, the government should take a holistic view of foreign policy spending. This entails recognizing the respective contributions that the Canadian Forces, CIDA programming and Foreign Affairs diplomacy make to foreign policy and security—and ensuring that foreign policy goals are served, not prejudiced by financial decisions. Without being rigid, the government should use a ratio of 20:7:3 as a rule of thumb for ensuring proportionality among our annual defence, aid, and diplomacy budgets. While military spending will always vastly outstrip diplomacy or aid budgets, because of the numbers of troops needed and the high cost of the equipment they use, the government should bear in mind that a dollar spent on diplomacy likely buys more security at the margin than a dollar spent on defence, and that the same is broadly true of foreign aid and defence. Diplomacy also helps extract the maximum international political return on the military and aid investment. Without effective diplomacy, military expenditures produce few political returns, as Mackenzie King's experience in the Second World War demonstrates.

12

JOB ONE:
The United States (and Mexico)

Geography has made us neighbors. History has made us friends.
Economics has made us partners, and necessity has made us allies.
—President John F. Kennedy in Ottawa, 1961

If the world is becoming increasingly multi-centric in character, the US will nevertheless remain the pivot of the international system for a long time to come, and its influence will be pervasive and often decisive. American culture will remain omnipresent. American science, especially medical science, will lead the world. American universities will continue to set international standards for excellence. The American economy will, despite the "great recession" and the structural changes it has brought in its wake, continue to generate unprecedented wealth for its people and for its trading partners. And the US military will remain without peer in terms of sheer hard power. The US will continue to be internationally pre-eminent, albeit financially beholden to China and others, and internally at "cultural war" with itself. The Obama administration has made it clear that it sees multilateral co-operation as a necessity, not a choice, if the US is to afford to fund its domestic priorities and international objectives. Even a superpower has limits.

Developing and maintaining an effective relationship with Washington remains "job one" for Canada. The US is our only neighbour, our irreplaceable market, our indispensable ally, and, for the reasonably foreseeable future, the most powerful country on earth. That it is these things and broadly shares the same values as we do is incalculably to Canada's advantage.

Relations with the United States must be managed both bilaterally and in a global context. The more effective our foreign policy is around the world, the more respect we get in Washington. The more respect we get in Washington, the more effective we can be around the world—and in Washington, as well—in promoting and protecting our interests, from the Afghanistan mission to softwood lumber. The report of the Canada-US project of Carleton University, led by Derek Burney, former Canadian ambassador to Washington and head of the Canada-US Free Trade Agreement negotiating team, and Fen Hampson of Carleton University, made the same point inversely: "Canada's capacity to move its bilateral agenda with the United States in productive directions will be considerably enhanced as a result of credible engagement in such forums as the United Nations, the World Trade Organization, and the Summit of the Americas." Good foreign policy is a virtuous circle; ultimately, it is good politics as well.

Relations with Mexico will also become increasingly important, as Mexico, already a member of the G20 largest economies, becomes a major international factor. Mexico's economy is already bigger than ours in terms of purchasing power parity (that is, what Mexicans can buy in Mexico with their pesos compared to what we can buy in Canada with our dollars), and Mexico's influence in Washington only grows stronger as the "Hispanization" of America expands. Mexico has a willing and capable diaspora in the US that delivers influence in Washington: Canada does not. In principle, that Mexican diaspora can be of help to Canada, too, in influencing Washington on trilateral issues.

Whether we need to influence Washington (and Mexico City)

is not in question. What is in question, eternally, is how to influence Washington, and for what purpose. What sort of relationship do we need to have with the US in order to exercise sufficient influence to protect our essential interests? And how do we most effectively manage relations with Mexico in the process?

THREE OPTIONS, SQUARED

There is an entire spectrum of views on how to manage relations with Washington, but—to the extent they are choices at all—they can generally be broken down into broadly the same options as were articulated in the days of Pierre Trudeau. The first option is to seek an actively integrationist relationship, getting as much inside the American tent facing outwards as possible, in order to try to shield Canada from the protectionist tendencies of American politics, and to make common cause against other trading blocks and competitors. The second option is to maintain our partnership with Washington as is, pragmatically and systematically improving processes and addressing problems as they arise. The third option is to seek counterweights to US power, through multilateral and other bilateral relationships, and, generally, to keep a wary distance. Interleaved with this debate is a second-order debate, but a scarcely less important one, also with three options: whether to manage relations in North America on a bilateral, a trilateral, or a kind of hybrid bi-trilateral basis. Managing North American relationships has become a "Rubik's Cube" of a challenge.

Since 9/11, the rate of trade growth among the three countries has slowed, our region's share of global GDP has declined significantly, Canadian trade with the US has slipped relatively, and legal entries of travellers into the US and Canada have decreased sharply, by a third.[1] All of this is prompting some to call for taking NAFTA further.

Advocates of deeper integration with the US, sometimes described as the "Big Bang" school, generally see the Canada-US FTA and NAFTA as way stations, not destinations. Partly to meet the offshore competition, partly to shield Canada from recurring American protectionism, the advocates would complete these agreements by totally eliminating tariffs and other border barriers, and pursuing deeper economic integration, such as a customs union, a common market, or a more political union[2]—albeit while respecting and preserving national sovereignty, to the extent that is possible. Some would also seek greater military cooperation, indeed integration, in managing Canadian coastal waters, although who they believe the enemy is, is not clear, and why military integration is necessary now when it was not in the Cold War is not obvious. [3]

Deeper integration with the US, along with Mexico or without it, would have some undoubted advantages, not least diminishing the costs of North American manufactures, which must surmount non-tariff barriers, adding costs, as they make their way back and forth across North America's borders on their way to becoming fully integrated final products. Offshore products cross the border only once (unless they too are incorporated into larger products). Making North America's coasts the continental security perimeter would facilitate creation of a North American, or at least a Canada-US, equivalent of the "Schengen area," the borderless zone created by twenty-five European countries, which would require harmonizing policies on immigration, visas, perimeter surveillance, and other such issues. The US's Western Hemisphere Travel Initiative, which requires all border crossers to have passports, is a large step in the opposite direction.

Former Canadian ambassador to the US Allan Gotlieb has written of building, as the Europeans have done among themselves, "a larger sense of community, a North American community that substitutes enforceable rights and obligations for political arbitrariness and the muscle of special interests."[4] Former deputy prime Minister John Manley and former US ambassador Gordon Giffin have called for a sequel to NAFTA, "a common market or at the least a customs union."[5] The independent trilateral Independent Task Force on Building a North American Community proposed that the North American community's "boundaries . . . be defined by a common external tariff and an outer security perimeter within which the movement of people, products, and capital would be legal, orderly, and safe."*

Where proponents of greater integration are divided, some in their own minds, is on the advisability of a bilateral or a trilateral deal. It is noteworthy that former Canadian officials with many years of experience on these files—John Manley and former Canadian ambassadors to the US Allan Gotlieb, Derek Burney, and Michael Kergin—all seem convinced that, when it comes to issue management, the Canada-US border and the Mexico-US border raise problems that are too different, both in their nature and in the extent and quality of the co-operation they require, to manage in a trilateral manner, with one-size-fits-all approaches. Some Mexicans and American experts[6] disagree, pointing out that the Canadian border is being treated as a real border by the Americans, as Secretary for Homeland Security Janet Napolitano described it on coming to office. As evidence, they cite the US Western Hemisphere Travel Initiative, which requires all travellers to produce a valid travel document or other biometric identification. Despite heavy lobbying, Canada received no dispensation from this policy. Andrés Rozental, a member of the Trilateral Task Force, observes that Canada's efforts to differentiate itself from Mexico have both affected Canada-Mexico relations very negatively and undermined progress in making NAFTA more competitive vis-à-vis the European Union and Asia-Pacific Economic Cooperation (APEC)—to say nothing of China, India, and Brazil.

It is one of the paradoxes of Canada-US-Mexico relations that the idea of greater North American integration unites the Canadian left and the American right in their fear of lost sovereignty. The arguments on each side suffer from a deficit of facts and a surplus

---

* The Task Force was chaired on the Canadian side by John Manley and co-chaired by the former head of the Canadian Council of Chief Executives, Tom D'Aquino, and included Wendy Dobson and Gotlieb.

of paranoia. While the American right was railing against the threat the now-defunct Security and Prosperity Partnership was said to have posed to American sovereignty, and the Canadian Left was doing the same on behalf of Canadian sovereignty, the three governments allowed the initiative quietly to disappear, for reasons apparently unrelated to the actions of any side. By all accounts, little of significance had been accomplished, in part because of the absence of high-level investment of political will, and perhaps the absence of oversight institutions in NAFTA itself. On the American side, officials had been directed to accomplish what they could within existing resources and without new legislation, which necessarily limited results.

Robert Pastor of the Center for North American Studies of American University, a former Carter White House official and member of the Independent Task Force on Building a North American Community, has asked why NAFTA has become "a veritable *piñata* for pandering pundits and politicians."[7] He answered his own question by responding that governance through NAFTA had not kept pace with the expansion of the continental market, in which new problems had emerged and old ones had been exacerbated. On that score, there seems to be a considerable commonality of view by experts in all three countries. Rozental has also lamented the reluctance of all three NAFTA partners to create any such institutions, rendering NAFTA inert and unable to respond to changing times and to meet external challenges.[8]

Advocates of less integration, for their part, also tend to put Washington at the centre of their foreign policy preoccupations, but where integrationists see benefits from closer relations, the opponents see costs. According to columnist and author Linda McQuaig, "NAFTA has done much to erode our sovereignty, denying us control over our own energy resources, creating a wide-ranging set of rights for corporations, and limiting our power to protect the environment and shape public programs. . . . We should simply bow out."[9] Maude Barlow,[10] chairperson of the Council of Canadians, has written extensively in the same vein.

In my experience, Canada's problem is not too much American

interest in Canada: it is too little, a reality observable in most US administrations going all the way back to Franklin Roosevelt, at least. When I first arrived for my posting in Washington in 1985, I was suspicious that at some level, "manifest destiny" lived, and that in some obscure, suburban corner of Washington, behind a razor-wire-topped chain-link fence, and with an innocuous sign on the door, there were Americans secretly developing designs on Canada. After four years in Washington, I concluded that, if there were such a conspiracy, it was an extraordinarily sophisticated one, because I had detected not the slightest evidence of it whatever—and distressingly little overt evidence of any interest in Canada at all. On the contrary, my colleagues and I at the embassy spent most of our time devising stratagems and spending our hospitality monies trying to get access to Reagan/Bush administration officials and congressmen and congresswomen and their staffers, so that we could defend and promote Canadian interests. Not much has changed in the interim. The Canadian embassy in Washington is still located at the corner of "Interdependence Avenue" and "Indifference Street."

In Trudeau's day, attempts to give substance to the "Third Option" policy and to find alternatives to the US in Europe and Japan failed. The North American economy proceeded to integrate willy-nilly, despite the international border running through it. For Canadian business, the American market was too rich, too close, and too open to pass up for political reasons. The "contractual link," a sort of trade deal that Trudeau pursued with Europe in order to encourage diversification, was the diplomatic equivalent of pushing on a rope, and delivered little of value.

Nearly forty years later, Canada and the European Union are once again negotiating, this time a Comprehensive Economic and Trade Agreement (CETA) that would complement our relationship with the US. If an agreement can be negotiated, and as trade and investment relations with Asia and Latin America grow, the US market will absorb a relatively smaller portion of our exports. Nonetheless, in the face of the realities of geography, the dynamism of the US economy, and the propinquity of the peoples on either side of the border, our economic and financial relations with the United States will continue to dwarf relations with others.

THE BIG BANG IDEA'S TIME HAS COME—AND GONE

For all the hope for greater integration into the United States by some, and the fear of getting too close by others, the reality is that neither is happening. There is little disposition to take major steps in the direction of deeper integration. "Muddling through" is the likeliest course of action—or inaction.

My own view is that the Big Bang idea of dramatically deeper integration with the US is fatally flawed, whether it be on a bilateral or on a trilateral basis, although the latter would deliver some protections to the two smaller partners that the former would not. The vision of a system that substitutes "enforceable rights and obligations for political arbitrariness and the muscle of special interests,"[11] as called for by Allan Gotlieb, holds enormous appeal in principle, but is likely to disappoint in practice. The FTA and NAFTA deliver many benefits, but their dispute resolution mechanisms have proven inadequate when push comes to shove. The softwood lumber experience, in which the Americans sought to limit Canadian lumber imports four times in twenty-five years, is instructive regarding the unwillingness of Congress and successive administrations to respect treaties that affect constituents' economic interests.

There is also a major American governance problem. Put simply, the US system is in tight gridlock because of deep ideological and partisan splits. In the US Senate, the centre is not holding, to paraphrase Yeats. In recent years, moderate senators, such as Bill Bradley of New Jersey and, more currently, Evan Bayh of Indiana, have given up on reforming a system in which ideological and partisan templates are applied to everything. A simple majority in the hundred-seat Senate is not enough to pass legislation, because the minority filibusters, or threatens to do so.

On the major issue of the huge US deficits—on international

trade and the federal budget—the US Congress is unable or unwilling to cut spending or raise taxes, or to do some of both. Paul Volcker, the distinguished and respected former head of the US Federal Reserve (the US central bank) and now a counsellor to President Obama, observed on CNN that "Capitol Hill and the Senate [are] dysfunctional . . . I'm very disturbed about the trend in the government generally and its inability to get together and do things. . . . I do think this is more dysfunctional than I've seen it." Former US secretary of state Jim Baker, a Republican stalwart for three decades, has made similar points in discussion with CNN.

The extreme character of the Tea Party Movement, the appeal of know-nothing personalities to the American right, and the xenophobia of ubiquitous talk show personalities do nothing to support arguments for a more formal relationship between Canada and the US. We have our own problems in Canada, and, as Marci McDonald has written in *The Armageddon Factor: The Rise of Christian Nationalism in Canada,* some of them are found in similar—albeit not yet as pronounced—culture wars. Perhaps that is why Canadians think, by a wide margin (more than 2:1), that Canada is "becoming more, rather than less, like the United States," according to polling done by Frank Graves of EKOS Research Associates for the Carleton University Canada-US Project. However, by an even larger margin (8:1), according to his survey, Canadians would like to become *less* like the United States.

Semantics also discourages greater integration. There is no common word with which Mexicans, Americans, and Canadians identify themselves. In Europe, it is possible for the citizens of every country on the continent to call themselves "Europeans," because Europe is a continent and a civilization; "Europe" is the Union, not one of the countries of the Union. People can be Dutch or Polish, for example, and European too. It is safe to say that there would have been no European unification if the Dutch or the Poles, let alone the British or the French, had been expected to use the noun "German" as the common nomenclature for the new entity. Nigerians can be Nigerian and African. Indians can be Indian and Asian. In North America, the Americans have long since appropriated the name of the continent. Canadians and Mexicans do not, therefore, think of themselves as Americans. Their identities do not merge into something larger. ("North American" seems artificial; moreover, that is not what the Americans call themselves.) In any case, more formal integration of North America comes at a cost to sovereignty, independence, and identity that many Canadians appear unwilling to pay.

The advocates of deeper integration tend to discount concerns about a loss of sovereignty. In this regard, their allusions to the European experience are neither reassuring nor persuasive. Europe comprises twenty-seven countries, five of which have broadly the same size of population and economic strength. No one European country dominates. Germany is the largest, but it is far from being to Europe what the US is to North America. The similarity of size and strength, which ensures a degree of fairness, is simply absent in asymmetric North America, short of a highly improbable reformulation of the continent on the basis of regional economies. Perhaps that's a project for the second half of the twenty-first century.

For now, North America has three significant political entities, disparate in population size, economic strength, cultural impact, and military power. In a political union, the asymmetry in size and power among the three countries would dictate not only harmonization of approach, which would be reasonable, but alignment of the smaller with the larger. The US Congress is unlikely in the extreme to acquiesce in equality for Canada or Mexico, or entertain the idea of shared sovereignty. Nor would a North American parliament, a counterpart to the European parliament, likely be acceptable to any of the three countries in any reasonably foreseeable time frame. All three countries, not least the United States, are too attached to their own myths.

In any case, the moment has passed. There seems to be little public interest in closer integration, and less political will on either side of the Canada-US border. There are many steps short of economic union that can be taken to improve things. But the Big Bang is an idea whose time has come and gone.

WHAT WE SHOULD DO

Without an institutional framework, the three countries will have to muddle through, fixing problems pragmatically where they can and when they can. The secret to success is effective personal diplomacy and leadership by the heads of government. Here are a few things we should do to make things better.

First, we should recognize that personal diplomacy at the top by the prime minister is indispensable to our getting important issues addressed at the highest level. The leaders don't have to love each other; as Trudeau and Nixon showed, respect of each other's capacity is enough. The prime minister should, if anything, step up his leadership of Canadian diplomacy vis-à-vis the United States. Other ministers—Foreign Affairs, Finance, Environment, Public Safety, Transport, National Defence, among others—would continue to play their supporting roles, of course. In addition, the business community and civil society should be more engaged, formally or informally, to ensure that their concerns are taken into account and that the system is transparent enough that scaremongering is ineffectual.

Second, we should formalize annual back-to-back bilateral and trilateral summit meetings, which should take place in Washington. In practice, annual trilateral summits have been the norm; they should become the rule. A predictable action-forcing event once a year is necessary for getting our issues on the US president's agenda, and for getting cabinet-level and lower-level officials in Washington to take them seriously. Holding the meeting in Washington (or Camp David) on a fixed day every year—for example, the second Monday in May—would add some form and formality to the process. A troika of personal representatives could establish the agenda and oversee the follow-up. Perhaps a small secretariat could be created to establish agendas, commission research, provide early warnings of trouble, supervise logistics, maintain websites, record decisions, facilitate accountability, and generally keep the bicycle on its wheels and rolling forward. Given the propensity to hold summits anywhere other than in the respective capital cities, making Washington the regular site would save the president travel time, and not increase the travel burdens of the others, who have had to go elsewhere anyway. This is not a trivial benefit in an age of non-stop summitry. It would also afford Canadian and Mexican leaders annual opportunities to interact with Congress on issues important to them, and with the Washington-based media as well, who are largely indifferent to Canada and most other foreign countries—except as foils for the US. Other summits at which the Canadian prime minister and the two presidents intersect throughout the year—such as the G20, the G8, APEC, and the UN, among others—would continue to provide occasions for brief meetings when a given issue becomes too "hot" to wait for the annual meeting. Used strategically, these annual summit meetings would afford the prime minister helpful opportunities to develop a personal working relationship with his American and Mexican counterparts, facilitating telephone contact between summits. Once every four or eight years, the newly-elected president of the US could pay the (nearly) customary first bilateral visit to Canada (and Mexico). In those years, the trilateral meeting could be dropped.

Third, we should ensure that the agenda of every bilateral summit meeting with the US president has a global section. Engagement on bilateral and trilateral issues is necessary, but not sufficient to build and maintain a successful relationship with Washington. The Obama world vision of co-operation is much more cordial to mainstream Canadian thinking than the national-security-obsessed, quasi-imperial world view of the neocons of the Bush era. If Obama is to surmount the forces of inertia prevalent in the US national security establishment in both parties, he will need help—and even advice. Canada has something to say, and do, on global governance, peacekeeping, peacemaking and peace-building, international financial monitoring and regulation, Afghanistan, Haiti, the Middle East, terrorism, climate change, and even non-proliferation. It is possible; Mulroney was, after all, a valued confidant of two US presidents.

Fourth, the prime minister and president should each appoint a distinguished trusted representative to examine what needs to be done jointly and separately to protect North American security in an age of terrorism, and to advise how to do so in light of our differing constitutional protections. It would be the terrorism equivalent of the Permanent Joint Board on Defence. The idea would be to advise on the steps that could be taken to try to make sure that any future bombs in Times Square do not have a Canadian connection. Making a major, public effort to get ahead of this particular curve has many things to commend it, both substantive and presentational. It took years to live down the urban myth that the 9/11 terrorists came from Canada, and it cost billions of dollars. How much more difficult and costly it could be if the next time the story were true.

Other issues for examination by trusted representatives working with their American and Mexican counterparts include the illegal drug trade and climate change. There is a North American crime and drug crisis. On the demand side, Canada is part of the problem, and on the supply side, we are suffering the consequences of infestations of organized crime, as gangs carve out territory in our major cities, with bullets flying in our streets. The same is true, only much more so, in the US, and Mexico is struggling to put down exceedingly violent gangs. Further, distinguished personal representatives could move forward the climate change file—which cuts across the portfolios of the Finance, Environment, Energy, Trade, and Transportation ministers—more effectively than any single minister could do.[12]

Fifth, we could appoint cabinet-level officials on both sides to be responsible for border co-operation, particularly infrastructure development and physical security.[13] This would be a new portfolio for border co-ordination affairs.

Last, but not least, we should make it a priority to speak to Washington with one voice—Ottawa's voice. For Canada, coherence and unity are crucial. Experience shows that it is difficult enough getting our single voice heard and our national interests accommodated without trying to do so while one province or another follows the beat of its own inner drummer. In any negotiation, even two Canadian voices, whether they are speaking in one language or two, imply disunity, any hint of which creates openings to be exploited. If we divide ourselves, we can hardly expect the Americans not to conquer us, figuratively speaking. We are not big enough or powerful enough to prosper in spite of ourselves. At the same time, speaking with one voice presumes a degree of federal leadership and national co-ordination that has been missing on some key files in recent years, notably on climate change.

13

JOB ONE (A):
Reforming and Innovating Global Governance

Can we all get along?
—Rodney King, after widespread rioting marked the acquittal of
Los Angeles police charged in his beating

W hy can't we all just get along? First and foremost, major
global issues resist resolution because of a profound lack of trust
and human solidarity. That is the case in the Middle East, where
war without end has poisoned relations and blocked a solution
whose outlines have been evident for years. The distrust seeps into
issues far removed from the Middle East. A further example is the
conflict in Darfur, where humanitarian principles cry out for
intervention, but where colonial legacies and contemporary self-
interest prevent it.

The second reason problems persist is that many are global in
scope and require global solutions, sometimes of extraordinary
complexity, for example climate change. Further, there is no global authority with the power to deliberate, decide on a solution, and
compel its implementation. International institutions like the UN
can bring the horses to water but the authority and resources to

make them drink remain vested in individual states. There is no sheriff the UN can call if signatories violate agreements. International law depends on consent.

Third, the world has become a more complex place and power is migrating to the newly emerging economies. There is a disconnect between the distribution of authority in existing international institutions and the distribution of military and economic power in the world. The UN Security Council reflects mid-twentieth century, not contemporary, power realities. Conversely, restricted forums like the G20 reflect current realities but are not fully legitimate. Because they are neither universal nor representative, they cannot bind others.

Fourth, the world has shifted on its axis, from East-West during the Cold War to North-South now. For the great bulk of UN members, which both gained independence from colonial rulers and acceded to UN membership well after the birth of the organization in 1945, the priorities of the UN are, or should be, economic and social development, not security. For the North, the primary purpose of the UN remains security.

Finally, despite all the evidence to the contrary, and the fact that the UN Charter, which every state endorses, outlaws aggression, the belief persists in some countries that war is an effective instrument of foreign policy, or to paraphrase Clausewitz, the nineteenth-century German general and military thinker, war is merely a continuation of politics, by other means. For example, there is no doubt that when the US invaded Iraq in 2003, all other non-violent options had not been canvassed and found wanting. In the process, Americans lost faith in the world body because it did not endorse the war, and Muslims, and others, lost faith in the UN because it could not prevent the war.

In a shrinking and integrating world, good global governance has become an end in itself, or very nearly. The means have become integral to the ends of security, safety, prosperity, and dignity, internationally as well as nationally. The West will not dominate the next sixty-five years of international affairs as it did the past sixty-five, so now is the time to reinforce, not jettison, the rule of law that is codified in the United Nations Charter, and to inculcate a culture of respect for the law and partnership in international relations. Under the leadership of President Obama, the US, the *primus inter pares* of the world body, has signalled its intention to engage with the UN and to enhance its effectiveness. But the US cannot do it alone. World leaders need to recapture a common—or at least a compatible—vision of the future, and of the place they see in it for the UN. It is important for Canada to respond and do its part.

The unique legitimacy of the United Nations derives from its universal membership. No other organization encompasses and gives voice to the entire world. But it also has problems that its membership must, in its own interests, solve. The UN's problems are the consequence of an increasingly integrated and complex world, in which power is shifting and consensus is scarce on just about everything but gravity. Washington, Beijing, Brasilia, Berlin, Brussels, London, Paris, Moscow, Delhi, Pretoria, Tokyo, Ottawa, and all the other leading capitals need to regain a modern shared vision, and engage constructively in the resolution of major issues. US leadership is key, as is Chinese engagement.

To find that common purpose, the West will need to recognize that the UN is not its wholly owned subsidiary. The G77/Non-Aligned Movement countries will need to find a way to wrest their leadership back from the ideologues and the spoilers among them. The emerging powers, China in particular, will need to accept that they have responsibilities for the globe—as well as rights. Ottawa, for its part, will need to re-engage purposefully, and not just sit in judgment of the world body.

REFORMING THE SECURITY COUNCIL: ARISTOCRACY OR ACCOUNTABILITY?

Reform of the UN has become near synonymous with reform of the Security Council, although there is considerably more to it than that. The degree of the Council's perceived legitimacy has a direct bearing on the standing of the UN as a whole.

So long as the members of the community of nations recognize themselves in the makeup of the Council and see the Council's decisions as expressions of the common will, the organization has a potential for effectiveness that no other can match. Many, including people in a particular position to know, such as former Secretary-General Kofi Annan and Deputy Secretary-General Louise Fréchette, worry that this vital asset is being eroded; that the Security Council, as currently constituted, has a representational deficit; that there will come a point at which the mismatch between the prerogatives of the permanent seat-holders and the real-world distribution of power becomes so wide that it destroys the legitimacy of the body—and, with it, its effectiveness. The disparity between the world of 1945, in which the major victorious powers and France awarded themselves permanent seats with the ability to veto Security Council decisions, and contemporary reality is wide, and will undoubtedly get wider.

The delegates who gathered in San Francisco in 1945 to negotiate the Charter had to accept that the US, the Soviet Union, and other permanent members would have the power to veto Security Council action, or there would have been no deal. The latter would not allow themselves to be outvoted on matters of war and peace. But the veto has often been used—or threatened, which is tantamount to the same thing—in circumstances that could not be said to jeopardize the particular state's vital national interests. A good example was the US veto of the continuation of the UN mission in Bosnia and Herzegovina (UNMIBH) in 2002, in a bare-knuckled attempt to insulate itself from the jurisdiction of the nascent International Criminal Court. The US held hostage the international community's multi-billion-dollar effort to ensure long-term peace in the Balkans, and ultimately vetoed the extension of the mission's mandate. It was a "black day for the UN," as I told the assembled press at the time. In the cramped and closed backroom at the UN where the council meets privately, there are many more examples of self-serving vetoes or threats of vetoes. For example, the Russian Permanent Representative at the time threatened to veto any resolution proposing UN military intervention in Kosovo. When I represented Canada on the council in the latter part of 2000, the only permanent member of the Security Council *not* to use its veto, or threaten to do so, was France. The practice of threatening a veto is insidious, because it is usually done behind closed doors, and thus escapes the scrutiny—and often the opprobrium—that follows from a veto cast in a formal public session.

Rising powers India and Brazil naturally want the distribution of permanent seats on the Council to reflect the realities of emerging power. South Africa and other African countries want their continent to be represented among the permanent members. They want permanent seats, and vetoes, too. Japan and Germany, respectively the second- and third-largest payers of dues,[1] want powers commensurate with their financial and other contributions, although they would probably settle for permanent seats without vetoes. Japan* pays about 17 percent of the budget and Germany about 9 percent.[1]

The countries that aspire to permanent seats regard an anachronistic council as only quasi-legitimate, and, equally bad, semi-effective. In their view, the council's decisions would be respected more and, therefore, implemented by others more readily and more fully, if the permanent members were more representative of the entire membership. That does raise the question of how to reconcile equity and accountability, and therein lies the rub. Not everyone equates enlargement with reform. Some member governments think the council's more significant problem is its performance and accountability deficit—Rwanda in 1994

---

* At a time when the regular budget ($2.5 billion) and peacekeeping budgets ($7.8 billion) have climbed to almost US $10.5 billion combined, Japanese and German interests cannot be ignored. The US, in contrast, pays about 22 percent of the regular budget (27 percent for peacekeeping), and enjoys both a permanent seat and a veto; China pays 2.67 percent and has a permanent seat and a veto. (Canada pays 2.98% and has neither a permanent seat nor a veto.)

and Darfur at the beginning of this century being tragic cases in point—and that creating a larger council would not fix that. A large but potent minority of UN members, nicknamed originally "the Coffee Club" and "the Espresso Group" after the beverage served at the first meetings hosted by the Italian founders, is opposed to the addition of further permanent seats. Their position is partly a matter of principle—they are for accountability and against privilege—and partly a matter of self-interest: they presume that they themselves would not get a permanent seat and, in some cases, that their historical, regional rivals (Pakistan and India, Italy and Germany, Brazil and Argentina, South Korea and Japan) would. Most members of the Coffee Club, Canada included, would stand resolutely by their principles right up to the point at which they themselves were offered a permanent seat, and then they would grab it. The hypocrisy is disguised of course; the Coffee Club has renamed itself "Uniting for Consensus." In reality, it is united only by opposition to adding new permanent members to the council other than themselves.

Efficiency is also a consideration. The Council is currently relatively efficient, especially as compared to other bodies with larger memberships, notably the forty-seven-member Human Rights Council, the fifty-four-member Economic and Social Council (ECOSOC), and the 192-member General Assembly. The greater the number of Council members, the more difficult it will be to reach agreement and the weaker the outcome—and the more certain it is that the five permanent members will effectively form a council within the Council to run things.

That was already happening in my time on the Council when I served there in 2000. The P5 liked meeting among themselves to "cook" the outcome of debate of a given issue. Bob Fowler, my predecessor, and I used to chide them for behaving like parents afraid to talk in front of the children. We particularly objected when the secretary-general participated in the exclusive gatherings, which is not precluded by the Charter, but not foreseen by it either. Sometimes we would taunt the P5 for fearing to discuss things in our intellectually intimidating presence. It made the point, albeit a bit truculently. But why go to the trouble of electing members if they are expected simply to rubber stamp the decisions of their betters?

In the periodic public debates that took place in my time at the UN, I used to argue that if five permanent seats were bad, ten were geometrically worse. I characterized the addition of further permanent seats with vetoes as the diplomatic equivalent of pouring sand into the UN's gas tank. It sounds less clever as a metaphor in retrospect, but it did convey the idea that the UN would grind to a halt.

Successive Canadian governments have given priority to accountability and effectiveness over representativeness. According to this view, which I share, the most important, readily achievable, reform is to improve the Council's working methods, which too often give short shrift to the needs of the broader UN membership. For example, when drafting mandates on military missions, it makes sense that the countries that will contribute the troops, and those that will pay the lion's share of the costs of the mission, participate fully and effectively in the discussion.

Further, the accountability inherent in recurring elections is intrinsically more democratic than the privilege of a once-and-forever peerage, which is what permanent seats amount to. Requiring countries to run for election periodically has the benefit of ensuring that Security Council members stay in touch with the needs and interests of the larger membership, rather than retreating into a self-interested enclave. While accepting that the council could be enlarged somewhat by the addition of non-permanent seats, the dissenting countries argue that granting additional permanent seats on the Security Council, which is the minimum the aspirants want (some want vetoes too), would compound the problem created in 1945. Permanency is immutable, but power is transitory. Even if change has been almost imperceptibly slow, the world is a much different place at the outset of the twenty-first century than it was sixty-five years ago when the UN was born—and it is likely to be an equally different place sixty-five years hence.

There are also practical drawbacks to awarding more permanent seats. If the UN were to create a class of permanent seats without vetoes, which is one compromise that finds considerable favour around the world, those who do not get permanent seats—regrettably almost certainly including Canada—would effectively become third-class UN citizens. Considering the extent of Canada's contribution over the years in terms of ideas and resources, and the contributions of others like the Scandinavians, the Benelux, and Australia and New Zealand, that seems an unwise, as well as an unfair, outcome.

WHAT WE SHOULD DO

Because of history and temperament and residual diplomatic skills, there are few challenges for which Canada is better placed to make an effective contribution than UN reform. And, with the accession to power of an American administration that is disposed to multilateral co-operation, there are likely to be few times better than now to try to do so.

First, we need to take a page from the British playbook and make ourselves indispensable at the UN, or at least so valuable that others seek our help. The world body provides us with a key platform for promoting our ideas and protecting our interests, and we should make the most of it, working there actively and constructively on the major global governance issues of our times, notably arms control and disarmament, climate change, human security, human rights, democracy, and poverty alleviation. To make ourselves valued, we should develop a coherent Canadian strategy for engaging the UN, starting with our term on the Security Council—presuming we win a seat. The last time we were elected to the Council in 1999, we had a pre-thought-out plan—the Human Security Agenda—that produced one of the most fruitful, albeit brief, chapters of Canadian diplomatic achievement at the UN since the Golden Age. We can make a positive impact again. It should be possible, for example, to advance the Harper government's maternal and children's health objectives through the Council, because it is in conflicts that the dangers to women and children are aggravated. At the same time, our agenda should be cognizant of US objectives, notably on nuclear weapons. Where it is in our interests to do so, we should deliberately promote progress that the US administration finds constructive.

Second, as it is in our interest that the UN work better, we should tackle the governance issues that impede progress and undermine the legitimacy of the Security Council, especially the vexed questions of permanent membership. We should aggressively promote the creation of elected seats with longer terms than the usual two years, perhaps six or seven seats with four- or five-year terms, without vetoes. Winners could run for re-election consecutively; if the membership wished, it could re-elect them ad infinitum.

At the same time, we should continue to oppose the creation of new permanent seats, with or without accompanying vetoes. Democratic accountability requires that seat-holders face their electorates from time to time. Creating a half-dozen new, extended-term elective seats would be an acknowledgement of changing power realities, while nevertheless ensuring the accountability of seat-holders to the membership. Such an approach would also be consistent with historic Canadian efforts to have middle powers recognized as such, and would, if done skillfully, open the door to extended service on the Council by Canada, too.

Third, we should press for restrictions on the use of the veto. In recognition of the increasingly unified character of European Union policy, we should urge that the British and French undertake formally to employ their vetoes only jointly. We should also urge them to cast their vetoes only with the acquiescence of the European Union membership as a whole. Further, we should continue to press for a formal undertaking by all five veto-holders that they will never employ vetoes to prevent collective action on genocide, crimes against humanity, and war crimes, and will exercise the veto only in cases of supreme national interest.

Fourth, we should promote a better and more transparent

way for choosing the secretary-general. Under Article 97 of the Charter, the broader membership has had no option in practice but to endorse a choice for secretary-general made in a process dominated by the US and other veto-holders, which is little more transparent than a papal enclave. Canada could lead other General Assembly members in a creative reinterpretation of the Charter (without amending it, which is scarcely less difficult to do than amending the Canadian constitution) that would permit, as a minimum, a formal vetting process of candidates—including, ideally, a formal vote for the next secretary-general.

Fifth, Ottawa should make it a priority to have qualified Canadians appointed to senior positions in the Secretariat, where they have become as rare as any endangered species. These senior people, while working dutifully for the UN, would bring Canadian perspectives and values to the issues they handle, which is often beneficial for Canada.

Sixth, Canada, the country that invented "The Responsibility to Protect," should participate again in UN-led military operations and contribute to their upgrading. Even if we counted our contribution to Afghanistan, professional and effective as it has been, we still would not rank in the top ten troop contributors to missions led or mandated by the UN. Further, post-Afghanistan, we have a high-quality military force, both combat-capable and operationally savvy. We should use it to good advantage. There are strategic advantages in working through the UN with its greater international legitimacy and its capacity for peacebuilding, which are absent in American-led coalitions of the willing, and even in NATO operations.

Seventh, and related to increased participation, we should get into the game and help to fix the problems with the UN's military operations. We could continue to simply remain on the sidelines and disparage the UN, but a more constructive response is to help. Enhancing the UN's military effectiveness is very much in the Canadian interest. If we engage more actively, it should also be possible to bring a greater sense of accountability to UN military and peace-building missions. We could also remind the Council to respect sound military principles when it deploys forces, and support the secretary-general in rejecting mandates that are diplomatically appealing but militarily and politically unachievable given the resources available. We could promote greater functional participation of non-members of the Council in the Council's work, notably participation of the troop-contributing countries in negotiations over military mandates.

GOVERNANCE INNOVATION

At its meeting in Pittsburgh in 2009, the G20 proclaimed itself "the premier forum for . . . international economic co-operation." The G20 is one of two major new institutions created since the economic meltdown of 2008; the other is the Financial Stability Forum. The G20 came into being in the wake of the "great recession," when it was realized that the UN and the IMF were too broad a base for resolving contemporary, global financial challenges—and for narrowing differences on other economic challenges—and that the G8 was not broad enough. It was necessary to include China, India, Brazil, Mexico, Korea, Turkey, and others in the search for solutions, if those solutions were to gain any traction. With the banking crisis threatening widespread damage, the time for the G20, which had been strongly promoted by Paul Martin, had come.

Despite the economic orientation of the G20, it is an intensely political group. The more technical work of renovating the international financial system is done in the Financial Stability Board, although many questions about the purposes and functioning of that group remain to be answered. In any case, the "elevation" of the G20 at Pittsburgh was the clearest sign that the Obama administration understood that some problems could only be resolved co-operatively, and that participation in the search for solutions by the emerging powers, especially China, was the new international reality. Whether the new powers are prepared "to pick up the cheque," that is to say, to share in the obligations as well as the rights, remains an important question.

The G20 is in its infancy, and its future is not guaranteed. Whether it can be sustained beyond the immediate crisis and be extended to cover other governance issues remains to be seen. The group will earn the trust and respect of all concerned if it succeeds in resolving the financial regulatory issues so that another such finance-triggered recession does not happen, and if it effectively co-ordinates the issues of economic policy the world faces. Failure would be a serious setback indeed. If it survives, its agenda seems likely to expand, albeit slowly. It took several years for the G7 to admit Russia and transform the group fully into the G8; in fact, the G7 finance ministers still meet without Russia.

The G20 can complement the UN, not substitute for it. By definition, the G20 lacks the legitimacy that universality of membership affords the UN. The G20 ought not, moreover, to become a kind of "concert of powers." When the world last tried that, at the Congress of Vienna, it ended badly—in two world wars and 100 million dead. Until such time as the UN surmounts its hoary ideology-driven processes, the G20 is, nevertheless, a welcome alternative avenue for making progress. So long as the G20 liaises sensitively and effectively with those who are not at its table, a little competition would likely do the UN good.

At least for the time being, the G8 will remain in existence to address issues, especially geo-strategic issues, that the G20 will not address—notably arms control and disarmament, certain development issues such as maternal and child health, international political issues, and the like. The time demands of international summits—exceeding a dozen per year for some leaders—the wear and tear of travel across time zones, and the redundancy of G8 and G20 meetings, however, seem likely to try leaders' patience and to result in a merging of the two groups sooner than later. Further, few of the G20 leaders are economists or financiers, and most will not forever be content with an exclusively economic focus to their meetings. As was the case with the G8, the likelihood is that they will want to discuss other major issues when they find themselves sitting with other world leaders around a single table. It is very much in Canada's interest to help the G20 succeed, if for no other reason than to forestall the creation of new groups in which Canada might not automatically be a member.

Beyond the purely practical reasons for consolidating the G8 and G20, there could be substantive benefits. The G20 accounts for 90 percent of global economic production, 80 percent of world trade, and 67 percent of the world's population. The G20 also accounts for about 80 percent of current greenhouse gas emissions, although who among the members bears the primary responsibility to act is hotly contested. When the group reaches agreement among its members, a large part of whatever the problem it is addressing is on the way to being solved. It cannot bind non-members by its decisions, but it can commend its decisions to others. It can import its agreement into other organizations, notably the UN, making universal agreement substantially easier to achieve.

WHAT WE SHOULD DO

First, we should regard G20 membership as the near equivalent of a permanent seat for Canada on the UN Security Council, and make the most of it. We should, therefore, get ahead of the G8-G20 consolidation curve and lead that process, both to cement Canadian membership in the G20 and to promote discussion of non-financial issues.

Second, the government should identify other issues for discussion and focus in the G20, notably the economic development of the world's poorer countries, climate change, energy security, trade, and terrorism. UN reform itself might be more easily achieved if differences were narrowed within a smaller group of countries whose own standings as members of the world's premier economic group were secure. Perhaps ultimately, the G20 could function as a kind of economic Security Council, formally or informally.

Third, Canada should champion a way of taking into account—genuinely—the views of the 170 countries that are not members. We have a long and respected record in the IMF, where we speak on behalf of a constituency of countries that includes the Caribbean and Ireland. The poorest are not represented at the G20. Nor are some of the most effective countries, notably the Nordics and the Netherlands. Canada should work towards finding a solution to the efficiency (fewer countries around the table) and inclusivity (more countries around the table) conundrum. At a minimum, we should invite the UN secretary-general to the table to act as the voice of the absent.

Last but not least, we should promote holding the annual G20 meeting at UN headquarters. All of the leaders come to New York for the General Debate in September anyway, and a major security infrastructure is already in place. They could stay an extra day or two in New York and meet, on UN grounds or off. The incremental costs would be trivial, the cost of a few extra nights in a hotel. A side benefit is that having the two organizations meet side by side would help to make the work of each more coherent.

14

JOB ONE (B):
Major League Issues

When the one great scorer comes to mark against your name, he
writes not that you won or lost, but how you played the game.
—Grantland Rice, "Alumnus Football," 1941

AFGHANISTAN

Canada is in Afghanistan for good policy reasons, in the company
of allies, on a mission sanctioned by the UN Security Council. We
have a national security interest in seeing the Afghan government
and Afghan security forces develop to the point at which the
country can defend itself from the Taliban, and not again become
susceptible to exploitation by al Qaeda and international terrorist
groups. We have a further national security interest in promoting
stability in a region with three nuclear-armed states—one of
which is under pressure from Islamist extremists (Pakistan)—and
a fourth aspirant (Iran). We have a humanitarian and human
security interest in the protection of women and children, notably
the access of women and girls to education and health care. Finally,
we have a governance interest in making multilateral co-operation
work, and demonstrating that the UN and NATO can successfully

assist failed and failing states and protect threatened populations. Further, bilaterally, the Afghan mission is a textbook example of how Canada, playing an effective international role, can increase the respect with which we are held in Washington and other key capitals, even if only temporarily.

In Afghanistan, our role is significant. Canada's military and civilian commitment there is the largest our country has mounted since the Korean War. Since 2001, Canada has contributed more than 2,800 military and over 100 civilian personnel at any one time, and aid totalling $1.3 billion. Many Canadian NGOs are also present. By playing a leading military role in Kandahar, Canada has earned a voice in the conduct of the conflict and in the pursuit of peace, although we have been little visible or audible in the international diplomacy managing the process.

The insurgency has stubbornly and steadily grown, triggering a new surge of 30,000 troops by the United States. American troops are to begin to withdraw by 2011, but the end date of American presence in Afghanistan is unknown, although President Obama has made very clear that the US is not there forever. At the same time, efforts have been made to reconcile Afghan authorities and those insurgents who are willing. Ultimately, there will have to be a political solution; it is not in the nature of this conflict for total victory to be achieved. The Taliban, with their medieval attitudes towards women's rights, especially regarding access to heath care and education, make a distasteful negotiating partner, but peace is made with enemies, not friends. A complicating factor is the Karzai government itself, with its electoral fraud, cronyism, and links to crime and the opium trade. It, too, is not an ideal partner.

Prime Minister Harper has been categorical that the Canadian forces will leave in 2011, the year established by a House of Commons motion passed in March 2008. The date is entirely arbitrary, part of a domestic political compromise, with little reference to the evolving situation on the ground or to the views of the Afghans or Canada's allies. Further, little pressure is coming from the Opposition in parliament to extend the military mission—or to transform it, as Minister of National Defence Peter

McKay had hinted might be done. The Special Parliamentary Committee on Afghanistan has, nevertheless, re-opened the door to keep some Canadian troops in the country after the current mission ends in the summer of 2011.

President Obama has said he is convinced that the US faces, in his words, "no idle danger... no hypothetical threat" in Afghanistan. The Obama administration believes that US security is at stake there and in Pakistan, the epicentre of violent extremism. Obama has argued further that the danger will only grow if the region slides backwards into Taliban control. To try to prevent that from happening, he set narrow and limited objectives: denying al Qaeda a safe haven, reversing the Taliban's momentum, and denying it the ability to overthrow the government, in part by strengthening the capacity of Afghanistan's security forces and government so that they can take primary responsibility for Afghanistan's future. Obama, who as a newly elected president had ample reasons for walking away from Afghanistan, has, nevertheless, staked the success of his administration on achieving an acceptable outcome. This is not a situation that Canada should treat in any way other than very seriously.

Secretary of State Hillary Clinton has made it clear, publicly in Ottawa, that while obviously the decision to stay or go is Canada's to make, the Obama administration would welcome the Canadian military's continued participation, even in a non-combat capacity, such as training Afghan forces. If the Canadian decision to leave is final, that will have important consequences, because of the loss to the NATO military effort of the high-quality Canadian military contribution in Kandahar province, because of the demonstration effect that such a departure would have for other allies, and because of the signal it would send to the American public. Secretary Clinton's comments are in line with those made over a period of months by various other American officials, from Secretary of Defense Robert Gates and Admiral Mike Mullen, Chairman of the Joint Chiefs of Staff; to Susan Rice, US ambassador to the UN; and Ivo Daalder, the US ambassador to NATO; as well as NATO Secretary General Anders Fogh Rasmussen.

Canada has held NATO's ground in Kandahar, the home turf of the Taliban, at a time when the US was distracted in Iraq, and has impeded the Taliban's ambitions. Further, we have learned how to fight an insurgency effectively; our knowledge and capability are respected by the Americans and others. Our leaving before NATO leaves is bound to cause disappointment among our allies, especially the US, and raises fundamental questions for us.

The point is not whether we have done our share. Rather, it is whether leaving or staying in 2011 serves our interests. Further, to what extent do we think that President Obama's conclusion—arrived at very painstakingly—that US security is at stake in Afghanistan and Pakistan applies to us? If we agree with Obama's assessment, how do we justify leaving on an arbitrary deadline while the effort continues? Is our presence part of the problem or part of the solution? We know from vast UN experience that fixing failed and fragile states is not done in a few years to pre-fixed deadlines. Why do we think it should be otherwise in Afghanistan? Or do we think Afghanistan is a fool's errand, or simply not worth the cost?

WHAT CANADA SHOULD DO

In military/humanitarian interventions, responsible countries do not set arbitrary deadlines that are unrelated to the situation on the ground. We should not retreat into the political expediency of a parliamentary ceasefire. Parliament will not serve the interests of Canadians by just running out the clock on a matter that will define Canada in the eyes of friends, allies, and enemies. We need to revisit the decision, at the least.

We should have a national discussion and a parliamentary debate on what to do in 2011. If, after consideration of all of the strategic and tactical considerations, we think that success, in the limited terms it has been defined, is important and still achievable, we should carry on. We could, if need be, reduce our military presence and maintain a force of perhaps 500 to 1,000 troops in Afghanistan to help to train the Afghan national army. In any case, we should continue our economic development efforts as long as security permits, in Kandahar and elsewhere in the country where possible. If, on the other hand, we conclude that the mission is a lost cause, we should pull out on schedule. The Americans reviewed their strategy. We owe it to ourselves to do the same. Urgently.

THE MIDDLE EAST

Canada has supported Israel's right to exist since the partition of Palestine and the creation of Israel by UN General Assembly Resolution 181 in 1947. In 1949, Canada voted in favour of UN General Assembly Resolution 273 supporting Israel's entry into the United Nations. Since then, Canada has recognized Israel's right to defend itself under international law.

In 1948, Canada also endorsed UN Resolution 194, which recognizes that Palestinian refugees from the 1948 war have, as do all refugees, the right to return to their homes, or to compensation. We have interpreted that resolution to mean a right of return or compensation in the context of a comprehensive peace agreement. Since 1967, when Israel occupied the West Bank and Gaza at the conclusion of the Six-Day War, successive Canadian governments have made it clear that Canada did not recognize Israel's permanent control of the territories it occupied, or Israel's right to build settlements in the West Bank and Gaza, which violate the Fourth Geneva Convention and are a serious obstacle to achieving a comprehensive, just, and, therefore, lasting peace.

Following the 1967 war, we supported UN Security Council Resolution 242, which emphasized, among other things, the inadmissibility of Israel's acquiring land by force. In the same vein, we also supported UN Security Council Resolution 338 following the 1973 Yom Kippur War. Together, these two resolutions constitute a basis for trading land for peace. Over time, Canada came to support the creation of a sovereign, independent Palestinian state, living in peace with Israel, that is, a two-state solution. Successive Canadian governments have considered that the 1993 Israel–Palestine Liberation Organization joint Declaration of Principles pursuant to the Oslo Process provided the basis for a comprehensive agreement.

Canada recognizes Israel's right to protect its citizens from terrorist attacks, including by restricting access to its territory by constructing a lengthy barrier. At the same time, Canada opposes constructing the barrier on occupied territories inside the West Bank and East Jerusalem, which is contrary to international law under the Fourth Geneva Convention. Canada also opposes Israel's unilateral annexation of East Jerusalem.

Successive Canadian governments have supported a series of attempts, mostly under US leadership, to negotiate peace—the Oslo Accord, the negotiations at Sharm el-Sheikh, the Camp David talks, the Taba discussions, the "Road Map," the Annapolis process, and so on. All have ultimately failed. The peace process on this most complex and intractable of issues has brought only process—no peace.

The crux of the matter is that Israel has occupied the West Bank since 1967 and has been building extensive and illegal settlements on Palestinian lands ever since, progressively reducing and restricting the territory left for the Palestinians, and rendering the achievement of a two-state solution increasingly remote. Palestinian extremists, for their part, have been resorting to terrorism in their resistance to occupation, both in contravention of international law and in defiance of the will of most of the international community. The pain on both sides has been extensive, but the Palestinians have suffered larger losses because of Israel's much greater military strength.

At the UN, the Israeli-Palestinian conflict is the diplomatic equivalent of low-intensity war, and is the subject of many Human Rights Council meetings in Geneva and General Assembly resolutions each fall in New York. The conflict manifests itself in the consideration of everything from human rights to management reform to budget allocations. Faced with the impossibility of moving the Security Council on Middle Eastern issues, largely because of the US veto, the Arabs, under Palestinian leadership, have made the General Assembly their default forum.

Why does the issue continue to have such traction among UN members? Partly because it defies resolution, and events on the ground are truly tragic, and partly because the Arabs, particularly the Palestinians, have doggedly and skilfully kept it on the agenda, using their numbers and appeals to G77 solidarity to control the diplomacy. The representatives of the G77 in New York and Geneva identify with the hardships of the Palestinians. For them, the forty-plus years of Israeli occupation of the West Bank evoke memories of the colonialism they themselves endured.

Israel is seen by many at the UN as a rich, militarily powerful country, more Goliath than David, backed up by the most powerful state on earth. Partly as a consequence, even Israel's legitimate security concerns are given short shrift. The South sees Israel as non-compliant on a whole series of UN resolutions: on the return of the refugees or compensation to them; on control of East Jerusalem; on the continuing occupation of the West Bank; on the continued building of illegal settlements and the construction of new housing units in existing settlements; and on the separation barrier built partly on Palestinian territory, rather than along the pre-1967 border, despite the findings of the International Court of Justice. The fact that the United States and some US allies, including Canada, are disposed to give Israel the benefit of the doubt, or provide uncritical support of Israel's policies no matter which government is in office in Jerusalem, reinforces judgments about the unfairness of the American—and latterly, the Canadian—position. As such, it does nothing to persuade Third World countries to temper their reflexive solidarity with the Palestinians. The Israelis dominate on the ground militarily, and the Palestinians dominate in New York and Geneva diplomatically. And the conflict grinds on.

The UN's legitimacy is challenged by both sides. The Israelis and the Jewish diasporas, especially in the US and in Canada, regard the organization as disproportionately critical of Israeli practices and policies, and insufficiently understanding of Israeli security needs. On the other hand, the perception in many, probably most, developing countries, especially in the Muslim world, is that the world body is a tool of the West, particularly of the US, which condones the West's oppression of Muslims from Palestine to Afghanistan and Pakistan, and beyond.

WHAT WE SHOULD DO

What should any Canadian government do in handling this most intractable of problems? In the first place, we should reaffirm the fundamentals of Canadian policy, including maintaining our strong support for Israel's right to exist and to live in peace with its neighbours and to defend itself within the limits of the law, as well as our strong support for the establishment of a viable Palestinian state at peace with Israel.

Second, we should start exercising our judgment again, calling them as we see them, and letting the chips fall where they may. This means neither supporting Israel right-or-wrong or Palestine right-or-wrong, nor presuming that Israel or Palestine can do no wrong. Neither side can always be right. We should be fair-minded and clear-spoken on human rights violations by both sides. This means giving neither democratically elected governments nor sentimental underdogs a general dispensation from scrutiny. History is replete with examples of resistance movements and democracies violating human rights laws and norms. The excesses of Guantanamo, Abu Ghraib, and Bagram, to say nothing of the "rendition" of Canadians to torture abroad, were perpetrated by the self-proclaimed greatest democracy. We should support reputable human rights organizations on both sides, and help them in the very difficult and trying work they do.

Third, we should anchor our positions in international law, including international humanitarian law. Doing so would not be welcomed, at times, by either party to the conflict or by their respective supporters in Canada. Nevertheless, the law is a rock on which to stand in the turbulent flow of Middle East politics. It would also be the surest way to remain "fair-minded and principled," in practice, as well as in rhetoric. At the same time, we should remind ourselves that innocent people on both sides are bearing the brunt of this confrontation, and basic human compassion should also inform our judgments.

Fourth, we should seek opportunities to contribute to international efforts led by the US or the UN or anyone else with the credibility to achieve a solution. Further, we should take the initiative ourselves to work with the parties to the conflict to resolve specific issues or to narrow differences, for example regarding the eventual disposition of the refugee issue and security in the Old City of Jerusalem. We should support research into these intractable issues. We should, also, begin to research the consequences for Israel, for Palestine, and for the rest of us, if a two-state solution becomes unachievable, which seems an increasingly likely outcome of continued settlement building. Further, we should bring Palestinians, who have relatively fewer means, to Canada to study, in order to build up Palestinian capacity to run a successful state over the long run.

And, fifth, we should never, ever, play domestic political games with this issue.

ARMS CONTROL AND DISARMAMENT

The success of the Non-Proliferation Treaty (NPT) is one of humanity's profoundly encouraging self-affirmations. It shows that, faced with an existential challenge, the world can change course away from its own destruction. While there remain major obstacles and miles to go, and there is a danger that Iran, India, Pakistan, North Korea, or Israel will yet derail the process, the world—or most of it—is set on the right path, a fact that should encourage us in meeting the governance challenges of other complex, existential threats. This is especially true of climate change and international finance, two other issues that threaten to overwhelm civilization.

In 1963, President Kennedy famously said, "I see the possibility in the 1970s of the President of the United States having to face a world in which 15 or 20 or 25 nations may have these [nuclear] weapons. I regard that as the greatest possible danger and hazard."[1] That danger was largely averted, because the world concluded the NPT in 1970. Instead of twenty-five states with nuclear weapons, there are now eight or nine. Chances are better now than at any time since the initial development of nuclear weapons that we can establish a course to reduce their numbers progressively—and one day to eliminate them altogether.

The NPT is an inherently unequal treaty. Those countries with nuclear weapons when the treaty was concluded in 1970 got to keep them for an indeterminate period, but those without such weapons, including Canada, were prohibited from acquiring them.* The treaty is a beneficial one, nonetheless, because despite its unfairness, it makes everyone safer, and because it codifies the rules for co-operation on peaceful uses of nuclear energy. States have been prepared to accept such inequality because they understand that the greater the number of states that possess these most dangerous of weapons, the greater the likelihood that someone will eventually use them, accidentally or on purpose.

Those states without nuclear weapons also expect that the nuclear-armed states will keep their ends of the bargain and disarm, if not immediately, then in some meaningfully foreseeable future. And, in fact, as the Cold War receded, Russia and the United States first limited the increase in nuclear weapons and then began to reduce the very large numbers of such weapons, although nuclear warhead destruction has not kept pace, and research on the upgrading of remaining weapons and delivery systems has

---

* This was a bigger sacrifice for Canada than for many others, because, as a participant in the original Manhattan Project that produced the first US bombs, Canada had the materiel and the know-how to develop such weapons too. Presuming American acquiescence, which might or might not have been forthcoming, doing so certainly would have changed the course of Canadian history.

continued. The UK and France have also reduced their comparatively smaller arsenals. However, China has augmented its weapons, albeit from a small base, as, perhaps, has Israel. North Korea remains a riddle wrapped in an enigma, to borrow from Churchill.

Opened for signature in 1968 and ratified by 188* out of 192 countries, the NPT is one of history's most successful and most consequential treaties, and remains central to the effort to prevent the proliferation of nuclear weapons and, eventually, to reduce and eliminate them. But the treaty is not perfect. States can, by assembling the elements of a future nuclear weapons program and declaring those elements to be for peaceful purposes, go a long way towards creating nuclear weapons while remaining ostensibly in compliance with the treaty, abrogating it when convenient. North Korea did so with impunity, having assimilated whatever technology and know-how had been transferred to it in good faith while it was still a party to the treaty. That is, effectively, the course that Iran is suspected of being on. Were Iran to cross the nuclear-weapons threshold, it could trigger a seriously destabilizing nuclear arms race in the Middle East, potentially involving several countries.

Convinced that 9/11 had changed everything, the Bush administration seemed to have concluded that nuclear proliferation could only be managed, not averted, that multilateral mechanisms to avoid the spread of weapons were ineffectual, and—equally bad—that they constrained American freedom of action. In comparatively short order, the Bush administration abrogated the Anti-Ballistic Missile Treaty (ABMT) and rejected the necessity and feasibility of verifying other key treaties, particularly the Biological and Toxin Weapons Convention (BWC); the projected Fissile Material Cut-Off Treaty (FMCT), designed to control the production and stockpiling of material for making nuclear

---

* India, Pakistan, and Israel did not sign the NPT; North Korea has withdrawn.

warheads; and the Strategic Offensive Reductions Treaty (SORT) with Russia. Verification of compliance had, in the past, increased confidence that the treaties were being respected; dropping the verification requirement rendered the treaties little more than statements of good intentions, and of little use in the eyes of many states. "Trust but verify," as President Reagan often said about arms negotiations with the Soviet Union.

For the Bush Jr. administration, the danger of nuclear weapons lay not in their unimaginable destructive power, but in the malevolent character of some of the regimes that possessed them or of the terrorists who might acquire and use them. This was the National Rifle Association's argument against gun registration—"guns don't kill people; people kill people"—taken to its logical conclusion.

In 2008, India and the United States concluded a strategic agreement that more closely allied India and the US. India obtained de facto US recognition of its status as a nuclear-weapons state, ending India's nuclear isolation while preserving India's weapons programs. India was not required to relinquish its nuclear weapons or agree to any meaningful non-proliferation or disarmament requirement, for example, signature and ratification of the Comprehensive Test Ban Treaty (CTBT), or an agreed moratorium on the production of fissile material, or a defined ceiling on its new arsenal or a legally binding commitment to enter into multilateral disarmament negotiations. New Delhi did agree to separate its civilian and military nuclear facilities and open the former to IAEA inspection, but this is unlikely to be much of a constraint on India from a weapons perspective. US benefits from the deal include the fact that India will become a potential counterweight to China, will move a bit closer to the NPT than heretofore, and will provide access for US companies to its growing nuclear energy market.

The US-India deal violated earlier undertakings made by members of the Nuclear Suppliers Group (countries in a position to export nuclear technology) to provide nuclear-related material/

technology only to those states with IAEA "fullscope safeguards"*
agreements in place. Nevertheless, a combination of old-fashioned,
commercial interest and US pressure, combined with Indian
tenacity, resulted in the group granting India an exemption. The
India-US deal and the exemption blew a significant hole in the
integrity of the NPT. What looked to Washington like reasonable
accommodation to the realities of India looked like double
standards to Iran and Pakistan. Equally bad, other countries that
agreed to abandon their nuclear weapons aspirations, like Brazil,
might review their decisions.

The Harper government welcomed the US-India deal, partly
to please the large and influential Indian diaspora in Canada,
partly to improve relations with the Indian government (which
had been cool since 1974, when India secretly used the technology
supplied by Canada and others to make a bomb and exploded
weapons again in 1998),† partly in the hope of selling previously
prohibited nuclear material and services to India, and partly to get
along with the Bush administration. Ironically, two of the four
benefits expected from Canadian acquiescence in the Bush
administration's deal were soon devalued; the Bush administration
is gone, and Canada remains constrained in what it can sell to
India in good conscience. We cannot sell nuclear technology to
India for the reactors that the Indians are using in their weapons
programs,‡ and India is sufficiently advanced technologically that

---

* Full-scope safeguards (FSS) are mandatory safeguards that are applied
to all nuclear materials in all peaceful nuclear activities within a country's
territory or under its control.

† Canadian "realists" argued that we were placing our values before our
commercial interests. Others maintained that we were placing our security
interests above our commercial interests.

‡ The Indian government has decided that six reactors derived from
technology Canada transferred in the 1960s will go on the list of
installations reserved for the production of nuclear weapons, according

it does not need Canadian know-how for its civilian program, although co-operation on reactor safety matters would be natural, because both countries' reactors are derived from CANDU technology. While the government is apparently hoping that the deal with India will generate nuclear service business and uranium sales, there may be constraints on the latter. The Australian government, for its part, has declined to sell uranium to India so long as India remains apart from the NPT. Canadians should wonder why the Australian government thinks that exporting uranium to India is inadvisable, while the Canadian government is untroubled about it. Meanwhile, in supporting the exemption from Nuclear Suppliers' Group rules for India, we sacrificed our nuclear non-proliferation principles and our strategic stability and arms-control goals.

While the Bush administration often paid lip service to the centrality of the NPT, and never actually repudiated it, its heavy reliance on American power and its disdain for treaties was morphing into a de facto abandonment of key parts of the arms-control and disarmament treaties regime. The NPT was considered valid to the extent that it helped prevent proliferation, but invalid as regards the constraints it imposed on the US.

Some "realists" argued that nuclear disarmament had always been little more than a delusion on the part of the states without nuclear weapons, a necessary fiction that there would, one day, be a quid for the quo they were giving in renouncing their own nuclear weapons aspirations. Further, this was a quid on which the states with weapons never really intended to make good, nor should they have. In this light, the argument went, everyone would be better off just to drop the pretence, and learn to love the bomb (of others).

The counter-argument, made eloquently by President Obama,

---

to Leonard Spector, deputy director (Washington, DC) of the Monterey Institute Center for Nonproliferation Studies and a former senior arms-control official at the US Department of Energy.

is that ridding the world of nuclear weapons might necessarily be a goal for the very long term, but that is no reason to abandon it. The commitment should be maintained against the possible day that political attitudes and security perceptions with respect to nuclear weapons may change. Maintaining the goal of eventual disarmament, however far in the future that happy day might be, means that near-term decisions will continue to be framed in such a way as not to preclude reaching the longer-term goal. Remove that goal, and everyone's decision calculus changes.

Disarmament is not a "romantic" pipe dream; the argument of the disarmers is prevailing. In January 2007, in a seminal article in the *Wall Street Journal*, former US secretaries Henry Kissinger, George Shultz, and William Perry, and former chairman of the Senate Armed Services Committee, Sam Nunn, conservatives all, called for both setting a goal of a world free of nuclear weapons and working energetically to achieve that goal. They repeated their call in January 2008. Obama has endorsed it.

US policy is only one part, albeit an extremely important part, of the arms-control and disarmament negotiations, and getting the world to co-operate will not be clear sailing. Others, notably the Chinese, the Indians, and the Pakistanis, have mutually incompatible interests and the diplomatic skills to protect them. Nevertheless, thanks mainly to leadership by the Obama administration, vitality has returned to the nuclear arms-control and disarmament agenda after several years of deadlock and retreat. This opens opportunities for Canada to advance policies that we have traditionally supported, but which have been held in abeyance pending a more propitious time. That time has come.

Although Canada has never had nuclear weapons, there is an abundance of expertise in this country in the nuclear field that enables us to contribute responsibly and constructively to the international management of arms-control and disarmament issues. We have sophisticated capacity in our nuclear energy, engineering, and uranium industries, residual talent among public servants to conceive and carry out policy, strong policy-oriented academics to conduct both policy and technical research, and an active and knowledgeable civil society to help generate public awareness and political support. The remaining ingredients for success are belief in these capabilities, the political will to make a positive difference, and the pocketbook to pay for it. This is an important field of diplomacy, and success will not be achieved by trying yet again to do more with less.

WHAT WE SHOULD DO

First, as the prospect of a world without nuclear weapons has rarely been more promising, we should put our figurative shoulder to the wheel on this crucial issue. We can use our significant assets to promote a few key ideas of our own, and we can support the international effort President Obama is leading.

Although the general public has lost sight of the issue, there are currently an estimated 22,000-plus[2] nuclear warheads in the world, of which nearly 8,000 are considered operational.[3] The explosion of any one of them over a major city would cost many thousands—perhaps many hundreds of thousands—of lives, and change the way we live forever. The events of 9/11 would seem quite trivial in comparison. The government should, therefore, issue a white paper, making it clear to Canadians and the world where Canada stands on this danger. As we have no weapons of our own, but would be the victims, direct or indirect, of the deliberate or accidental use of nuclear weapons, we would unavoidably, but legitimately, be in a position of urging others to act.

Second, we should endorse the idea of an international nuclear weapons convention, which would prohibit the development and production of all nuclear weapons by all countries. Further, we should urge the US and Russia to establish a program of phased reductions of nuclear weapons that would see stockpiles shrink to a small fraction of their current holdings. At the same time, we should urge the Russians and the Americans to reduce the number of nuclear weapons—apparently almost 2,000—on hair-trigger status, and to separate warheads from missiles. We should press both of the major nuclear powers, especially the US, because it is more advanced, to endorse the goal of a weapons-free outer space and to refrain from basing weapons systems in space. We should work for the conclusion, within five years of a treaty, to cut off the creation of fissile material and to reduce the existing stocks of such material, in order to "suffocate" the supply of weapons-grade fissile material for nuclear weapons. As well, we should press for reform of NATO's strategic doctrine, including supporting the repatriation of US nuclear bombs from Europe and the reduction of the numbers of tactical nuclear weapons available to NATO and Russia.

Second, institutional reforms are needed as part of any comprehensive strategy. We should join with like-minded countries in strengthening the capabilities of the International Atomic Energy Agency by doubling its budget. To pre-empt others from following the Iranian and North Korean path of using civilian enrichment and reprocessing facilities to create weapons-grade material, we should endorse some version of a multilaterally owned or run nuclear fuel bank. Such a "bank" would reduce the need for countries to produce their own nuclear fuel. Further, we should work with others to enhance the effectiveness of the NPT by equipping it with a secretariat and a members committee to respond to crises arising between five-year-review conferences. We should promote agreement for NPT signatories to meet in annual "conference of states" parties and agreement on more systematic reporting by member states on their implementation of the treaty; both would be valuable steps in strengthening the treaty.

Third, we should strongly and visibly support President Obama's efforts to cut back US nuclear-weapons systems significantly and to persuade Congress to ratify nuclear treaties. Not all of the Washington security establishment, on either side of the political divide, supports Obama's nuclear policies, just as they and their like-minded predecessors did not support President Reagan's efforts to eliminate nuclear weapons in the 1980s. Inertia, complacency, ideology, and self-interest are real and serious obstacles. Support from key, nuclear-savvy allies like Canada can be a helpful factor in the debate. In our relations with Congress, we should promote US ratification of the Comprehensive Test Ban Treaty.

The Global Partnership Program Against the Spread of Weapons and Materials of Mass Destruction was created at the 2002 Kananaskis G8 summit, and was designed to help Russia and others safely reduce their arsenals of weapons of mass destruction. The Chrétien government committed Canada to contribute about $1 billion to this $10 billion G8 program over ten years. Successive governments have largely kept that promise. Prime Minister Harper used the 2010 Nuclear Security Summit in Washington and the G8 meeting in Muskoka to urge participants to extend the duration of the program and expand the number of participants. We should commit ourselves to contributing a further $1 billion to a renewed $10 billion program over the coming ten years to help pay for the disposal of what is likely to be the accumulating numbers of surplus warheads, nuclear materials, and weapons systems. Of that $1 billion, a small fraction, perhaps $20 million, should be set aside to rebuild Canada's once-vaunted treaty verification research program.

Last, but not least, unless we can satisfy ourselves that Canadian uranium will not end up contributing indirectly to the Indian nuclear-weapons program, we should not sell any to India. Nostrums about India's reliability are unpersuasive; the Indians are making nuclear weapons; their doing so takes us further from the goal of a world without nuclear weapons.

CLIMATE CHANGE

No one said fixing the climate change problem was going to be easy. It is undoubtedly the most difficult international governance challenge we face. It presents the mother of all "tragedies of the commons": all countries have an interest in seeing the global temperature not rise to the point at which it triggers dangerous climatic consequences, but all also have an interest in conducting activities that, while individually beneficial, collectively can destroy the commons—in this case the earth. Canada is as conflicted as any other country on this issue, and perhaps more so than most.

. I led the Canadian negotiating team for the Kyoto Protocol (of the UN Framework Convention on Climate Change). On instructions from Ottawa, we committed Canada to reduce Canadian greenhouse gasses to 6 percent below the emission levels that existed in the base year that had been agreed upon, 1990. We also agreed to a timetable that included an agreed-upon deadline of 2012.

The implementation efforts by the Liberal government of the Kyoto Protocol were, however, too little and too late. It tried for years to tiptoe into the cold political waters of compliance, consulting every industrial and interest group repeatedly, until all had been said and said again, but little had been done. Largely because of the National Energy Program experience in the 1980s, the Liberals did not want to risk imposing policies that disaffected the Alberta and Saskatchewan governments—and, more particularly, their voters—any further. While Canada dithered, Canadian carbon dioxide emissions *increased* by 33 percent, according to a 2009 report by the International Energy Agency. On coming to office, the Conservative government abandoned the Kyoto commitment and initiated its own plan. It departed from some of the basic features agreed to by all at Kyoto, choosing a baseline year (2006) completely different than that agreed to by 187 other countries, and proposing targets considerably less demanding than those committed to under Kyoto. But the Conservatives never implemented the plan and have been "ragging the puck" ever since, negotiating defensively, waiting on Washington.

There is no doubt of the need, and the responsibility, to act. According to the 2007 Synthesis Report of the Intergovernmental Panel on Climate Change, the scientific body that is charged with interpreting the science, climate warming is now a fact, based on observations of increases in global average air and ocean temperatures, widespread melting of snow and ice, and rising average sea levels globally. Global atmospheric concentrations of carbon dioxide, methane, and nitrous oxide have increased markedly as a result of human activities since 1750, and now far exceed pre-industrial-age levels, as has been determined by examining ice cores that span many thousands of years. Currently, the concentration of carbon dioxide—the most prevalent greenhouse gas—is about 400 parts per million, which is a 38 percent increase since pre-industrial times. Humanity, especially its richer members, has clearly taken the atmosphere into uncharted territory.

Despite the alleged transgressions of some of the scientists associated with the issue, the consensus about the science itself is that it is very sound. There is growing agreement that the world should try to avoid a temperature increase of 2 degrees Celsius above pre-industrial-age levels, in order to avoid "dangerous interference with the climate system." We might already have reached an increase of 1.3 degrees Celsius because of what we have done to change the atmosphere.

The fundamental issues are how to increase global efforts to reduce the emission of greenhouse gases sufficiently to head off further dangerous change, how to adapt to the change that is now unavoidable, and how to share the financial and economic burden of doing both equitably. Some countries, notably Canada and the US, have insisted, as a condition of acting themselves, that major emitters of carbon dioxide among the developing countries, especially China and India, participate in the effort. However, China and India and other developing countries have taken the view, understandably, that, because greenhouse gases have been accumulating in the atmosphere over decades and centuries, ever since the Industrial Revolution began, the bulk[4] of today's problem has been created by the rich countries, and it is they who have the responsibility to lead in fixing it. They see the West's demands on them as akin to rich countries arranging for a sumptuous dinner for themselves, inviting the poorer countries to come afterwards just for coffee, and then suggesting splitting the bill equally when it comes time to settle up.

This argument is true as far as it goes, and the West, including Canada, should certainly lead. But the argument does not go far enough. The greenhouse gas emissions of the poorer, emerging countries are now growing at a rate that means they will account for the larger proportion of emissions going forward. China overtook the US in 2007 as the world's largest emitter of carbon dioxide, and India, which trails China, is growing fast. China and India argue that, on a per-capita basis, both remain far behind most industrial countries. But it is states which sign international treaties, not individuals, and the scale of the emissions from China, India, and others will be such that, mathematically, they must be part of the solution, albeit differentially, or their growth will more than nullify the reductions made by others, and climate change will accelerate. The realization is sinking in around the world that we are all in the same boat, and we will prosper or perish together.

The optimists see progress in some of the steps agreed to in the Copenhagen Accord on climate change, which "recognizes" the scientific case to limit a rise in global temperatures to below 2 degrees Celsius above pre-industrial-era levels. They see the fact that poorer, developing countries are participating voluntarily in mitigation efforts as an important precedent. The Copenhagen Accord sets a short-term goal for the period from 2010–2012 of $30 billion in aid from the richer countries to the poorer countries, to help offset the costs of mitigating the effects of climate change and adapting to them. The accord also establishes a longer-term goal of $100 billion a year, starting in 2020. Most of the richer, developed countries have subsequently established national targets for emission reductions, and many poorer, developing countries have committed themselves to "nationally appropriate" mitigation actions, some without specific targets.

Canada has set itself a target of reducing national greenhouse gas emissions by 17 percent from 2005 levels by 2020, which, in the government's own words, is completely aligned with the US target. The US target, as endorsed by the House Clean Energy and Security Bill, is a 17 percent reduction by 2020, based on 2005 levels—the equivalent of a 3 percent reduction from 1990 levels. Canada's target is contingent on all major emitters "associating themselves" with the accord.

Critics, including the respected Canadian environmentalist Jim

MacNeill, former director of the OECD's environmental program and the lead author of the landmark *Brundtland Commission Report* on sustainable development, consider Copenhagen to have been a major step backwards to the days before the Kyoto Protocol. The Copenhagen Accord lacks internationally agreed binding targets and timetables for emission reductions, relying instead on national targets supported by national legislation. It is vague on the promises of financing to poorer countries, puts large carbon emitters in the driver's seat of international negotiations, and sidelines the many poorer countries who will suffer a great deal, despite having contributed only a little to the problem. Both optimists and pessimists have a point, but I fear MacNeill is largely right.

Canada does not come to this international debate in a strong position. Domestically, Canadian governments have been dilatory in dealing with climate change, and internationally, they have been seen to be acting irresponsibly. Canada ranks seventh in the world in total greenhouse gas emissions. Despite our relatively small population, we are a world-class polluter. Even though the Harper government enjoys a very strong political position in Alberta and Saskatchewan, and could afford to make a gesture, Ottawa made it very clear in Copenhagen that Canada was going to stay in tandem with Washington.

There are lessons from the near past that are applicable to current circumstances. In the 1980s, when Ottawa was pressing Washington for action on acid rain, the economic risks of Canada acting before the US did were broadly similar—albeit more regionally limited—to what they are now. The Mulroney government acted first anyway, and took steps to ensure that Canadian emissions of sulfur dioxide and nitrous oxide were reduced. That leadership was crucial in persuading Washington to follow suit, and to conclude an acid rain agreement with Canada. If we had waited for Washington to go first on acid rain, we might still be waiting.

For now, we are waiting for the US to move effectively on climate change. Neither Canada nor the US is trusted by our international partners on this issue, by virtue—if that is the right word—of our respective non-performances in implementing Kyoto. The world is waiting to see if the Obama administration and the US Congress can find the political will to meet even the modest obligations the US assumed under the Copenhagen agreement.

Trust is an indispensable factor in conducting international negotiations. We will regain it only when the many foreign embassies in Ottawa, and the many Canadian and foreign NGOs interested in the issue, begin to report that we are implementing our obligations responsibly and effectively.

WHAT WE SHOULD DO

First, in co-operation with the provincial governments, Ottawa should lay out Canada's own climate change action plan—a Green Plan II—and implement it. Doing so will begin to restore our image in this area, and our influence. Obviously, the degree to which Canada can subject Canadian industry to made-in-Canada rules and regulations that are more demanding than those imposed by Washington on American firms is limited. (As the former head of the negotiating team, I actually advocated *not* ratifying the Kyoto Protocol when the Americans simply walked away from it, because I did not think we could carry the support of the provinces and industry if the US were to become a "free rider.") At the same time, the structure of the Canadian economy is not identical to that of the US, and there is room for Canadian national action.

Second, we need to work "bottom-up" with the provincial governments, industry, university researchers, and constructive NGOs, supporting the "Western Initiative" (WI), the program of western states and Canadian provinces to cut greenhouse gas emissions from power plants, manufacturers, and vehicles, as well as the Regional Greenhouse Gas Initiative, a co-operative undertaking by northeast and mid-Atlantic states of the US, supported by some Canadian provinces. We should encourage any other sub-national schemes that seem likely to help. At the same time, there is no substitute for leadership by Ottawa. The federal government should work top-down to cap allowable emissions and facilitate the creation of a market for trading carbon emissions credits, or to initiate a carbon tax, as has been done in British Columbia, or to impose industry-specific regulations, or, most usefully, to do some combination of all three.

Third, internationally, we should move aggressively on implementing those aspects of the Copenhagen Accord that are not dependent on our self-imposed tandem with the US. In particular, we can establish timetables and targets for meeting our share of the commitment made by the richer countries to provide $30 billion to the poorer countries, in order to fund mitigation and adaptation programs over the years 2010–2012. Doing so would be consistent with CIDA's programming theme of "stimulating sustainable economic growth." It could also bolster Canada's International Development Research Centre programs that are working to improve the capacity of African countries to adapt to climate change. We can also begin to plan how we intend to meet our share of the goal agreed to by the richer countries at Copenhagen to mobilize $100 billion per year by 2020, to address the needs of developing countries for mitigation and adaptation.

Fourth, we need to try to fix the negotiating process. The UN's consensus-based decision-making means that every one of the UN's 192 members has its own veto. At Copenhagen, a small group of ideological spoilers was able to block progress. New negotiating mechanisms or processes are needed to prevent minorities from blocking the great majority who wish to advance. If this problem is not resolved, and if the world is prevented from managing global issues through the UN, the organization will be bypassed, and the vetoes will disappear altogether—which is effectively what happened at Copenhagen. There, a very small group of very large countries—China, India, South Africa, Brazil, and the US— produced an agreement and presented it to the broader membership on a take-it-or-leave-it basis. If the UN's deliberative process is not reformed, increasing recourse to such restricted processes will be pursued, either inside or outside of the organization, undermining the world body in the process.

Fifth, we should complement our work to improve UN processes by promoting the use of the G20, of which we are a member, as the group in which vital and contentious matters can be aired—and, where possible, ironed out. The G20 will not be a magic wand, partly because India and China prefer to keep climate change negotiations inside the UN, where they have more cover, and partly because there are genuine differences of view among the twenty of what needs to be done. The G20, nevertheless, has the ideal membership for reducing differences among the major countries and for bypassing spoilers. Just the threat that they *might* do so would be salutary. If a critical mass of the major countries could reach agreement through the G20, the spoilers would find it more difficult to block progress. Of course, to be legitimate, any outcome would need to be brought back into a universal setting under UN auspices for endorsement.

Sixth, whichever restricted group might come into play, inside the UN negotiating process or outside it, we need to move heaven and earth diplomatically to make sure we are "at the table." At Copenhagen, we appear to have been left to take or leave the deal reached by the US and others, on a matter that has a potentially crucial impact on our environment and our economy. To the extent that we left our interests in the hands of the US, deliberately or involuntarily, we fed a dangerous practice. Our interests are not, in every case, the same as US interests, and we simply cannot afford to hand Washington our proxy. That really is behaving like the fifty-first state of the union, albeit without representation.

15

TIME TO GET BACK IN THE GAME

It's not the size of the dog in the fight that matters;
it's the size of the fight in the dog.
—Mark Twain, General Dwight D. Eisenhower, others

GETTING BACK IN THE GAME

Our world is changing before our eyes, dramatically, rapidly, irreversibly, and—the doom and gloom of current news cycles notwithstanding—very largely for the better. People around the world are richer, healthier, and living longer; they are better educated, more literate, and better connected to each other; they are more democratic in their governance, and most are living in peace. It is true that many are still being left behind economically, but the world can meet that challenge too, if it can muster the will to do so. Almost half a billion people have climbed out of poverty since 1990, the great majority of them in Asia.

The change from generation to generation, which shows few signs of slowing down, has been breathtaking. From 1950 to 2005, gross world product has increased from US$7.4 trillion to $61 trillion and per-capita income has increased from US$2,923 to $9,440.[1] Growing volumes and varieties of cross-border flows of investment, goods, and services have accelerated economic interdependence. Prosperity has broadened and deepened as a consequence, the "great recession" notwithstanding. For example, almost two out of every three people around the world—4.1 billion—have access to cell phones, an invention that is scarcely twenty-five years old.[2] Illiteracy has fallen from 37 percent (in 1970) to 20.3 percent. In the poorer countries, the decline in illiteracy has been even more dramatic, from 52.3 percent to 26.4 percent, and life expectancy has increased from forty-seven years to sixty-eight years.[3]

The world's advancing economic integration, the advent of mass, affordable travel, the accelerating diffusion of technologies worldwide—especially Internet-based communications—medical technology, and the progressive creation of a rules-based system for international commerce and interstate relations have, together, been hugely beneficial. Globalization has helped vast numbers of people, even if its benefits have been unevenly distributed within and between countries, and if it has universalized risks, as the "great recession" demonstrated.

Canadians are arguably the luckiest people on the planet. We live in one of the richest and most respected countries in the world, in extraordinarily favourable times. We have benefited enormously from vast improvements in our standard of living and lifestyle. We are also fortunate in our friends, especially the giant superpower next door. The US has its problems, but it is one of the most resilient societies on earth. It has elected arguably its most sophisticated leader ever, who is embracing the world, not seeking to dominate it, and is privileging co-operation over coercion and partnership over autocracy. He has singlehandedly transformed the way the world sees his country.

Beyond America, the news is also good. Countries that were poor and isolated a generation or two ago are engaged and prospering and, in doing so, they are largely embracing the existing international order rather than rejecting it. Never have we enjoyed more opportunities to prosper—or had a greater responsibility to contribute to making our rapidly changing world a better place, or a stronger interest in doing so.

It is all the harder to accept, then, that Canada has been in retreat from international engagement for nearly a generation. Even counting our contribution to Afghanistan, we have slipped far down the list of contributors to UN missions, below countries with a small fraction of our population and wealth. Despite growth in our foreign-aid budget, we rank closer to the bottom of the donor generosity list than to the top. With our aid funding set to be capped starting in 2011, we will continue our descent. Once considered the international leader on environmental protection, we are now regarded as a laggard, at best, and a spoiler, at worst; on climate change, we have come to be seen as an obstacle to action. Once a human-rights champion, we are now selective about whom we protect. At the same time as Ottawa is spending nearly $20 billion on defence to procure (mostly) much-needed modern equipment, funding for diplomacy, where the marginal return on expenditures is much higher, has not kept pace with need and opportunity. We have been closing embassies abroad and selling off precious diplomatic assets to relieve budgetary pressures, handicapping our diplomacy at the very moment when we most need it. Our still highly capable Foreign Affairs department, starved for core funds, consumes itself in "process," and turns itself into a service provider to better-funded domestic departments.

It does not have to be that way. Canada's wallet is not the problem. Despite the "great recession," never in our history have we been richer or better able to afford an effective, responsible, independent foreign policy. To govern is to choose. There is no inherent reason why we cannot choose to be more effective diplomatically, as we have rightly chosen to be more effective militarily, and to give ourselves the diplomatic capacity to speak up—and more important, to stand up—for what we believe in. There is a world of good to be done, and Canadians are eager that Canada do it. We can also augment and revamp our foreign-aid program. Few countries can match us at policy innovation, perhaps because our governments have been more willing to think about foreign policy than to pay for it. But, we have it in our power to do better.

There have been objective reasons for our flagging performance, starting with the need through the 1990s to get our financial
house in order. With the restoration of the government's fiscal
health since the turn of the twenty-first century, however, we have
declined further, a consequence of fragmented parliaments,
minority governments, internecine warfare in our political parties,
and stunted and warped ambitions. More recently, our government
seems to have come to regard engagement in the world as elective,
apparently not really sure we can play the international game.

We *can* play. Though power is a zero-sum game, capacity is
not. We are a country of extraordinary assets—tangible and
intangible. The world needs us to take a larger, more responsible,
share in the management of international relations. The message
coming out of Washington, loud and clear, is that the Americans
cannot run the world and afford their domestic priorities at the
same time. On crucial issues such as nuclear arms control, climate
change, Afghanistan, the Middle East, failed and fragile states,
terrorism, the alleviation of poverty in poorer countries, and the
promotion and consolidation of human rights, to cite only the
obvious, they need and want help. At the UN, in NATO, at the IMF
and World Bank, around the G20 table, Canada's contribution is
valued and desired. Further, it is in our own interests to "step up."

As we saw in the Copenhagen climate change negotiations
and at the Doha trade negotiations, you cannot protect your
interests, let alone advance your values, if you are not at the table
where the decisions are being made. It is always better to be a
policy "maker"—even if co-operatively—than a policy "taker." No
one can carry our proxy effectively. We need creative and insightful
diplomacy, and our diplomats need the tools to act on our behalf
at the major decision-making tables.

It all begins with Canadians. In a democracy, citizens get
what they deserve, and, as the wag said, usually good and hard.
We get the government a minority of us vote for, and the foreign
policy we demand—or don't demand. If we do not ask for much,
that, we can be sure, is precisely what we will get. We would not
be satisfied with bronze performances from our hockey players;

we should not accept that from our political representatives, either.

We need to be more demanding. We should start by demanding that our leaders have international experience when they come to office—or at least have some reasonably persuasive idea of how they plan to represent us and advance our interests in the world. It is no coincidence that our most successful prime ministers have been those with the most international experience. We should also demand more of ourselves. From civil society in church basements and community centres to aid workers in distant shanty towns, from diplomats seeking to understand our world to entrepreneurs trying to transform it, we can all do better. We can help to make the world a better place. And we should do so. From whom so much has been given, much is expected.

Canadians see their country as capable, constructive, and compassionate. They want Team Canada back on the world field, playing, not on the sidelines, watching. The world is changing and other players are emerging, but we can meet that competition. We are not a superpower, but we are a super country. And, in any case, it's not the size of the dog in the fight that matters; it's the size of the fight in the dog.

ENDNOTES

CHAPTER I: OPTIMISM BEATS PESSIMISM

1 National Oceanic and Atmospheric Administration (NOAA), "Carbon Dioxide Emissions (CO2), thousand metric tons of CO2 (CDIAC) July 2009," cited in "UN Millennium Development Goals Indicators," 2010.

2 Germanwatch, "The Climate Change Performance Index." 2010: 6.

3 Organisation for Economic Co-operation and Development (OECD),"Table 1: Net Official Development Assistance in 2009, Preliminary Data for 2009," DAC Aid Statistics, 2010.

CHAPTER 2: CANADA: THE SIZE OF THE DOG IN THE FIGHT

1 United Nations, *Population and Vital Statistics Report*, United Nations, Vol. LXI, No. 2. July 2009.

2 UK Census 38,328,000, 1901.

3 *Times Higher Education* (British), "Top 200 World Universities," 2009.

4 United Nations Development Program (UNDP), Human Development Report, 2009.

5 Swiss Federal Institute of Technology, "2010 KOF Index of Globalization," 2010: 1.

6 World Bank, "World Development Indicators Database," October 2009.

7 Wilson, Dominic, and Anna Stupnytska, "The N-11: More Than an Acronym," Goldman Sachs, Global Economics Paper No. 153, March 2007.

8 World Trade Organization (WTO), International Trade Statistics, 2009.

9 Schwab, Klaus, ed., *The Global Competitiveness Report: 2009–2010*, World Economic Forum, (2010): 14.

10 Organisation for Economic Co-operation and Development, Research and Development, OECD *Factbook 2009*: *Economic, Environmental and Social Statistics*.

11 Canada's Corporate Innovation Leaders, RE$EARCH Infosource Inc., November 6, 2009.

12 OECD, Research and Development, Factbook 2009.

13 Statistics Canada, "*2006 Census: Immigration in Canada: A Portrait of the Foreign-born Population: 2006 Census: Findings.*"

14 Perlo-Freeman, S., C. Perdomo, E. Skoens, and P. Staalenheim, Stockholm International Peace Research Institute. *SIRPI Yearbook 2009: Armaments, Disarmament and International Security* (Oxford: Oxford University, 2009), 182. Also in *Population and dwelling counts:*

A Portrait of the Canadian Population, www12.statcan.ca/census-recensement/2006/rt-td/pd-pl-eng.cfm.

15   As of March 2010.

16   Gotlieb, Allan, Romanticism and Realism in Canada's Foreign Policy, C. D. Howe Institute, Benefactors' Lecture, 2004.

17   Dymond, Bill and Michael Hart, "The Potemkin village of Canadian foreign policy," *Policy Options*, IRPP, December–January, 2003–4. Similar sentiments were expressed by Roy Rempel in *Dreamland: How Canada's Pretend Foreign Policy Has Undermined Sovereignty*. (McGill–Queen's University Press, 2006).

18   Landmine Monitor Report 2009, *Toward a Mine-Free World. International Campaign to Ban Landmines*, November 2009.

19   Granatstein, Jack, "Yankee go home? Is Canadian anti-Americanism dead?" *Behind the Headlines*, CIIA, 1996.

20   Hart, Michael, *From Pride to Influence: Towards a New Canadian Foreign Policy* (Vancouver: University of British Columbia Press, 2008), 335.

21   Katzenstein, Peter and Robert Keohane, *Anti-Americanisms in World Politics* (New York: Cornell University Press, 2006).

22   Deputy Minister Leonard Edwards' statement to the Standing Committee on Foreign Affairs, house of Commons, Ottawa, August 26, 2009.

23   Environics poll conducted for the NGO Canada's World, 2008.

CHAPTER 3: A FOREIGN POLICY OF OUR OWN

1   Brown, Robert Craig, *Dictionary of Canadian Biography Online*, Government of Canada, (2010).

2   United States Department of State "Foreign Relations of the United States," Conferences at Washington and Québec, 1943 and 1944.

3   Stairs, Denis, "Founding the United Nations: Canada at San Francisco, 1945," *Policy Options*, Vol. 26, No. 07 (September 2005): 16.

4   Bothwell, Robert, Ian Drummond, and John English, *Power, Politics and Provincialism* (Toronto: University of Toronto Press, 1989), 39.

5   Armstrong-Reid, Susan and David Murray, *Armies of Peace: Canada and the UNRRA Years* (Toronto: University of Toronto Press, 2008).

CHAPTER 4: FROM THE GOLDEN AGE TO THE MODERN AGE: LESSONS LEARNED

1   Pearson, Lester B, *Mike: The Memoirs of the Right Honourable Lester B. Pearson, Volume II*, Munro, John A. and Alex I. Inglis, eds, (Toronto: University of Toronto Press, 1973), 28.

2   *Ibid.*, 28.

3   Helleiner, Eric, *Towards North American Monetary Union? The Politics and History of Canada's Exchange Rate Regime* (Montreal: McGill–Queen's University Press, 2006), 79.

4   Pearson, *Mike*, 36.

5   English, John, *The Life of Lester Pearson: The Worldly Years* (Toronto: Vintage Canada, 1993), 364.

6   Cohen, Andrew, *Extraordinary Canadians: Lester B. Pearson* (Toronto: Penguin Canada, 2008), 188.

7   *Ibid.*, 114.

8   English, *The Worldly Years*, 385.

9   Kinsman, Jeremy, "Who Is My Neighbour: Trudeau and Foreign Policy," *London Journal Of Canadian Studies* (2002-3) Vol. 18, 103-120.

10   MacGuigan, Mark. *An Inside Look at External Affairs During the Trudeau Years* (Calgary: University of Calgary Press, 2002), 13.

11   English, John, *Just Watch Me: The Life of Pierre Elliott Trudeau* (New York: Knopf Canada, 2009), 168-70. Nixon also called Trudeau "an asshole."

12   Head, Ivan and Pierre Trudeau, *The Canadian Way: Shaping Canada's Foreign Policy, 1968-84* (Toronto: McClelland and Stewart, 1995), 159.

13   *Ibid.*, 216.

14   *Ibid.*, 212.

15   *Ibid.*, 300.

16   *Ibid.*, 305.

17   English, *Just Watch Me*, 601.

18   MacGuigan, *An Inside Look*, 124.

19   Mulroney, Brian, *Memoirs: 1939–1993* (Toronto: Douglas Gibson Books, 2007).

20   All figures from NAFTANOW, a site jointly run by the governments of Canada, the US, and Mexico: http://naftanow.org

21   Kohl, Helmut, Commission of Inquiry into the History and Results of the SED dictatorship in Germany, November 4, 1993.

22   See also: Mulroney, *Memoirs*, 908.

23   Mulroney, *Memoirs*, 690.

24   Stewart, Brian, "When Brian Mulroney Was Great," CBC website, May 15, 2009, and personal conversation with the author, April 9, 2010.

25   Chrétien, Jean, *My Years as Prime Minister* (Toronto: Knopf Canada, 2007), 309.

26   *Ibid.*, 315.

27   *Ibid.*, 313.

28   Harper, Stephen and Stockwell Day, *The Wall Street Journal*, March 2003.

29   Chrétien, *My Years as Prime Minister*, 87.

30   *Ibid.*, 139.

31   *Ibid.*, 140–41.

32   *Ibid.*, 331.

33   *Ibid.*, 340.

34   Evans, Gareth and Mohamed Sahnoun, *The Responsibility to Protect: Report of the International Commission on Intervention and State Sovereignty* (Ottawa: International Development Research Centre, 2001).

35   Chrétien, *My Years as Prime Minister*, 90.

CHAPTER 5: THE UNITED NATIONS: THE MOTHERBOARD OF GLOBAL GOVERNANCE IN A CHANGING WORLD

1   Clinton, Hillary, "A Discussion with Secretary of State Hillary Clinton," Brookings Institute, Washington, September 19, 2009.

2   See Polling done for BBC *World News* by Globescan and the University of Maryland PIPA, 2006, along with the Pew Global Attitudes Project, 2009.

3   Leitenberg, Milton, "Death in Wars and Conflict in the 20th Century," Cornell University Peace Studies Program, Occasional Paper 29 (2006).

4   See the 2005 *Human Security Report* of the University of British Columbia and, latterly, of Simon Fraser University.

5   Perlo-Freeman, et al., SIPRI *Yearbook 2009*.

6   United Nations, "United Nations Peacekeeping Operations." (February 2010): http://www.un.org/en/peacekeeping/bnote.htm.

7   James Dobbins, et al., "The UN's Role in Nation-Building: From the Congo to Iraq," RAND Corporation, 2005.

8   Annan, Kofi, "We the Peoples: the Role of the United Nations in the 21stth Century," April 3, 2000, 48.

CHAPTER 6: AMERICAN NATIONAL SECURITY: THE QUEST FOR INVULNERABILITY

1   MacMillan, Margaret, *Paris 1919: Six Months that Changed the World* (New York: Random House, Inc., 2003).

2   Government of the United States, NSC 68: *United States Objectives and Programs for National Security, A Report to the President Pursuant to the President's Directive of January 31, 1950.* (April 7, 1950).

3   Bacevich, Andrew, *The Limits of Power: The End of American Exceptionalism* (New York: Metropolitan Books, 2008), 111.

4   Preble, Christopher, *The Power Problem: How American Military Dominance Makes Us Less Safe, Less Prosperous, and Less Free* (New York: Cornell University Press, 2009), 47.

5   See, for example, Christopher Preble in *The Power Problem*, 29, and Patrick Tyler and Leonard Silk in *The New York Times*, March 8, 1992.

6   "Executive Summary of the Report of the Commission to Assess the
     Ballistic Missile Threat to the United States." Available at Federation of
     American Scientists (2010): http://www.fas.org/irp/threat/bm-threat.htm.

7   The list includes *Empire*, *On Empire*, *Incoherent Empire*, *Inadvertent
     Empire*, *Sorrow's Empire*, *Fear's Empire*, *After the Empire*, *Colossus*, *The
     Case for Goliath*, *The New Imperialism*, *Imperial Tense*, *Resurrecting
     Empire*, *Day of Empire*, etcetera.

8   Transcript of President Bush's Speech on Terrorism, *New York Times*,
     September 6, 2006, as provided by CQ Transcriptions, Inc.

9   Report on the Treatment of Fourteen "High Value Detainees" in CIA Cus-
     tody, by the International Committee of the Red Cross, February 2007, as
     excerpted in "US Torture: Voices from the Black Sites," by Mark Danner,
     New York Review of Books, April 2009.

10   The legal advice given to the president is available on the *Slate*
     magazine website at http://slate.msn.com/features/whatistorture/
     LegalMemos.html.

11   Johnston, David and Scott Shane, "Memo Sheds New Light on Torture
     Issue," *New York Times*, April 3, 2008.

12   Kennedy, Ted, Massachusetts State Democratic Convention, August
     2009, reported in the *Huffington Post*, August 29, 2009.

13   Chrétien, *My Years as Prime Minister*, 313.

14   Colin Powell in discussion with George Carey, "Building Trust, Peace
     and Reconciliation," *World Economic Forum*, 2003.

15   Secretary of State Colin Powell to the UN Security Council, February 5,
     2003.

16   George Kennan interview in the *New York Review of Books*, 1999.

CHAPTER 7: THE US UNDER NEW MANAGEMENT: PARAGON REGAINED?

1   *The Mini-Atlas of Human Security*. World Bank and the Human
     Security Report Project (2009).

2   "Confidence in Obama Lifts U.S. Image Around the World," Pew
     Global Attitudes Project (2009): http://pewglobal.org/2009/07/23/
     confidence-in-obama-lifts-us-image-around-the-world/.

3   "American is Now the Most Admired Country Globally—Jumping to
     the Top of the 2009 Anholt-GfK Roper Nation Brands Index." Anholt-
     GfK Roper, (2009): http://www.gfk.com/group/press_information/
     press_releases/004734/index.en.html.

4   Danner, Mark, "The Red Cross Torture Report: What it Means," The
     New York Review of Books, April 30, 2009.

5   Promoted by Christopher Preble in *The Power Problem*.
6   Bacevich, *The Limits of Power*, 169.
7   The National Coalition on Health Care and the Henry J. Kaiser Family Foundation Focus on Health Reform, July 2009.
8   Wills, Gary, "Entangled Giant," *New York Review of Books* (October 2009).
9   Baker, Kevin, "Barack Hoover Obama: The best and the brightest blow it again," *Harper's* (July 2009).
10   Brzezinski, Zbigniew, "From Hope to Audacity: Appraising Obama's Foreign Policy," *Foreign Affairs* (January–February 2010).

CHAPTER 8: A MULTI-CENTRIC WORLD?

1   http://en.wikipedia.org/wiki/list_of_Nobel_laureates_by_country.
2   Schwab, Klaus, ed., *The Global Competitiveness Report: 2009–2010*, World Economic Forum, (2010): 14.
3   Mahbubani, Kishore, "The Case Against the West," *Foreign Affairs* (May–June 2008).
4   Statement by President Obama, White House website, January 10, 2010, www.whitehouse.gov/the_press-office.
5   Jaeger, Markus, "BRIC outward FDI—the dragon will outpace the jaguar, the tiger and the bear," *Talking Points,* Deutsche Bank, (2009).
6   IMF, World Bank and CIA Factbook at http://en.wikipedia.org.
7   Goldman Sachs, *The N-11: More than AN Acronym*, March 2007.
8   *Ibid.*
9   Mahbubani, Kishore, *The New Asian Empire: The Irresistible Shift of Global Power to the East* (New York: Public Affairs, 2008), 10.
10   And security cost is much more in Vancouver than in Beijing.
11   "Fear of the Dragon," *The Economist* (January 7, 2010).
12   "China Top Holder of US Debt, After All," Agence France Presse, February 27, 2010.
13   The World Bank estimates that more than 60 percent of the population was living under its $1 per day (PPP) poverty line at the beginning of economic reform. That poverty head-count ratio had declined to 10 percent by 2004.
14   United Nations, *Statistics of the Human Development Report*, (2010): http://hdr.undp.org/en/statistics/.
15   Kahn, Joseph and Jim Yardley, "Choking on Growth," *New York Times*, August 26, 2007.
16   Transparency International ranks China seventy-ninth in the world. (Canada is tied for eighth with Australia; New Zealand tops the list.) "Corruption Perceptions Index (CPI)," Transparency International

(2009): http://www.transparency.org/policy_research/surveys_indices/
cpi/2009/cpi_2009_table.

17   Premier Wen to Fareed Zakaria, CNN, September 2008.

18   As quoted by Fareed Zakaria in *The Post America World* (New York: W.
      W. Norton & Company, 2008).

19   Op-ed by Zhong Shan, Vice Minister of Commerce of the People's
      Republic of China, *Wall Street Journal*, March 26, 2010.

20   World Bank, IMF and CIA *World Fact Book*.

21   India ranks 134th in the world in human development. *Statistics of the
      Human Development Report*. United Nations, (2010): http://hdr.undp.
      org/en/statistics/.

22   Transparency International ranks India 84th in the world on its 2009
      Corruption Perceptions Index scale. "Corruption Perceptions Index
      (CPI)," Transparency International, (2009): http://www.transparency.
      org/policy_research/surveys_indices/cpi/2009/cpi_2009_table.

23   Tabuchi, Hiroko, "Rising Debt a Threat to Japanese Economy," *New
      York Times*, October 20, 2009.

24   Emmott, Bill, *Rivals: How the Power Struggle Between China, India and
      Japan Will Shape Our Next Decade* (Orlando: Harcourt Books, 2008).

25   "The US and the World: An Interview with George Kennan," *The New
      York Review of Books*, 1999.

26   CIA *World Fact Book*, 2010.

27   *Ibid.*

28   President Dimitry Medvedev, as quoted by Dmitri Trenin, "Russia
      Reborn: Reimagining Moscow's Foreign Policy," *Foreign Affairs*,
      (November–December, 2009).

29   Perlo-Freeman et al., *SIPRI Yearbook 2009*, and Cirincione, Joseph, Jon
      Wolfsthal, and Miriam Rajkumar, *Deadly Arsenals: Nuclear, Biological,
      and Chemical Threats 2nd ed. Revised and Expanded* (Washington:
      Carnegie).

30   "World Economic Outlook," IMF, 2009.

31   Ash, Timothy, "The agonies of the eurozone reflect a far more signifi-
      cant hidden deficit," *The Guardian*, February 24, 2010.

32   Schwab, Klaus ed.,*The Global Competitiveness Report 2009–2010*,
      World Economic Forum (2010).

33   "World trade developments in 2008: International Trade Statistics,"
      World Trade Organization (2009).

34   "Financing for Development," European Commission (2010).

35   "Strength in Numbers? Comparing EU Military Capabilities in 2009
      with 1999," EU Institute for Security Studies, Policy Brief No. 5 (2009), 1.

36   "A Policy-Driven, Multispeed Recovery," International Monetary Fund,
      World Economic Outlook Update, January 26, 2010.

CHAPTER 9: CANADIAN FOREIGN POLICY AND DIPLOMACY

1   Burney, Derek, *Getting It Done: Memoirs* (McGill–Queen's University Press, 2005).

CHAPTER 10: THE HARPER GOVERNMENT: NOT "BACK" YET

1   *The Lancet*, Volume 375, Issue 9726, P. 1580, May 8, 2010.

2   According to Frank Dimant, the Executive Vice-President of B'nai Brith Canada, speaking about the Conservative Party and Israel on the cbcs *The National*, February 3, "This group of politicians have (sic) come with a background, and in some cases a religious background, which help them make their determinations in terms of the Middle East, in terms of justice."

3   See the statement by Prime Minister Harper on the occasion of receiving the Simon Wiesenthal Leadership Award, Office of the Prime Minister, May 31, 2009.

4   Statement by Prime Minister Harper on the occasion of Israel's 60th Anniversary, Office of the Prime Minister, May 8, 2010, http://www.pm.gc.ca/eng/media.asp?id=2097.

5   See: "B'Tselem's investigation of fatalities in Operation Cast Lead," The Israeli Information Center for Human Rights in the Occupied Territories, (2009), and "Guidelines for Israel's Investigation into Operation Cast Lead," The Israeli Information Center for Human Rights in the Occupied Territories, (2009).

6   A/64/351-S/2009/464, *Report of the Secretary General on the Peaceful Settlement of the Question of Palestine*, September 15, 2009.

7   Graham, John, "Canadian Policy in the Americas: Between Rhetoric and Reality—A Needless Dance" in Hampson, Fen, and Paul Heinbecker eds., *Canada Among Nations 2009–10: As Others See Us* (Montreal: McGill–Queen's University Press, 2010).

8   Mei Ping, "Return to Realism and Restart the Relationship" in *Canada Among Nations*.

9   Andrés Rozental, "A Mexican Perspective" in *Canada Among Nations*.

10   Fréchette, Louise, "Canada and the United Nations: A Shadow of its Former Self" in *Canada Among Nations*.

11   un website, June 2010: http://www.un.org/en/peacekeeping/contributors/2010/may10_2.pdf.

CHAPTER II: GETTING OUR HOUSE IN ORDER: THE NEED FOR POLICY COHERENCE

1   Green, Ian, and André Côté, "Leading by Example: 50 Prominent
    Canadians Talk to us About the Federal Public Service and why
    Leadership Matters," Public Policy Forum, (2007): http://www.
    ppforum.ca/sites/default/files/Leading_e.pdf.

2   Mulroney, Memoirs, 398.

3   Head and Trudeau, The Canadian Way, 253.

4   MacDonald, Ian, "Mulroney tips hat to foreign service," Toronto Sun,
    February 19, 2010.

5   Statistics Canada, International travellers, seasonally adjusted, 2009.

6   Gates, Robert, "A Balanced Strategy," Foreign Affairs (January–February
    2009).

7   Treasury Board Main Estimates, 2009–10.

8   "Federal government quietly releases $490B military plan," CBC News,
    June 20, 2008: http://www.cbc.ca/canada/story/2008/06/20/military-
    plan.html.

9   Ibid.

10 McAskie, Carolyn, "Canadian Aid—More, Not Less, Is Needed," in
    Canada Among Nations.

11 "Secretary of State Hillary Rodham Clinton Congressional Testimony
    House Appropriations Committee Subcommittee on State and
    Foreign Operations," Committee on Appropriations, 25 February
    2010: http://appropriations.house.gov/images/stories/pdf/ew/Hillary_
    Clinton-2-25-10.pdf.

CHAPTER I2: JOB ONE: THE UNITED STATES (AND MEXICO)

1   Pastor, Robert, "Should Canada, Mexico, and the United States Replace
    Two Dysfunctional Bilateral Relationships with a North American
    Community?" Conference on North American Futures: Canadian and
    U.S. Perspectives, Berkeley, March 2010. See also Statistics Canada.

2   Dobson, Wendy, "Beyond FTAS: Deepening North American
    Integration," SSRN (2005).

3   "Open Canada: Global Positioning for a Networked Age," Canadian
    International Council, June 2010.

4   Gotlieb, Allan, "Romanticism and Realism in Canada's Foreign Policy,"
    Benefactor's Lecture, C. D. Howe Institute, November 2004 39.

5   Manley, John and Gordon Giffin, "Bilateral Trilateralism" in Canada
    Among Nations.

6   See especially Andrés Rozental, former Mexican Deputy Foreign
     Minister, and Robert Pastor, formerly of the US National Security
     Council in *Canada Among Nations.*

7   Pastor, Robert, "North American's View of the Old NAFTA and the New
     North American Agendas" in *Canada Among Nations.*

8   Rozental in *Canada Among Nations.*

9   McQuaig, Linda, "We should revert to use of global trade rules,"
     Toronto Star, August 28, 2005.

10   Barlow, Maude, *Too Close for Comfort: Canada's Future within Fortress
     North America* (Toronto: McClelland & Stewart, 2005).

11   Gotlieb, Allan, "Benefactor's Lecture," C. D. Howe Institute (November
     2004).

12   Former Ambassador Derek Burney has also proposed appointing
     personal representatives for climate change, citing the Mulroney
     precedent on acid rain.

13   Former Canadian Ambassador to the US Michael Kergin proposed
     two similar such commissions, one to co-ordinate a longer-term
     strategy to address border security, North American competitiveness,
     significant rule-making, and a transportation infrastructure strategy,
     notably regarding bridges over the Detroit River. Former Ambassador
     Derek Burney suggested a bi-national border commission,
     empowered to streamline customs and entry regulations, reduce
     regulatory overlap and competition, harmonize immigration and
     visa policies, examine a common external tariff, and intensify police
     collaboration along the border.

CHAPTER 13: JOB ONE (A): REFORMING AND INNOVATING GLOBAL GOVERNANCE

1   *Report of the Committee on Contributions: A/64/11.* United
     Nations (2009): http://www.un.org/ga/search/view_doc.
     asp?symbol=A/64/11(SUPP).

CHAPTER 14: JOB ONE (B): MAJOR LEAGUE ISSUES

1   Quotations of John F. Kennedy, John F. Kennedy Presidential Library
     and Museum.

2   Evans, Gareth, and Yoriko Kawaguchi, eds., *Eliminating Nuclear Threats:
     A Practical Agenda for Global Policymakers.* International Commission
     on Nuclear Non-Proliferation and Disarmament, (2010), 3.

3 "Status of World Nuclear Forces," Federation of American Scientists (Accessed May, 2010): http://www.fas.org/programs/ssp/nukes/ nuclearweapons/nukestatus.html.

4 The richer countries are the source of about 70 percent of the emissions since 1950. Nicholas Stern, *The Global Deal* (New York: Public Affairs, 2009).

CHAPTER 15: TIME TO GET BACK IN THE GAME

1 Source: Compiled by Earth Policy Institute with 1950–1979 from Worldwatch Institute, Signposts 2001, CD-Rom (Washington, DC: 2001) (Worldwatch update of Angus Maddison, Monitoring the World Economy 1820-1992 [Paris: OECD, 1995]); 1980–2005 from International Monetary Fund, World Economic Outlook Database, at www.imf.org/ external/pubs/ft/weo/2006/02/data/index.htm, updated September 2006; United Nations, World Population Prospects: The 2004 Revision (New York: 2005); U.S. Commerce Department, Bureau of Economic Analysis, "Implicit Price Deflators for Gross Domestic Product," Table 1.1.9, revised August 30, 2006, at www.bea.gov.

2 ITU world telecommunication/ICT indicators database.

3 Unesco Institute for Statistics, Data on Illiteracy, for Population Age Fifteen and Older: http://www.uis.unesco.org; Economic and Social Council E/CN.9/2010/3, January 28, 2010.

ACKNOWLEDGEMENTS

It is appropriate that I acknowledge the contribution of many people, without whose help this book would never have been written. I am thinking first and foremost of my wife, Ayşe, who has suffered almost as much as I have in the production of the book. She is my indispensable partner in our nearly life-long foreign-affairs enterprise, and contributes immeasurably to its success. Writing this book has been more difficult than I ever thought possible, and I would not have finished it without her forbearance and explicit encouragement at a time when she had every entitlement to love, support, and undivided attention herself. Our daughters, Yasemin and Céline, have long been pressing me to write a book about my experiences. This is not *that* book, but at least it is *a* book, and I hope that pleases them. As they work in the foreign-policy business, I wish to make clear that I have not consulted them on the substance or the advice offered. If the judgments in this book offend, it is my fault, not theirs.

Finally, I thank Polly, our sadly deceased and terribly missed Otterhound, who sacrificed many a walk to sleep at my feet so I could get this book written.

INDEX

PAUL HEINBECKER is a veteran of a dozen international summits and is a former career diplomat who has served in Ottawa as chief foreign-policy adviser to Brian Mulroney, as point man for Canada's human security agenda, and as head of the Canadian climate change delegation in Kyoto. He was posted abroad in Ankara, Bonn, Paris, Stockholm, and Washington, D.C. In 2000, Heinbecker was appointed ambassador and Permanent Representative of Canada to the United Nations, where he represented Canada on the UN Security Council. At the UN, he was a leading opponent of the war in Iraq and a defender of the International Criminal Court. Heinbecker is a distinguished fellow at the Centre for International Governance Innovation in Waterloo, Ontario, and the inaugural director of the Centre for Global Relations at Wilfrid Laurier University. He lives in Ottawa. For more information, visit www.heinbecker.ca.